D1356649

Exploring Arab Folk Literature

Pierre Cachia

Edinburgh University Press

Edinburgh University Press Ltd
22 George Square, Edinburgh
www.euppublishing.com

Typeset in in Times New Roman by
Koinonia, Manchester, and
printed and bound in Great Britain by
CPI Group (UK) Ltd, Croydon CR0 4YY

A CIP record for this book is available from the British Library

ISBN 978 0 7486 4086 7 (hardback)

Published with the support of the Edinburgh University Scholarly Publishing
Initiative Fund

Contents

Part 3. Cultural and Social Implications

Acknowledgements

The material I have to offer in this volume has a long history. All but two of the twenty items included have had a life in print before this one. The journals, books and conference proceedings that gave them shelter are all named in the table of Contents, and to the editors and compilers of these I offer heartfelt thanks. For it is the responses of their readers that gradually gave some impetus and some scope, perhaps even some direction, to the study of a vast but long ignored aspect of Arab literary life.

The Table of Contents identifies who the adoptive parent of each article was. From as many as I could trace I sought a blessing for this rebirth, and many earned renewed thanks by the readiness and generosity of their responses. Failures to get such responses have to me been akin to the loss of old friends. Particularly keenly felt has been the frustration of all efforts to renew contact with my former student Ali Obali, who more than twenty years ago espoused my project of familiarising Western readers with the long ballad of 'Karam il-Yatīm' as an example of an Egyptian folk singer's narrative skills, so he buckled down to transcribing the entire text while I worked on its translation, and the results of both our labours were published together.

I am certain that if we had managed to make contact we would both have enjoyed reliving our months of collaboration, and that he would now agree to put his piece through the limited but indispensable revision which all the other items in this book have undergone. Since he alone has the right to re-edit his work, I have had to consider whether I would be doing it good service by including it in a collection where it would be out of step with all others even in the method of transcription it uses. In the end, I deemed it best to point the reader to where it was first published and is still available, but not to include in this volume one item that does not conform with the system of transcription used everywhere else. The inconvenience to the reader is not great, for my main purpose had been to illustrate the folk artist's narrative skills, and these can be detected in the translation, whereas the text would demonstrate verbal and rhetorical tastes amply illustrated elsewhere in the book. If I have erred in my judgement, I hope that Ali will forgive.

Since the material that was to be made into a book had already been through editorial and critical processes akin to a ruminant's digestion, the only foreseeable problem was that there was as yet no widely accepted system for the transcription into Latin characters of *oral* Arabic texts. Over the years, I had experimented extensively, and in different articles had tried various formulae designed to fill the need. A case might have been made for the retention of this harlequin feature as illustrative of an inevitable historical process. I consulted James Dale – who in the absence on leave of Nicola Ramsey, Edinburgh University Press's perceptive, decisive and unobtrusively expeditious Senior Commissioning Editor – was the appointed guardian angel of the project. Both to him and to me, it seemed intolerable that the reader should be faced with different transcription formulae in different parts of the book. On the contrary, here it seemed was an opportunity to put forward a transcription scheme that could command wide acceptance. The decision was taken to bring all the earlier folk texts into line with what later experience favoured.

I am not of a practical turn of mind, and the marvels of modern technology, including the resources of computers, dazzle rather than illumine me. In all my previous publications I had never had to do more than provide a readable typescript, leaving it to the publisher to solve problems of production; but this sensible division of labour is no longer the rule. More than half the articles that I wanted to reissue had survived only as printed texts. I had been given reason to believe that scanning could turn them back into editable material, but I soon discovered that the process was no more magical and immediate than that of feeding sausages backward through a meat grinder to produce a live lamb. I may plead in mitigation of my simple-minded expectation that even experienced computer mavens were unprepared for the distortion that occurs when what is fed into a scanner is a medium of expression for which no dictionary exists. Somehow the gibberish actually produced would have to be remoulded. I had set myself a back-breaking task which for months kept me at the computer substituting characters for characters. Even this began to fail me as my limited visual disability got progressively more severe.

I appealed for help, and help did come, generously. It came from Edinburgh University Press, where Eddie Clark mobilised more resources and oversaw the expenditure of more time and labour than had initially been promised to bring distorted texts closer to their pristine form. It came from Columbia University, where at the behest of its Director Professor Peter Awn, the School of International and Public Affairs provided funds for the part-time employment of copyreaders to achieve even greater refinement. Of these Andy Knight proved to be extraordinarily sharp-eyed and capable of sustained hard work, and Mariam Bazeed acquired a lively interest in the subject matter and proved to be a keen and dependable reviser. To all of these I offer fervent thanks.

During the long months spent updating and correcting errors in the transcription of Arabic texts my eyesight was steadily getting worse. If as a result more typographical errors have escaped my notice than I would normally tolerate in someone else's work I acknowledge that the responsibility is entirely mine and beg the reader's forgiveness.

Ultimately, my sustenance has come from two personally close individuals.

One is my wife, Merle. It has so long been her practice unfussily to see to my pettiest as well as my most basic needs that I might easily have taken her help for granted were it not that my typing has become so erratic that she has to check and refine every trivial communication as well as every ponderous pronouncement that I make. That her almost knee-jerk solicitude is of long standing has been earmarked by my dedication to her of a much earlier book.

My other benefactor is 'just a friend', not a colleague who shares my interests, not a childhood pal whose memories are blended with mine, not a wartime comrade-in-arms whose traumas are fused with mine, but just an individual whose path crossed mine late in life.

When – like most of my other acquaintances – he became aware of my growing disabilities and the difficulties they created in the production of my book, he unreservedly took charge of the entire technical side of the project, often anticipating and always finding ways to surmount what seemed an endless series of obstacles. Intensely practical and gifted in computer lore, he has day after day and month after month used all the hours he could spare in advising me, acting for me, investigating new technical resources that could be of use to me. In the end, he assumed all but my editorial duties in connection with the book's production, personally creating the final text for submission to my publisher, so that the only feature of this book that will be a surprise to him is the entry on the next page.

Dedicated to
Simon Heifetz
who patiently and expertly
piloted me between
the Scylla
of partial visual impairment
and the Charybdis
of total blindness to computer technology
to bring me and this book
to safe harbour

Foreword

It is a signal honour to have been invited to write the Foreword to this collection of papers by the doyen of Arabic folk literature, Professor Pierre Cachia, the 'honorary Sa'īdī'. Although now well into his eighties, Professor Cachia still continues to produce perceptive editions, translations, commentaries and analyses of folk literature as practiced in his beloved Egypt. All who toil in this and related fields sincerely hope that, despite the infirmities of age, he will continue to do so for many years to come.

The present collection gathers together some of Professor Cachia's most important journal-length contributions to Arabic folk literature and allied subjects, published over roughly the last forty years. Although only two of the twenty articles have not been previously published, collecting them together in a single volume is a great service to other researchers, many of whom may not have access to all of the journals in which they originally came out. While Professor Cachia's interest in folk literature is long-standing, he has never been a one-club golfer, and he has made significant contributions to Classical Arabic Literature and Arabic linguistics over his long career. In fact, it is his vast hinterland of Arabic linguistic and literary knowledge that is one of the main reasons why his contributions in the field of popular culture are so authoritative: the breadth and depth of his scholarship enables him to bring a sense of context and proportion, and a cultural understanding of both high culture and the grass roots which nowadays is rare in Arabic studies, in which the trend, as in other disciplines, is to specialise in an ever narrower field and say more and more about less and less. Professor Cachia knows Egypt's folk traditions better than anyone, but he has never gone in for half-baked theorising about a field in which we still know so relatively little. Where he does stick his neck out and generalise, his statements are judicious and provisional until such time as further empirical evidence refines or refutes them: the mark of a true scholar.

Professor Cachia's familiarity with Egypt's social and geographical fault-lines is evident on every page of the present work, whether in its 'fact-finding', 'textual' or 'social and cultural implications' sections. An upbringing, including schooling, in Egypt gave him a highly unusual asset for researchers into Arabic culture: a native-like competence in the language from an early age, and an intimate acquaintance through first-hand observation of the rhythms, practices and beliefs of ordinary Egyptians, and not just those of the relatively Westernised large cities, but of the countryside too. It is obvious from both his translations and expositions that he is a lover of language, displaying a well-honed sensitivity to subtlety and allusion, whether in English, Arabic, Maltese or inter-textually. I particularly enjoyed his Hamletesque observations on how social values are reflected in Egyptian popular ballads like Shafī'a and Mitwallī, and Ḥasan and Na'īma:

> Not one of the stories hinges on an inner conflict, on a choice between two honourable obligations or two painful courses of action ... But the consensus thus implied is a consensus of opinion only. To judge by these ballads, it was only in the halcyon days of the Prophet and his Companions that men vied with one another in noble and generous behaviour. Our times are out of joint, and it is everyone's cursed spite to find himself in a position demanding that he set it right.

There is much discussion throughout the book of how the verbal artistry and ingenuity described in it should be labelled. Professor Cachia favours 'folk' as the correct word, arguing that it is primarily the type of audience that they attract that should define literary genres. In this case, that is overwhelmingly the ordinary population of rural Egypt, to whom may be added the inhabitants of the poor quarters of the cities who have had an education along traditional religious rather than modern secular lines – in short, those who wear the *gallabiyya*, rather than the Western clothes of the *afandiyya* class of lower middle-class Egyptians and those above them in the social pyramid. The performers of the art come from the same background as those who consume it, and the moral universe which they all inhabit has a fixed set of reference points: an unquestioning belief in the traditional forms and practice of popular Islam; an unbending honour code of crime and punishment which, it could be argued, is to a great extent pre-Islamic; and an inbred suspicion, if not an open hostility, to the agents of central government, which is seen as at best distant, at worst arbitrary and uncaring to the lives of the *ibn il-balad.* The narrative content of the materials is based partly on legend, partly on embroidered versions of real events; but the whole oeuvre of Egyptian folk literature has an overwhelmingly religious patina, and an abiding concern with honourable conduct and its opposite, as seen through the eyes of the Egyptian peasantry. Summing this up, Professor Cachia comments: 'Indeed, one could trace in them [= folk ballads] almost the entire history and destiny of mankind as understood in popular Islam, from the Creation to the Day of Judgment.' The literary tropes employed by the balladeers and singers are also *sui generis*, notably what is known as *zahr*, literally 'flower', a type of punning paronomasia in which the poet ends his lines with what are seemingly homonyms, but which, if the syllables are divided differently, and the vowels tweaked, actually mean different things. It is one of the audience's tasks – and pleasures – to try to divine the performer's real meaning (*tazhīr* 'opening the flower'). To those who are not aficionados, even Egyptians, the lines seem naively repetitive, but nothing could be further from the truth.

Excluded from this definition of 'folk' literature are Egyptian 'popular' poets, such as Mahmūd Bayram al-Tūnsī and his artistic heir Ahmad Fu'ād Nigm, who also write in the vernacular – although it could be argued, in the case of Nigm especially, that his background is similar to that of Professor Cachia's most eminent folk poet, Mustafā Ibrāhīm 'Ajāj. The difference between them is the audience at whom they aimed their work. Most of Nigm's work is 'modern' in a sense that 'Ajāj's is not: it addresses contemporary social and political issues, on both the national and international level, and attempts to show the listener/reader how they encroach on his existence *as an Egyptian*, and in a sense, convince him of the need for action. Nigm is *multazim*, 'committed', a man with a well-defined political agenda which is anti-foreigner, anti-middle-class, anti-religious establishment (insofar as he mentions religion at all) and pro-Egyptian working class. The work of 'Ajāj and others like him from sixty or seventy years ago, on the other hand, completely ignores such matters. Only when the doings of those outside the immediate world of rural Egypt impinged directly on them – such as in the infamous Danshaway incident of 1906 when several Egyptian peasants were executed by the British after an altercation and skirmish with a party of British army officers – does that world become an element in the repertoire of the folk balladeer. National crises involving powerful but remote actors are hardly reflected at all in 'folk' poetic activity, and, where they are, as Professor Cachia shows, the poems are ephemeral and soon forgotten, while the themes of proper conduct, honouring one's religion and acting in accordance with its precepts are timeless. The indifference of the 'folk' tradition to national and international political issues, compared with the 'popular' tradition of Nigm and his ilk, could not be more stark than in its treatment of the Suez Crisis of 1956. Where Professor Cachia managed to find only one, half-forgotten ballad composed by one of his 'folk' balladeers (Abū Dhrā'), no less than eighteen pen-and-paper compositions on this theme by many 'working-class' poets appeared in the Cairo newspaper *al-Masā'* between November 1956 and March 1957 (see M. Booth: 'Colloquial Arabic Poetry, Politics, and the Press in Modern Egypt', *International Journal of Middle Eastern Studies*, 24 [1992], 419–40). It is hard to believe that at least some of these outpourings, describing, for example, how the 'plane' and 'hammer' of the carpenter were now being laid down for the rifle and hand-grenade of the infantry, were not commissioned (perhaps even rewarded by) the Nasserist 'alliance of popular forces' of the time.

Likewise, it is instructive to compare both this populist, urban tradition and Professor Cachia's essentially Nile Valley folk literature with that of the Sinai Bedouin, who, after all, are Egyptians too. The oeuvre of 'Unayz Abū Sālim al-Turbānī (c. 1920–99), Sinai's most renowned Bedouin poet, includes half-a-dozen poems on the wars of 1956, 1967, 1973 and even one on the Gulf War of 1991. These are definitely 'folk' poems according to Professor Cachia's criteria, being composed by a semi-literate artist ('Unayz had no formal education, learning the rudiments of formal Arabic only at the age of forty when in prison for smuggling) and for the delectation of fellow tribesmen from the immediate area. Yet they are all to some degree politically nuanced, as in the famous one on the Suez Crisis, which records 'Unayz's feelings as he witnessed the Israeli army crossing the *dīra* of the

Tarābīn on 30 October 1956. Far from the jingoism of the 'working-class' poets of *al-Masa'*, the poem concludes with a couplet expressing barely concealed resentment at the fact that Nasser's government had refused to arm the Sinai Bedouin in its fight with Israel because it didn't trust them (see Holes and Abu Athera, *Poetry and Politics in Contemporary Bedouin Society*, New York, 2009, pp. 47–66). It is, of course, true that the Sinai Bedouin, because of their geographical location, witnessed 'up close and personal' the three wars with Israel that convulsed Egypt between 1956 and 1973, which may be one reason why they feature more prominently in the poems of illiterate 'folk' poets of the area than is the case with Professor Cachia's Nile Valley material. A second reason, of course, is that the theme of war is part and parcel of the Bedouin poetic tradition in a way that it is not true of that of the *fallāhīn*, whom the Bedouin contemptuously refer to as *Banī Far'ōn* 'the sons of the Pharaoh' (viz. 'Pharaoh's slaves'). But in other respects there are similarities: both the Nile Valley literature described by Professor Cachia, and that of the Sinai Bedouin are profoundly suspicious of central authority and all its works, especially when they intrude on the local scene. A parallel with the 'folk' ballad on the Danshaway incident of 1906, for example, which Professor Cachia notes was still being sung fifty or sixty years later, is a poem by an illiterate poet from central Sinai, Husēn bin 'Īd bin 'Āmir al-Tayāhā, composed in 1985, in which he complains at length about the extremely rough treatment meted out by the Egyptian police to hundreds of Sinai Bedouin, following the shooting of a UN peace-keeper who had been propositioning local women (Holes and Abu Athera, *op. cit.*, pp. 68–70). After describing the cruelty and abasement to which the Bedouin women in particular had been subjected, the poet calls down divine retribution on its perpetrators and those who control them, including the Egyptian President Husni Mubarak, who is contemptuously dismissed as 'that dumb peasant who wields a spade'. In both cases, the poems deal with a situation in which the world of the folk balladeer/poet and his audience collides with alien or outside forces.

Although things now appear to be changing for the better, one can only echo Professor Cachia's sentiment that 'There must be an end to "surveys of modern Arabic literature" that make not even a tangential reference to this other vast field of Arab creativity.' However, it appears that a main motivation for increased interest in 'folk' and 'popular' Arabic literature is the discovery by historians and social scientists in the West that there is a fund of untapped resources here which can deepen their understanding of matters like social class. One thinks in the Egyptian context, for example, of the writings of scholars like Joel Beinin and Walter Armbrust. But, apart from Pierre Cachia, literary, linguistic and cultural analysis of Arabic literature composed in the colloquial is still the interest of only a tiny minority of scholars such as Marcel Kurpershoek, who has produced a masterly five-volume enquiry (1994–2005) into the 'Nabatī' tribal poetry of Saudi Arabia, and Nadia Yaqub, who has recently (2007) published a detailed analysis of Palestinian duelling poetry. Classical Arabic literature still rules the roost. One is not asking for that to change necessarily, just for a more holistic approach. It is becoming clearer that there are many areas of cross-over between the two, particularly in the field of poetry, but this goes largely unrecognised. In the West, the reason is partly a matter of academic training, which has only relatively recently begun to include fostering a usable competence in spoken Arabic as one of its goals. This would be an unthinkable lacuna in the teaching of languages like French, Spanish or Russian, yet has long been regarded with apparent equanimity by many Western scholars of Arabic literature, culture and history, either because they think the study of the language people actually use to speak to each other has no place in the academic curriculum (the 'gutter Arabic' argument), or because, more cynically, they wish to 'defend their patch'. In the Arab world, the academic prejudice against 'folk' and 'popular' literature is as old as the hills, and the reasons for it – religious and political as well as cultural – are too well known for me to need to go into them here. I would just add this: six centuries ago, writing about the Bedouin oral poetry of his time, Ibn Khaldūn, that great historian and polymath of North Africa, made the following observations:

> Most contemporary scholars, philologists in particular, disapprove of these types of poems … and refuse to consider them poetry. They believe that their literary taste recoils from them because they are linguistically incorrect and lack vowel endings … But vowel endings have nothing to do with eloquence. Eloquence is the conformity of speech to what one wants to express and to the requirements of a given situation, regardless of whether the u-ending indicates the subject or the a-ending the object, or vice versa … If the indicated meaning is in conformity with the requirements of the situation, we have sound eloquence. The rules of the grammarians have nothing to do with it. (*Muqaddima* ['Introduction to History'], Rosenthal's translation, vol. 3, pp. 414–15)

Perhaps that statement should be engraved in stone and suspended over the entrance to every university Arabic department in the Arab world (and in the West, for that matter). But things are changing in the Arab world too. The pioneering research into the literary aspects of folk and popular literature of scholars like the Saudi anthropologist and critic Saad Sowayan has been as unexpected as it has been impressive, particularly his 600–page analysis of the non-Classical Nabatī tradition of Arabia, written in Arabic and published in 2000 by Al-Saqi Books, which delineates in elaborate textual detail the similarities in language, imagery and topoi between the ancient Classical poetry and that of the Nabatī tradition. The textual evidence Sowayan amasses enables him to definitively refute the prevailing Arab view of the Nabatī tradition as a corrupt, recent excrescence, which he describes as 'ahistorical and elitist'. Sowayan sees it rather as the naturally evolved heir of the pre-Islamic tradition over a period of fifteen centuries. Hardly surprising, really, when one considers the relative imperviousness of Arabia to the outside world until recently, and that the two traditions appear to have originated in the same geographical space. That is because they are in essence one and the same. But one wonders how many scholars of Classical Arabic poetry, Arab or Western, have read

Sowayan's book, such is the lamentable and self-defeating compartmentalisation of Arabic literary studies.

The publication of this collection of essays by Edinburgh University Press deserves a very warm welcome, and is a fitting recognition of the enormous contribution that Pierre Cachia has made to the study of a neglected yet important field of study. Let us hope that it inspires a new generation of scholars to emulate his example, which is that of open-minded, unprejudiced, scholarly engagement with the rich artistic sensibilities of ordinary folk – which, when all is said and done, is what all of us, excepting a few *nawābigh* like Shawqī, are. And yet even Shawqī, the very paragon of classicism, also composed poetry in the vernacular, however hard his editors try to conceal the fact!

Professor Clive Holes, FBA
Khālid bin 'Abdullah Āl Sa'ūd Chair
for the Study of the Contemporary World
Magdalen College, Oxford

Introduction

I was born and grew up in Egypt as a British (colonial) subject. This made me part of the privileged European community which – especially in its largest concentrations in Alexandria and Cairo – could function largely in isolation from Egyptian society. Not so my own family: my father's occupation as a bank official entailed residence in provincial towns where European families were counted by the tens rather than by the thousands, and by disposition both he and even more my mother were open to friendly relations with Egyptians; and as far as I have been able to ascertain they were the very first foreigners to decide that their sons should attend Egyptian schools where Arabic was the medium of instruction.

This did not shatter all barriers. When later I wrote a memoir combining my mother's reminiscences with an account of my own intellectual formation, the title I gave it was *Landlocked Islands* (American University in Cairo Press, 1999), for my home language and cultural leanings were French, and I was well aware that although we had daily, casual and good-natured contacts with Egyptians, there were unmapped gulfs between us. But what is significant in the present context is that I was at ease with my friends' literary perceptions, and for leisurely reading I turned as comfortably to a book of Arabic fiction as I might to a collection of French poetry.

Yet my encounter with the local folk literature in my late teens was a discovery for me, for it had never commanded attention or respect from the foreign community or from the educated city-dwelling Egyptians with whom I associated. Certainly, none of my teachers had ever had a word to breathe about it. To me it now was a treasure house of quaint perceptions, startling valuations, novel twists of expression. I took to travelling to saints' festivals, haunting tiny holes in the wall that functioned as bookshops in the poorer quarters of Cairo, persuading singers to dictate their lyrics to me. And I took notes.

Then, abruptly, the Second World War snatched me away from all this. I served – mainly with a Scottish division – in North Africa and Italy, and when that was over, as soon as I had saved enough money, I headed for the University of Edinburgh to work for a PhD. This was to launch me into a long teaching career first in Edinburgh, then in Columbia University.

There I first had to get acquainted with European Orientalism before it acquired a bad name. Its pioneers had set about uncovering the character and achievements of the Arab-Islamic civilisation in its heyday; they acquainted themselves with classical Arabic and delved into the writings of pre-fifteenth-century Arab thinkers and scholars. By what they achieved in the field they chose for themselves I was impressed, but in what Arab contemporaries thought and even less what the Arab man-in-the-street said or how he said it, they had little concern.

By 1950, which is when I started teaching in Edinburgh, priorities had not changed significantly. Some translations of modern Arabic prose had appeared in French, and a handful of articles on Arab short stories were available in English, but there was not a single book-length study of any aspect of modern Arabic literature in any European language. Here was I freshly come from where Arab self-expression at all levels was commonplace to where it was a discovery waiting to be made. Of course, it was classical Arabic that I was expected to teach, and with this I had no quarrel, for it was the basic, well-regulated early form of Arabic with which the student should be first acquainted; but the new courses I instituted and my own publications were aimed at giving parity to modern developments.

Change was very slow to come. Enrolment in my new courses was sluggish at first, partly because so little was offered in university courses to combine with them or to direct attention to them. Although it was reissued much later, my first book – on a leading Egyptian modernist who was later nominated for the Nobel Prize in Literature – appeared in an edition of only five hundred, and most of the copies were sold in Southeast Asia where Muslims who could not read Arabic yet hoped for a lead from the Arabs on how to cope with modern conditions. Even the publisher had been so ill-equipped to meet the demands of the subject that every word that was to appear in the Arabic script had to be reproduced from my handwriting. Once wakened, however, the giant was quick to stir his limbs, and by 1973 the editors of the *Journal of Arabic Literature* were getting more submissions on modern than on classical Arabic writings.

I was in my fifties then, and feeling remiss at having left folk literature out of the reckoning as an integral part of Arab literary creativity, a part which, in fact displayed – despite a fractured record – a wider range of genres than one encounters in the writings of the elite. I dug up the material I had collected in my youth and was heartened to find that even the notes were sound. During the 1970s and early 1980s I rummaged among the works of early Arab scholars who wrote apologetically of their dabbling in an inferior linguistic medium. They were fascinated almost exclusively by the new verse forms generated by the common people. More directly informative was extensive field work I now undertook in Egypt. Before long, I acquired a special interest in narrative ballads, largely because there was nothing comparable in the literature of the elite; but I also collected a great deal of incidental information, because more often than not I let my informant choose what he wanted to say as I wanted him to reveal his priorities. Some of the disparate items of information I also garnered went into a number of articles. But once I had cumulated enough information on narrative ballads to give a well rounded and self-consistent account of the genre, I attempted this in a book titled *Popular Narrative Ballads of Modern Egypt* published by the Clarendon Press in 1989, only two years before my retirement. It was never intended for the bestseller list, but it scored enough of a *succès d'estime* for the publisher to decide to keep it permanently in print.

This did not put an end to my curiosity. What I had discovered left me feeling as if I was on the shore of a wide sea in which a few islands stood out invitingly and much else remained uncharted. Less mobile now, I have continued to record information as it reached me and to write up my observations. What motivated and shaped my activity was not a pre-conceived thesis that I wanted to test or to establish, but an awareness that there is still a multitude of elementary facts to ascertain before the character and range of Arab folk literature can be defined, that there is no Aladdin's cave of assembled information to tap, so that there is something to be gained by scouting here and there in semi-darkness until (as happened in my previous work when the theme of the narrative ballad became a focus) enough of the terrain is perceived to make more purposeful thrusts worthwhile.

In the book I now offer the reader, I admit that there is no new revelation. If there is one prescriptive feature sustained right through the book, it is a demonstration and defence of a system of transcription of Arabic both as written and as spoken which I believe is essential to advanced work in this field. As for the substance, chance and browsing brought it to me, and circumstances shaped the treatment I gave it. Opportunities to do so came my way through conferences I attended, colloquia to which I was invited, the detection of whiffs of change brought about by technological devices such as the recording cassette, or by one of those magic moments in a researcher's life when, in the course of casual reading or listening, two stubborn problems suddenly coalesce into a luminous solution. These were so many probes into a reality that still needs to be refined.

It is twenty of these probes – all but two of which have already appeared in academic journals and collections – that I wish to bring together in one volume. Unplanned though my probes may have been, they do fall into a self-consistent framework, with innumerable cross references to bind them. They fall into three groups.

The first consists of efforts to ascertain historical developments in the relationship between the literature of common folk in Arab lands and that of the elite, of tracing the gradual elaboration of certain genres, and of compiling information about the producers of folk literature.

By far the longest section deals with single or related texts, mostly dwelling on their artistic features, but also providing evidence germane to the questions raised in the other sections.

The last of these groupings searches for evidence of social and cultural implications, and for differences in the attitudes of folk and elite towards sensitive issues.

All this is done in the hope that another score of like-minded researchers will each add a further score of their loaves and fishes, so that together we may give substance and definition to our understanding of Arab folk literature, perhaps reassessing the role it has long been assigned vis-à-vis the 'high' literature of the Arab elite, and reaching a new valuation of an integrated Arab literary creativity.

The Transcription of Both Classical and Colloquial Arabic

When – following a precept of the Prophet's and the orders of Egypt's ruler – Rifā<a Rāfi< aṭ-Ṭahṭāwī (1801–73) undertook to acquaint his co-religionists with useful knowledge amassed even by obdurate unbelievers, he focused his considerable talents on France. In the third chapter of the Introduction of his oft-published and republished *Taxlīṣu l->Ibrīz fī Talxīṣi Bārīz*, he attempted a quick survey of leading centres of civilisation all over the globe. In so doing, he stumbled on languages which, unlike Arabic, tolerated digraphs that sometimes produce a sound unlike that of either component, and words that crowd strings of consonants into a single syllable, as in his carefully vocalised Was-hin-x̱i-tūn in al->Ītzūniyā. Yet the direction taken made it inevitable that he or his immediate successors would have to familiarise themselves with a widening range of Western writers on kindred subjects, such as David Chisholme. What manual of orthography or morphology would enable any of them to work out how such a name was to be pronounced? Might they have been tempted to spare themselves the guesswork by resorting to transliteration instead of transcription? And would the result have been any less befuddling?

The European pioneers of Arabic studies had more enticing reasons for adopting transliteration.

Enshrined in Scriptures, classical Arabic had been stable for centuries, its syntax and morphology meticulously codified, and – though this was precept rather than reality – it was to be spoken exactly as it was written. And in it had been written all the masterpieces of Arab-Islamic culture that were the main attraction to scholarly Arabists. It was therefore to Standard Arabic, letter for letter, that the European pioneers of Arabic studies bound themselves.

And the transliteralists served their purposes well, not least when they allowed common sense to sideline the principal article of their faith. None so lost sight – or hearing – of the realities of language that he found it necessary to provide a parallel for the silent >*alif* which literate Arabs add to the masculine plural parts of the conjugation of verbs, or to insert a long ā in the name of Allāh where no >*alif* is written into its Arabic form. But the truly committed transliterator, even at the cost of disrupting the metre if he is dealing with verse, will write *fī al-šams* for 'in the sun' even if he knows that no Arab has ever pronounced it except as *fi š-šams*.

The great gap in the work of the transliterators is their cold-shouldering of the distinctive features of spoken Arabic, although echoes of it were sometimes committed to writing. Here again the Arab elite must bear some of the responsibility for the omission, for they were well aware of the many regional vernaculars, but they looked upon them as corruptions unworthy of serious attention.

But, as I expound in 'Arabic Literatures, "Elite" and "Folk": Junctions and Disjunctions' (the first item included in the present book), since at least as early as the thirteenth century the Arab elite has given nods of recognition – though no admission to the literary canon – to some folk verse forms and some folk prose narratives; and since the nineteenth century new trends have appeared in the literature of the Arab elite which have led to the recognition of Arab folk literature at least as a valid subject for academic study. Besides, the use of the colloquial, though still opposed, has gained a foothold at least in the dialogue of plays and of works of fiction of undeniable literary quality.

These developments make it imperative that account be taken of the regional vernaculars of Arabic. Even Arabists who intend to deal mainly with texts in Standard Arabic are likely increasingly to come across illustrative or comparative material drawn from spoken sources, and for these traditional transliteration will not do. At the same time, researchers who wish to confine themselves to Arab folk literature may look upon each regional vernacular as an independent self-subsistent linguistic register, and need only have its phonetic system approximated in Latin characters. I hope to be able to demonstrate that there are instances in which recalling its classical ancestry can be of practical benefit. A new system of transcription that makes accurate differentiation possible must become part of the equipment of any serious Arabist.

I have experimented for years with alternative solutions, and inflicted my fumblings on colleagues and students. I have no illusion that so broad a change from a long-established pattern will be immediately welcomed, but I have no doubt that in time some scheme along the lines of what I now propose will have to be adopted.

Let me first set forth what I have tried to do and why.

To facilitate standardisation, I have drawn all symbols from the Times New Roman Unicode table.

I find digraphs clumsy, and if used without ligatures confusing, for the constituents of many digraphs also appear as contiguous but separate phonemes, as in *adham*, *ashum*, etc.

To retain as much as possible of what is familiar to colleagues, I have built on the foundation laid by Brockelmann, retaining all his symbols except four.

The first two of these exceptions were aimed at cutting down the number of symbols based on 'g' or 'h' but differentiated by added diacritics. To serve new needs, I detached from the 'g' range the plain 'g' which has a direct role to play in distinguishing classical from vernacular usage, for 'g' (as in 'go') is the way ج, is pronounced in some regional vernaculars (notably in Lower Egypt) whereas 'j' replaces it in other regions (in Upper Egypt and Syria) and is also widely accepted as the correct classical usage. I therefore found it economical to use these two plain letters as handy symbols for alternative pronunciations of ج.

Next, from the ‘h’ range of Brockelmann’s symbols, I excise his ‘ẖ’, which stands for خ, borrowing instead ‘x’ from the International Phonetic Alphabet; and for its voiced equivalent غ I extend the use of the ‘x’ by underlining it, in accordance with an established practice.

My last defection from Brockelmann’s ranks is a double one, and it will hit many as all but iconoclastic: I wish to depose a long-established and widely accepted pair of symbols: ʾ for *hamza* and ʿ for ع. My main objection is to their being superscript, for they are not diacritics but letters of the Arabic alphabet that represent phonemes and that may be radical and may be geminated, although they may not have hit the ears of early Arabists as the equals of good honest English consonants. They also have the disadvantage that they may be hard to pick out in print and difficult to distinguish from apostrophes and single quotations marks – how easily can one tell whether *ʿaḏrāʾ* is the Arabic for ‘virgin’ or the verb *aḏrā* between single quotation marks? I have searched hard for alternatives correctly aligned, and found none more suitable than ‘<’ and ‘>’, which have the advantage of being accessible straight from the keyboard.

The question now arises: how spoken Arabic is to be integrated into this system of transcription.

The fact that the vernaculars of Arabic are uninflected affects their syntax and especially their word order considerably, but between the classical and the colloquial vocabularies the gap is not wide. Each region has created coinages and adopted loan words of its own, and gross distortions of pedigreed Arabic words occasionally occur, as when classical *wajh*, ‘face’ becomes *wišš*; but this happens because the abandonment of declension has brought j and h, which should have been in different syllables, into awkward contiguity. Their kinship, however, is restored in the plural *wujūh*. In the mass, what the regional linguistic variants attest is the liveliness of their common core and the continued prestige of its ancestral form.

Directly relevant to our concern here is a large category of words which differ from the classical only in that one consonant is substituted for another. The change is regular within each regional vernacular: it is not conditional on some specific context and it is always the same consonant that replaces a particular classical one. The words so produced are not temporary formations. They have a life of their own at the colloquial level, and may be thought of as verbal avatars.

Their regularity widens the use that the transcriber can make of them. Thus, ‘q’ is widely used for classical ق, and it should continue to do so in the handling of standard texts; but in the Arabic spoken in some regions (such as Lower Egypt and the Levant) ق, is uttered as a glottal stop, and in yet other regions (such as Upper Egypt) it becomes a hard g, as in ‘go’. In the Arabic script, which has not yet been modified to serve the spoken language, ق, is still often used to stand for any of the three phonemes it represents, and under the long dominance of transliteration some Western Arabists are tempted to force the same multiple role on q. This one may be forced to do if one is dealing with a folk text available only in the Arabic script, with no indication of the region that produced it. Otherwise the temptation must be resisted for it is surely the primary purpose of transcription to produce the closest approximation of the sounds actually uttered. For the regional variants of q I would therefore choose > and g; but I would also warn the reader that these are departures from standard pronunciation, and this I do by adding a tilde to each of the symbols, producing >̃ and g̃. Accordingly, the word which in Standard Arabic would be transcribed as *waqafa* 'he stood' should be *wa>̃af* if it occurs in a Lower Egyptian text, and *wag̃af* in an Upper Egyptian one. And without the symbols that I favour confusion could be twice confused when a folk poet picks a Lower Egyptian *gat luh* 'she came to him' and an Upper Egyptian *g̃atluh* 'killing him' and binds them unequally in a punning yoke!

The benefit of this marker to the reader is that it alerts him to the possibility of searching for the meaning of the word in a standard dictionary, where aids to regional vernaculars are extremely rare. The marker also distinguishes between homonyms, which may be favoured for punning but may be misunderstood.

I have opted to use the tilde (provided it is typographically congruent with the letter to which it is to be attached) to signal departures from Standard Arabic practice. My reason for the choice is that we are as yet familiar with only a few regional vernaculars. As our knowledge expands, we are likely to come across many more local usages to record, and the tilde is the most convenient symbol to use because it is the only available diacritic that may be placed above a letter, below it, or at its midpoint, a bar across the consonant being a suitable alternative if the tilde does not fit in satisfactorily.

Among the avatars, there are several parallels to the transformations that q undergoes. For example, ḏ and ṯ are hardly ever heard in spoken Arabic. Instead ḏ becomes either d (to be transcribed as đ) in some words, as in *đakar*, 'male'; or (unpredictably) as z (transcribed as ƶ) in others, such as in *ƶākira*, 'memory'. Similarly, ṯ becomes ŧ in some words, such as *ŧalta*, 'three' in some instances, and s̃ as in *s̃ābit*, 'firm' in others.

Of the same order, though not so wide in its application, is the fact that when the *hamza* is the first radical of a word, it often – but not always – turns into a w, which should then be transcribed as w̃. This differentiates *wakkal*, which is from the standard root *w-k-l* and means 'he appointed an agent' from *w̃akkal*, which is a variant of >*akkal* from the root >-k-l and means 'he fed'.

Vowels, especially short ones, do not command much attention in this context as they are chameleon-like in ordinary speech and are never part of the root anyway. Mostly, it is enough if their length as determined by usage is indicated by surmounting them with a macron while leaving the shorter ones unmarked. Only exceptionally – as, for example, in the discussion of the scansion of a passage of verse – one may need to single out vowels shortened where standard syntax requires them to be long; one need only add a tilde to the offending vowel.

Not often invoked, but impossible to ignore, is the distinction between a front and a back 'a'. They may then be differentiated by placing a dot beneath the back one. Such 'a's occur whenever the vowel combines with any of the so-called 'dark' or pharyngalised consonants or when it precedes ru or ra, but not ri. All this has long been known to scholars and functions *per se* as a phonetic phenomenon. It is therefore not necessary to signal it in the transcription. It may also be worth noting mentally that exceptionally in *Allāh* the 'ā' is pronounced as a back vowel unless the word is preceded by 'i': compare *bi l-lāhi* and *wal-lạ̄hi.* More important and not to be overlooked in the transcription are instances in which it is the quality of the 'a' that determines the meaning of a word, as in the difference between *jārī*, 'current', and *jạ̄rī*, 'my neighbour'. The phenomenon in fact has a phonemic function in nursery words like *bạ̄bạ* and *mạ̄mạ* for 'daddy' and 'mummy', in the colloquial word for 'water,' *mạyya*, or in neologisms accepted in formal language, such as the Pope's title: *al-bạ̄bạ̄.* In all these instances, it is the entire word that has been coloured, but the vowel is the most distinctively audible, and the dot under it is enough to alert the reader to the phenomenon.

Let us now examine some practices long established in transliteration.

Initial *hamzas* are almost always omitted by the transliterators. They are also often elided in the vernaculars. One of many distinctions between the different levels of Arabic is that in the colloquial an initial *hamza* may be and often is elided, whereas in Standard Arabic there are precise norms that determine which may and which may not. A *hamzat waṣl* may therefore be disregarded, but a *hamzat qaṭ<* ought therefore to be represented by > in transcription, although a long-sustained precedent makes dropping it tolerable where the distinction between standard and colloquial usages does not need to be stressed.

A bone of contention now is the *tā> marbūṭah*, the feminine ending in its pausal form, the silent 'h' signalling that, but for the pause, it would have been a 't' carrying a desinential vowel. It has long been transcribed as such, but the third edition of the *Encyclopaedia of Islam* has decided to drop the 'h'. It is true that since the 'h' is in fact silent, the 'a' is sufficient to identify the suffix in most cases, but not if it is appended to a word ending in a long ā. The word *fatā*, 'young man', could then have no feminine form. To avoid such awkwardness, let the old 'h' be restored either throughout or at least after long vowels. An incidental effect worth noting is that if the suffix had been declined it would have acquired an additional syllable and the stress (seldom noticed in grammatical discussions of Arabic) would have moved forward; here it does move and remain forward even when the desinence is suppressed.

The same effect occurs in an entirely different construction that also ends with a silent 'h' after a long vowel. This is when a verb with a *wāw* for a third radical takes a third person masculine singular attached pronoun as its object, and this then goes into its pausal form. The sequence may be *>arjū* 'I wish' → *>arjūhu* 'I entreat him' → *>arjūh* with the stress moving from the first to the second syllable. Once again, a long vowel followed by an 'h' at the end of a word signals a shift in the stress. Although no rule has been formulated, the arrangement is used even in coining words from foreign sources. Thus, *māyū*, with the stress on *mā* is the month of May, and *mayūh* (Fr. 'maillot') with the stress on *yūh* is a bathing costume. The formula of a long vowel followed by an h was accidentally reached, but it seems worth retaining.

My last contribution to this panoply of symbols is a ghost. Arabic does not tolerate contiguous consonants in the same syllable, and in the Standard idiom there are almost always enough desinential vowels to insulate consonants from one another. Not so in the colloquial. Words ending in two consonant are not rare, and if the next begins with yet another – 'a long rope', for example, would be *ḥabl ṭawīl* – a speaker would insert a neutral vowel between the two words. For this addition the Arabic script has not yet devised a character, but in an utterance it is unmistakable, and if in verse it would be necessary to the metre. I believe it should appear in a transcription, and to represent it I have considered the Turkish undotted 'i' or the phonetic alphabet's inverted 'e', but I finally opted for ı as being neither too elusive nor too intrusive; hence: *ḥablı ṭawīl.*

Here, then, is a table of all the symbols – additional to Brockelmann's list or differing from it – needed for the transcription of Arabic. I have, however, taken a liberty with the IPA symbols which mark the pharyngalisation of the 'dark' consonants by superimposing a tilde above each. This is typographically awkward, so I have placed the tilde below each consonant instead.

Colleagues who choose to try out these innovations will find that they give access to new destinations without departing far from the beaten path.

Symbol	*Unicode*	*IPA*	*Arabic*	*Description*
>		ʔ	ء	Glottal stop
>̃	>+0303	ʔ	ء ← ق	Regional pronunciation of ق, as in >*a>̃ūl*, 'I say'
<		ʕ	ع	Standard ع
a		a-ɑ	fatḥa	Back or front short vowel
ạ	1EA1	ɑ	fatḥa	Back 'a', as in Egyptian *mạyya*, 'water'
ā	0101	a:-ɑ:	>alif	Back or front long vowel
ã	00E3	a	fatḥa	Long in Standard Arabic but shortened colloquially
ạ̄	0101+0323	ɑ:	>alif	As in *jạ̄rī*, 'my neighbour'

Symbol	*Unicode*	*IPA*	*Arabic*	*Description*
ḍ	1E0D+0303	ḍ̰	ض	Pharyngalised 'd'
ḍ̃	1E0D+0303	ḍ̰	ض ← ظ	Colloquial substitution of ḍ for ẓ as in Egyptian *ḍuhr*, 'noon'
ḏ	1E0F	ð	ذ	Like 'th' in *this*
đ	0111	d	د ← ذ	Regional ذ, pronounced 'd' as in *đabaḥ*, 'he slaughtered'
ē	0113	ɛ:	اي	Colloquial rendering of 'ay' as in *bēt*, 'house'
ẽ	1EBD	ɛ		Diphthong in Standard Arabic but short vowel colloquially
g		g	ج	Cairene ج as in *gabal*, 'mountain'
g̃	g+0303	g	ج ← ق	Regional ق as in Upper Egyptian >*ag̃ūl*, 'I say'
ḥ	1E25	ħ	ح	As in *ḥajj*, 'pilgrimage'
ī	012B	i:	ي	Long 'e' as in '*fīh*', in it
ĩ	i+0303	i		Shortened form of a long 'e' as in *git lak*, 'I came to you'
ɪ	026A	ə		Neutral vowel added to break a consonantal cluster, as in Egyptian *il-bintı gāt*, 'the girl came'
j		ʤ	ج	Pronounced ʒ in the Levant
ō	014C	o:	و	Colloquial rendering of 'aw', as in *yōm*, 'day'
õ	o+0303	o	و	Shortened form of long 'o' as in *loztē*, 'two almonds'
q		q	ق	Standard (classical) pronunciation of ق
s		s	س	Standard س

Symbol	*Unicode*	*IPA*	*Arabic*	*Description*
s̃	s+0303	s̃	ث ← س	Colloquial ث as in *s̃ābit*, ‘firm’
š	0161	ʃ	ش	Standard ش
ṣ	1E73	s̴	ص	Pharyngalised s
t		t	ت	Standard ت
ŧ	0166	t		Colloquial rendering of ث as t: e.g. *tār*, ‘revenge’
ṯ	0167	θ	ث	Standard ث
ṭ	1E6D	t̴	ط	Pharyngalised t
ū	016B	u:	و	و preceded by *ḍamma*
ũ	0169	u	و	Shortened form of long ‘u’
w̃	w+0303		ء ← و	Initial *hamza* changed to w, as in *wakkal*, ‘he fed’
x		x	خ	As in >*axīr*, ‘last’
x̱		ɣ	غ	As in *x̱ēr*, ‘other’
z̃	z+0303	z	ذ ← ز	Colloquial pronunciation of ذ as in <*uz̃r*, ‘excuse’
ƶ	01B6	z	ذ ← ز	Alternative to ذ as in <*uz̃r*, ‘excuse’
ẓ	1E93	z̴	ظ	Standard ظ
ẓ̃	1E93+0303	z̴	ظ ← ض	Colloquial substitute for ض, as in Egyptian *ẓ̃ābiṭ*, ‘officer’

PART 1

Fact Finding

1

Arabic Literatures, 'Elite' and 'Folk' – Junctions and Disjunctions

The pre-Islamic Arab's strongest loyalty was to a tribe. This was essential to his everyday concerns; but already before Islam he was aware that he and his fellow tribesmen were part of a wider entity. What was the mainstay of this entity? It was not a geographic unit: there is no single word for Arabia in Arabic; instead, one speaks of *bilād al-<arab*, 'the settlements (in the plural) of the Arabs'. If not territory, what? Ethnicity, no doubt, as is indicated by the fact that not only tribes but also some tribal groups claimed a common forefather. But I hold the view – which I admit is not widely shared by my colleagues – that, to a larger extent than is true of other peoples, language has been and remains a key constituent of the Arabs' self-view and self-esteem. My evidence is that when they spoke of their ancestry, the Arabs distinguished between the 'Arabiser' and the 'Arabised' Arabs (*al-<arab al-<āribah* and *al-<arab al-musta<ribah*), terms that, when used in conjunction have virtually always been glossed as denoting a linguistic process. Furthermore, most of the commonly used derivatives from the *<-r-b* root denote expressiveness, even when speech is not involved, as when a woman displaying affection for her husband is said to be *<arūb*. In contrast *<ajam*, the word that pre-Islamic Arabs used for 'foreigners' or more specifically 'Persians', comes from a root the primary sense of which is 'to chew', presumably implying that they seem to chew their words, and most of the other derivatives from <-j-m carry the sense of 'indistinctiveness', or 'obscurity'. And in early Islam, when Arabs had expanded their reach and had the opportunity to evaluate and assimilate the achievements of other peoples, one finds in various contexts a readiness to credit each group with high attainments in one field of human endeavour or another – the Greeks, for example, being praised for their eminence in philosophy – but always the Arabs are said to be supreme in eloquence and the ready command of language.[1]

At all events, linguistic considerations play a decisive part in the distinctions we need to make and the inter-relationship we want to trace between the 'elite' and the 'folk' forms of Arabic literature.

This language was first honed in an impressive corpus of orally transmitted pre-Islamic poetry, some reputedly dating back to the middle of the fifth century CE, yet already bearing the marks of a long development. And early in the seventh century it was hallowed in the *Holy Book of Islam*, which repeatedly describes itself as an Arabic Qur>ān whose exact wording is never to be altered. Furthermore, Muslim Orthodoxy from the ninth century onwards asserts it to be the uncreate

Word of God and therefore in no way subject to the forces of historic time. The fact that the poetry was pagan did not result in disqualification: bowdlerisation ensured that no favourable reference to false gods survived. Linguistically, it was indispensable for elucidating some of the vocabulary of the Qur>ān. And both together were mined by philologists and grammarians to establish the norms of what is known as classical Arabic.

Yet even before Islam two features of poetic practice raise the question of whether there already was a linguistic stratification.

One of these features is that odes ascribed to poets of different tribes show none of the dialectal differences which are known to have existed. Here the use of an acceptable common idiom even at so early a stage is not unlikely. Encounters between tribes were not always on a field of battle. There were widely accepted months of truce, there were fairs at which all gathered, some even reputed to involve formal poetic displays, competitions and even adjudications. A parallel of some relevance here is that present-day regional linguistic differences are matters of fairly wide common knowledge – such as the fact that in one region of Egypt the classical *qāf* and in another the classical *jīm* are both pronounced 'g' – and some folk poets exploit this for punning purposes.

The other feature implying a split literary tradition is that of several metrical patterns that came into use; one known as the *rajaz* was treated as a distinct and apparently inferior form of poetic expression. Reasons for the discrimination have long troubled scholars,[2] but the most obvious – such as the fact that it allows for a multiplicity of rhymes and that like doggerel it was often used for mnemonic records of scientific or historical facts – are characteristic only of later practices. This particular issue is therefore as yet unresolved.

The Linguistic Bifurcation

In the existing poetry and in the Revelation, therefore, classical Arabic had a firmer anchorage than is common in other languages. Yet the pressure for change was all the greater in early Islam as the Arabs rapidly built an empire and to no small extent integrated into their faith peoples who had linguistic and literary traditions of their own. <Amr ibn-Baḥr al-Jāḥiẓ (c. 776–868 or 9) gives us strong evidence of extensive change by recording jokes about misunderstandings between the Bedouins, who still used grammatical inflections in their everyday speech, and city-dwellers, who no longer did. Such variations he recognised as natural and valid, and, indeed – mainly with oral communication in mind, although it is not impossible to convey some of the flavour in writing – he deemed them relevant to literary expression:[3]

> People's language is stratified, just as the people themselves are stratified. Discourse may be chaste or it may be loose; it may be tangy and fine or it may be loathsome and foul; it may be light or it may be heavy – but it is all Arabic, and [by Arabs] all these varieties have been used to communicate with one another, to praise or dispraise one another.

> When – may God have you in His keeping – you hear a witticism uttered by Bedouins, beware of repeating it except with all its inflections and all its characteristic consonantal sounds. If you alter it by introducing into it any of the solecisms or mispronunciations common among the half-breeds and the city-dwellers, you will come out of your attempt at recounting it with much dispraise. Similarly, if you hear one of the common people's *bons mots*, a pleasantry peculiar to the plebeian masses, beware of introducing syntactic desinences into it, of choosing elegant words, or of allowing your mouth to endow it with easy-flowing articulation. That would spoil the delight that might be taken in it, distort its image, remove it from what it was meant to achieve, and do away with people's appreciation of it and delight in it.

Al-Jāḥiẓ's linguistic tolerance appears to have been shared by at least some of his contemporaries and near-contemporaries, for literary histories echo one another in telling us that Baššār ibn-Burd (c. 714–84) used 'Nabatean' – that is, 'vulgar' – words in his verse, and >Abū l-<Atāhiya (748–828) is said to have 'brought the language of the marketplace into poetry'. Yet one searches in vain for such malfeasance in their collected works. Why?

The reason is that soon after this generation a *sine qua non* for admission to the literary canon came into being, too absolute and too widely accepted to need formulation until it was challenged in modern times by writers attracted to European literary practice where the idiom of everyday speech is also the literary medium, the most outspoken and eminent proponent of the new dispensation being Maḥmūd Taymūr (1894–1973),[4] although he later converted to the opposite view. The debate was often vehement, such labels as 'linguistic heresy' – *kufr luxawī*[5] – being attached to any proposed departure from classical grammar. But it fell to the leading modernist of his generation, Ṭāhā Ḥusayn (1889–1973), to articulate most cogently and persistently the case for the retention of age-old standards, which he deemed necessary for the preservation of the Arab cultural heritage and capable of meeting modern needs, whereas he branded its colloquial form as a corrupt dialect incapable of giving voice to the concerns of advanced intellectual life.[6]

In fact – as we shall see when we come to modern times – almost by default, the vernacular has gained a foothold in the theatre and in the dialogue of novels and short stories, but it is still resisted, especially in poetry.

The Formation of an Elite

Such ardent and long-lasting attachment to classical norms was necessarily the appanage of an elite that was not always free of contempt for the common herd. >Abū Ḥayyān at-Tawḥīdī (b. between 922 and 932, d. 1023), though he found some excuse for them in their extreme poverty, could write of the vulgar and mean that they 'have no virtues worth mentioning, no vices worth proclaiming ... So small-minded are they and so mean-spirited, so sordid by nature, that they could not possibly achieve any kind of fame or notoriety.'[7]

There is not even a similar palliative to the heavy sarcasm of Yūsuf ibn-Muḥammad aš-Širbīnī's (d. 1687), *Hazz al-Quḥūf fī Šarḥ Qaṣīd >Abī-Šādūf*, a punning title which may mean either '"the shaking of heads" or "the stirring of the yokels" – purporting to be a commentary on the poetry of >Abū Šādūf'. Its opening lines are:

> Praise be to God Who has honoured mankind with an articulate tongue ... Who has made natures different and manners divergent over the ages, distinguishing the men of good taste by subtlety of character and sweetness of tongue, and reserving ill-disposition and thick temperament to their opposites, the common country folk and vile denizens of animal pens.

Its centrepiece is a mock ode with an equally inept commentary said to have been composed by a peasant ludicrously named 'Father of a shadoof', and this is supplemented with innumerable anecdotes mostly deriding peasants who try to ape their betters. Some modern commentators want to see in it a disguised denunciation of a minority's sense of self-importance; but the humorous tone is not enough to discount the condemnatory intent, for the text is larded with authoritative quotations. One anecdote, for example, tells of a king who is moved to pity at the sight of a miserable peasant and considers redeeming the peasant's son by educating him. The vizier, who is ultimately proved right, tries to dissuade him with a quotation attributed to <Alī: 'Do not bestow learning on the children of the low-born (*safalah*), for once they have attained it they seek high positions, and if they obtain them they apply themselves to humiliating the noble (*ašrāf*).'[8]

Even more extreme and more difficult to ignore in this respect is Abū-Bakr Muḥammad ibn-Ṭufayl's (c. 1100–85), *Ḥayy ibn Yaqẓān*. Cast in the form of a long narrative about a child who grows up on an island where he has no contact with any human being and who solely by the exercise of his cognitive powers gets to know all that sensory experience, scientific observation, philosophic reasoning and mystical experience can teach. When at last he comes into contact with a Muslim community, he finds that the conclusions he has reached are congruent with what has been revealed to them *as it is understood by the most perceptive of them*, but trying to take others beyond the literal meaning of the teachings they previously received merely irritates and antagonises them. He realises that 'the sole benefit most people could derive from religion was for this world, in that it helped them lead decent lives without others encroaching on what belonged to them'. Concluding that most men are 'no better than unreasoning animals', he does not merely leave them in their inadequate understanding but confirms them in it. 'He told them that he had seen the light and realised that they were right. He urged them to hold fast to their observance of all the statutes regulating outward behaviour … [and] submissively to accept all the most problematical elements of the tradition.'[9]

The significance of these attitudes is not to be discounted, but neither is it to be taken as the final characterisation of a culture. So imposing a scholar as <Abd ar-Raḥmān Ibn-Xaldūn (1332–1406) perceived quality in the poetry composed by Bedouins of his day in their own dialect.[10] And even as he argued against the admis-

sion of folk texts to the literary canon, Ṭāhā Ḥusayn conceded that they could be enjoyable,[11] and enjoyed they were at all levels of society.

Two Literatures

(1) Early Manifestations

Nevertheless, the unyielding distinction made between the intellectual and artistic activities of the elite and comparable pursuits of the common folk solely on the ground of their mediums of expression ensured that they ran separate courses and left separate records.

Both grew out of the same root. Both functioned in the same society, although in different strata; both professed the same faith, although they understood it with different degrees of penetration and subtlety.

On the literary scene, the pre-Islamic poetry that was one of the two props of the elitist writers' linguistic commitment also functioned as their aesthetic measuring rod, its prosody and conventions commanding such approbation that it became known as 'the tent-pole of poetry', not substantially challenged or modified until the middle of the twentieth century. Until radical change was forced upon it by European penetration, confident of its grounding, resistant but not immune to innovations, the elite went on to build a mighty and decorative edifice the main lines of which are too extensive and too well known to be surveyed here; but germane to the present discussion is a complex of observations consonant with the importance given to language per se. It is that – as evidenced in pre-modern Arab literary criticism – (1) poetry was treated as the heart of all literary expression, (2) content and style were deemed to be entirely separable, as is implied, for example, in the introduction of Ibn-Qutayba's (828–89), *Kitāb aš-Ši<r wa š-Šu<arā>*, and precedence was given to expression rather than content, and (3) a taste for verbal ornamentation grew, and led to the creation of an entire branch of rhetoric known as *badī<*, which was concerned not with imagery but with wordplay, recognising or devising some 180 'embellishments'.[12] And though many deserved subtler treatment, it is mainly for their mastery of words that poets were praised or condemned.

Also consistent with the key position given to poetry is that few prose writers commanded the attention of the critics, and when they did it was again for their skill in handling words that they were celebrated. As for features distinctive of prose genres, such as narrative structure, they attracted no critical attention of any kind.

The entire record of folk literature, on the other hand, has suffered from neglect, not to say disdain.

It was, of course, primarily oral, and as such unstable and impermanent, and on the rare occasions when a folk composition was committed to writing, this was by some anonymous scribe, perhaps at the behest of a private collector or to meet a limited demand among the literate. Such manuscripts had an even slimmer chance than those of learned authors of being handed on from generation to generation.

Furthermore, they were subject to some distortion as they passed through the filter of an educated scribe's tastes and prejudices, for they were made at least minimally conformable with classical syntax. This process was less obtrusive when applied to prose compositions than to verse, where scansion and rhyme would have had to be adjusted. Yet from an early stage there must have been at least work songs, love songs, wedding songs, but none has come to light that we can confidently ascribe to the earliest stage of this survey.

This is to say that the very process by which the development of folk literature could become known was bound to produce a fragmented and skewed record, and at the outset the role of folk poetry was obscured.

The prose genres, especially the narrative, were better served.

In the early material that formed the shared heritage of the elite and the common folk there was a good deal that could feed this genre at either the high or the low level. The deeds, historical or legendary, of pre-Islamic and early Islamic heroes were a powerful source of inspiration. So were beliefs in superhuman agencies, some supported by the Revelation and some of older origin, such as that each poet had a familiar spirit, or that there were *jinn* and sorcerers capable of metamorphosis, and wielding great powers over humans. One may even include flashes of the popular imagination, such as travellers' tales and descriptions of fantastic animals that found their way into a succession of treatises started by al-Jāḥiẓ's *Kitāb al-Ḥayawān.*

There was even material accepted as factual – as *axbār* – that (if only it had been couched in a regional vernacular) might have been recognised as folklore. Such are the early Islamic accounts of the lives of the *<uḏrī* poets, each of whom suffered the pangs of unfulfilled love because social convention debarred a man from marrying his beloved if his love had been made public. Ṭāhā Ḥusayn was first to observe that such a convention is not attested anywhere else, and that the stories told of different poets are suspiciously similar; he was particularly sceptical about the elaborations concerning Qays ibn al-Mulawwaḥ, who was said to have gone mad for love of Laylā and to have chosen to live in the wild consorting with gazelles.[13]

But the literary establishment was uneasy about any narrative fiction intended only for entertainment, if only because of a derogatory reference in the Qur>ān (31:6) to 'one who buys idle stories in order to lead men astray from the path of God'. Accordingly, pedigreed writers made abundant use of anecdotes, but these were presented as historical or edifying. Yet the appeal of storytelling is so universal and self-justifying that the pretence that it was motivated by loftier purposes was sometimes dropped, as in Abū-<Alī at-Tanūxī's (940–84), *al-Faraj ba<d aš-Šidda* ('Relief after Hardship'), where some of the narratives bear a close resemblance to those we find in the universally known folk collection, *The Thousand and One Nights*, with nothing to indicate whether either served as a model for the other. The elite's interest in narration is also attested by <Abd-Allāh Ibn-al-Muqaffa<'s (early eighth century) translation of *Kalīla wa Dimna* and in edifying imitations that followed, whereas Muḥammad Ibn-<Abdūs al-Jahšiyārī's (d. 942–3) attempt

to collect Arabic, Persian and Greek stories did not command the same approbation and his work in this respect did not survive.

In the end, the only narrative genre established and creatively pursued in pre-modern elite literature was the *maqāma*. Badī< az-Zamān al-Hamaḏānī (968–1008) was long credited with having invented it; but his contribution is better understood as having given an artful and highly ornate expression to a kind of anecdote long popular about the *ṭufayliyyūn*, characters who used their wits to make a living off their betters; and the devices they are said by al-Hamaḏānī to use in achieving their ends – petty frauds, deft trickery and clever use of words – are characteristically folk.

The folk artists, on the other hand, had no inhibition about drawing freely from any source or resource available. The Arabic book most widely known among non-specialists of Arabic literature is *The Thousand and One Nights*, an admirable collection of fables, tales, romances and humorous anecdotes skilfully told. The rare survival of a manuscript fragment[14] enables us to trace its beginnings to a translation of Persian stories in the eighth century, but it was to go through a number of transformations before it took the shape of the fourteenth-century manuscript which was edited by Professor Muḥsin Mahdī (1926–2007) in 1984. Such documentation of an early development in folk literature is a matter of luck, for the tendency of the elite was to ignore developments outside the range of its own interests.

Nowhere was the gap wider than in two areas of creativity in which the elite writers took no part at all. One was the epic, in which folk artists have created more than ten narrative cycles,[15] which some scholars regard as romances, but each of which is centred in the exploits of a warlike hero who may be pre-Islamic, such as the poet-warrior <Antarah ibn-Šaddād, whose name is shortened to <Antar, or a much later historical figure, such as Abū-Zayd al-Hilālī, whose tribe fought on behalf of the Fatimid ruler of Egypt in the eleventh century in protracted efforts to subdue the North African Zanātah tribe. These epics, though they have no fixed text but are told or sung in each performer's words, have enjoyed more than a passing vogue: a manuscript titled '*<Antar*' is listed – and described as 'coarse' – in the tenth-century *Fihrist* of Ibn an-Nadīm,[16] and the Hilālī saga is still recounted in Egypt, and has been acknowledged by UNESCO as 'a masterpiece of the intangible heritage'.

The other creative endeavour peculiar to folk artists was a variety of theatrical activities, possibly starting as early as in the eighth century and ranging from pageants to shadow plays to dramatised monologues to rudimentary playlets.[17] These left no literary record other than three bawdy shadow plays by Šams ad-Dīn Muḥammad ibn-Dāniyāl (d. 1310), mostly in classical Arabic.

(2) The Andalusian Experience

Yet in time folk literature did break the surface of literary history. That was in Islamic Spain, and the service rendered is but one part of the notably distinctive contribution Andalusia made to Arabic literature, presumably because the region was never as thoroughly Islamised or Arabised as were territories in North Africa or the Middle East. Many of the people known to Europeans as Moors were Iberians who adopted Islam as their faith and Arabic as their language, and of them those who were steeped in the new culture produced verse and prose compositions scarcely distinguishable from those that reached them from the heartlands. But they had relatives and friends who no doubt were to various degrees conversant with, and appreciative of, both the local surviving and the imported dominant cultures. So it is that texts that must have been known, and indeed been generated, further east, such as the legend of Alexander and a popular account of the Prophet's ascent to the heavens,[18] surfaced only in Andalusia and have survived not in their Arabic originals but in European translations.

More directly relevant here is that Andalusia gave full recognition to Abū Bakr ibn <Abd al-Malik ibn Quzmān (c. 1086–1160), a man of some learning, well connected and well acquainted with classical poetry, but celebrated for his multi-rhymed compositions in the vernacular, some clearly intended to be accompanied by comic theatrical activity.[19] The specific prosodic form he used was known as *zajal*, but later the term stretched to cover all verse compositions in the regional vernaculars of the Arabic-speaking world.

This openness of Andalusian society to cultural cross-fertilisation also made its mark on the literature of the elite. Obviously related to the *zajal* is the *muwaššaḥ*, a stanzaic verse form in classical Arabic, except that the concluding couplet, the *xarja*, was sometimes in a mixture of Arabic and Romance and could in fact be borrowed from an existing popular song. It was long assumed that the lowly *zajal* derived from the loftier *muwaššaḥ*, but an indication that both were tarred with the same brush is that such a pillar of the Andalusian elite as >Abū l-Ḥasan ibn-Bassām (1084–1147) in his *aḏ-Ḏaxīra* excluded both *zajal* and its putative parent from the canon, and recent scholarly opinion has been veering towards a reversal of this chicken-and-egg relationship,[20] also raising the question as to whether they both derive from earlier sources.

And is it too far-fetched to attribute the appearance of other features of Andalusian literature unparalleled elsewhere to the same readiness to overstep conventional limitations? One such feature is the use of a narrative framework (as is not unknown to folk artists) to serve an expository purpose. A rather pedestrian example of this is *Ḥadīṯ Bayāḍ wa Riyāḍ*,[21] which strings together the commonplaces of Arabic love poetry into a narrative of the ups and downs of a pair of named lovers. More impressive is >Abū <Āmir Aḥmad ibn-Šuhayd's (992 or 993–1035), *Risālat at-Tawābi< wa z-Zawābi<*,[22] in which the author exploits the pre-Islamic folk belief that each poet has his own familiar to perform a fine piece of literary criticism by describing the author's otherworldly encounters with these spirits of ancient poets, emulating their styles and comparing them with his own. And unique in pre-modern Arab literature is Ibn Ṭufayl's *Ḥayy ibn Yaqẓān*, which has already been cited above for its elitist assessment of the common man, but which deserves greater attention as a book-length sustained and self-consistent narrative with a philosophical purpose: it starts with a folk tale of a child who is reared by a gazelle in isolation from humans, then the story is developed to show how, solely by the exercise of his human faculties, he goes on to reach the highest stages of scientific and religious cognition before finally getting the opportunity to compare his attainments with those of others who have had a divine revelation.

(3) Hybrid Forms

What needs to be stressed here is that the distinctiveness of the Andalusian literary scene is not that it created unprecedented literary forms, but that it led the way to scholarly recognition of a phenomenon active throughout the Arab world.

Indeed, once Ibn Quzmān had opened the door to literary activities that overstepped the strict limits of the literary canon, eminent authors in the heartlands began to catalogue parallel genres long known to them. First of these authors was Ṣafiyy ad-Dīn al-Ḥillī (1278–c. 1349),[23] who described and illustrated – mainly by compositions of his own – five long current genres distinguished mainly by their prosodic forms, but to some extent also by their function. Together with classical poetry and the *zajal*, these came to be known as 'the seven arts' even after followers of al-Ḥillī had added several to the list. The beginnings of these 'arts' are fancifully described rather than documented, but the labels attached to some of them, such as the *mawāliyā* (now more commonly known as the *mawwāl*) and even more obviously the *dūbayt* hint at a non-Arab element in their ancestry.

This – and perhaps some socio-economic readjustments that developed as trade guilds prospered and the Arabic language lost its supremacy in the Mamlūk age – diminished somewhat the elite's antipathy to all but strictly classical standards. A few well-born and educated men, such as >Abū l-Ḥasan <Alī ibn-Sūdūn(1407–64),[24] made a living and something of a name for themselves by catering for the lowbrow. A more consistent and significant trend is that it became acceptable for an established poet occasionally to compose some verse in the vernacular; but such exercises were looked upon as mere witticisms, and were usually excluded from the poet's *dīwān*. Possibly exceptional was <Abd Allāh Xalaf ibn Muḥammad al-X̱ubārī, who flourished in the second half of the fourteenth century. He was a highly respected traditionalist who was also reputed to have compiled an entire *dīwān* of his contributions to vernacular poetry, but of this there is no hard evidence, and only a handful of his compositions in the vernacular, all on conventional themes, has survived.[25]

It must be stressed that none of this – neither Andalusian *zajal* nor its parallels in the heartlands – is folk literature, nor does it signal an acceptance of folk compositions into the literary canon. At most it may reflect some aspects, mainly prosodic, of the practice of folk artists, but always with reservations. Some of the leading exponents of the 'seven arts' were apologetic about the direction taken. Al-Ḥillī himself wrote,[26] 'I did in my youthful days compose a great deal in three of the "seven arts", but I set no great store by these and had not intended to incorporate them in writing-books', and he went on to imply that it was only at a patron's request that he had retained just enough to illustrate the various forms. Folk narratives in prose, epics and theatrical representations inspired no parallel developments in elite writing. And from Arab literary critics neither prose nor verse compositions of lowly origin received any attention before the twentieth century.

(4) The Moderns

In modern times, the old elite attached to traditional Islamic values subsists, but it has been elbowed into second place by a new one that has come to accept – in a modified form – most of the literary and many of the social values of the West. Influenced by Western political 'isms' too, it sees itself as the guardian of the common people's interests, the guarantor of their future. It remains an elite, however, albeit a benevolent one.

And its attachment to the classical language remains strong. At most it has tacitly accepted that the vernacular has a justifiable place in the theatre and in the dialogue of works of fiction. The point was made when Maḥmūd Taymūr was elected to the Egyptian Academy of the Arabic Language that it was only what he had written in the classical language that qualified him for the honour; but a generation later no critic would exclude the plays which Yūsuf Idrīs (1927–91) wrote in a lively vernacular from what is now often called *adab rasmī* ('official' or 'formal' literature). Poetry, however, remains the inner sanctum of classicism: as late as 2000, a collection of the poems by >Aḥmad Šawqī (1868–1932), entitled *aš-Šawqiyyāt* and edited by <Alī <Abd al-Mun<im <Abd al-Ḥamīd, excludes all his *zajal* compositions.

Otherwise the use of the vernacular by literate authors is relegated to a category known as *>adab <āmmī*, in which the word *>adab* denotes recognition as literature of a kind, and the modifier *<āmmī* identifies the language as 'vernacular' or 'colloquial', but may also carry the sense of 'common' or 'general'. And this *<adab <āmmī* is widely accepted at all levels of society as a valid and enjoyable, but separate form of expression, especially as it has expanded to include much humour and biting social satire. It is a convenient grey area which may serve as limbo for what is inadmissible to the canon, sometimes also as purgatory for what may be on its way to promotion.

An example of how accommodating this grey area of *<adab <āmmī* can be, merging material from different sources and perhaps easing passage to different levels of acceptance is that when in the nineteenth century theatrical performances on European models became popular without as yet being regarded as literary, the *Thousand and One Nights* provided the subject matter for virtually all the comedies and musical plays of <Aḥmad >Abū Xalīl al-Qabbānī (1841–1902). The *Nights* have since earned fuller acceptance largely – as was conceded by Ṭāhā Ḥusayn in 1948 – because they commanded unstinted admiration in the West.[27] In numerous dramatic and fictional works, Šahrazād has now acquired a new function as a champion of the weak – not only women but also disadvantaged men – again advancing modernistic values. Two half-breed forms of literary expression seem to have risen in status by joining forces.

Folk literature also is now dignified as *>adab*, but qualified as *ša<bī*, literally 'popular'. And since the middle of the twentieth century it is accepted at least as a valid subject for academic enquiry, although not as an integral part of Arab perception or artistry. Even contributors to their study – like al-Ḥillī before them – are sometimes apologetic about their interest in it, as was <Alī al-Xāqānī (1912–79) who launched the publication of a series of folk texts with an introduction bewailing the fact that their language was the result of seven centuries of decadence.[28]

Their Interactions

This delineation of the historical record opens the way to a consideration of how the two literatures have interacted.

Before the nineteenth century, the Arab elite drew directly on its inheritance and borrowed judiciously from the Greek, the Persian, and the Indian civilisations it encountered, empowering itself to give eloquent and increasingly decorative expression to the highest attainments of Arab-Islamic civilisation. But having set up a rigid barrier against linguistic corruption, it scarcely heard the rumblings in its underbelly. And its very success made it resistant to change. Yet on the few occasions when it lowered its guard against seepage from the lower levels of society, its literature was enriched – with the development of the *maqāma* and with the adoption of multi-rhymed verse forms pioneered in Andalusia.

Modern developments – as we have seen –included a measure of recognition of the folk literature, but not its integration into a common cultural process. Modernists like Ṭāhā Ḥusayn and Tawfīq al-Ḥakīm (1898–1987) were familiar since childhood with Arab folklore, but their knowledge of it was at best subliminal, as is indicated by the fact that when comparing their literary heritage with that of Europeans they sought – and found – plausible reasons why the Arabs had produced no epic and no dramatic works, as if folk achievements in these fields did not exist.

The folk literature, on the other hand, dips into any source that flows its way. One encounters in it elements akin to Pharaonic, Persian, Indic, Hebrew, even occasionally European culture.[29] It is, of course, no less receptive of what trickles down to it from on high. Its carriers are respectful of the elite, sharing with it its basic religious tenets and mostly yielding to it the regulation of the social order. But did the linguistic barrier set up by this elite hinder communication in both directions? The Sufi brotherhoods have been a major conduit for interchanges. Accounts of their holy men have been bread and butter for folk artists. Even illiterate adherents of the Orders learn some litanies to be repeated by rote. The most celebrated Sufi poet, <Umar ibn al-Fāriḍ (1181–1235), composed verses in the vernacular. Did any compositions by elite poets, at least when they stooped to using the vernacular, actually pass into the repertoire of folk artists? If only because the authorship of a folk text is seldom recorded, direct evidence of indebtedness is not to be expected

except on rare occasions. But one such rare and precious occasion occurred when Mayy Ziyādah (1886–1941) recorded the texts of several popular songs that Syrians and Egyptians sang unaware that the lyrics had been composed by the established poet Ismā<īl Ṣabrī Pasha (1854–1923) or by the aristocratic, secluded, and highly cultured <Ā>išahTaymūr, daughter of a Pasha and wife of a Pasha, who wrote poetry in Arabic, Persian and Turkish, but also in the Egyptian vernacular.[30]

This does not amount to a great deal of cross-fertilisation. There is, however, a broader sense in which, through the medium of expression, the two literatures may be said to have been interactive. For all that they are decried as debased forms of the language, the regional vernaculars derive some benefit from the umbilical cord that still connects them to the mother tongue. Any religious activity, any dealing with the authorities, the merest modicum of formal education will engender some awareness of the classical language, of its authority, its prestige, its relevance. Only where these circumstances cease to apply, as in Malta, has the local form of Arabic developed into a separate language. Elsewhere the spoken forms of Arabic have remained relatively stable, fairly intelligible in neighbouring regions, their peculiarities sufficiently well known as to lend themselves to humorous or to stylistic wordplay exploiting differences encountered across borders.

Already mentioned as pertinent to the importance given to language per se is the pre-modern elite's delight in wordplay, the most prominent variety being the paronomasia, the *jinās*, which became increasingly elaborate and increasingly recherché. Whether by conscious imitation or by a parallel unfolding of an attitude to language, the folk poets have created a similar device which they call *zahr*, 'the flower', a favourite especially in the rhyming of the genre known as *mawwāl*. It consists of a multisyllabic pun, but one achieved by a deliberate distortion of the pronunciation, in which only the consonants remain true and anything may happen to the vowels, to the *hamza*, or to gemination. This I have called 'consonantal paronomasia', but Professor Dan Varisco has coined for it a far more aptly descriptive word: 'disenvoweled'.

Two short examples of the two practices will show both the kinship and the divergences between the two. The first occurs in <Abd al-X̱anī an-Nābulusī's (1641–1731), *badī<iyyah*[31] – that is, a poem in praise of the Prophet which, together with an ample commentary, is intended to illustrate and define all the varieties of *bad<* that have been devised. In it this pillar of the establishment roundly condemns the lowly *zahr* as a paltry distortion of the language; but the following three lines are quoted, without naming the author, to illustrate his entry on *al-jinās al-murakkab*, 'the 'conjunct paronomasia' in which a word is echoed by a combination of two. They run:

سألتُ وصـالًـها فأبتْ وصالى　　وآلَـتْ أنـها لا كلمتْنى
لقدْ صدقتْ وبرتْ غير أني　　رأيت لحاظها قدْ كلمتْنى
فقلتُ لـها دعي صدي وهجْري　　فعن حَمْل التجافي كَلَ متْني

I asked for union with her but she refused
And vowed she would not speak to me.
She has been truthful and kept her word, but
I find that her glances have scarred me.
So I told her, 'Desist from rejecting and abandoning me,
For of the burden of estrangement my back has wearied.

Compare with this tercet part of a somewhat irregular *mawwāl*:[32]

ṭabīb ya x̲ālī ta<ālā-lī w sallimnī
Physician, O dear one, come to me and make me whole
lamā kān ma<āy māl kānit kull in-nās tikallimni [tākul mannī]
When I had money, all people used to feed off my bounty.
>andah a>ūl yā walad, miyya tisallimnī
I had only to call out: 'Boy, hand me a hundred [coins]!'
lammā xaffı jēbī >andah <alā xūya bnı wāldī
Now my pocket is light, I call my brother, my father's son,
<imil aṭraš mā riḍīš yikallimnī
He pretended to be deaf and would not speak to me.
ra>adtı <ayyān lammā l-faršı kallimni [kallı minnī]
So I lay down ill until my bed wearied of me.

All these marks of linguistic kinship and divergence, however, loom large mainly because the old elite made language – indeed, a form of the language inseparable from a formal education – the sole criterion for the differentiation of the two literatures, and its modern successor has not entirely freed itself from the consequent priorities. This has had the effect of eclipsing vitally relevant issues, including intellectual, social and aesthetic perceptions.

The opening of folk material to modern academic research may be relied on to remedy this lack – eventually. But a great many more texts from different parts of the Arabic-speaking world will need to be unearthed and studied before clear patterns can be detected and described. In the meantime one cannot fail to notice – and to be disturbed by – instances of estrangement between the producers of the two literatures, as one stratum of society goes through a marked revision of its values and the other does not. Both the elite and the common people profess their adherence to Islam, but the elite has stressed its peaceable disposition and compatibility with the other Semitic revealed religions,[33] at the same time disclosing a more positive orientation by referring to Freud, or Marx, or Picasso or the exponents of structuralism as moulders of modern thought.[34] Of all this, very little has trickled to the masses.

One live issue affecting all levels of society will serve as a measuring stick: the status of women. The first Arabic book advocating the emancipation of women, for example – Qāsim >Amīn's (1863–1908), *Taḥrīr al-Mar>ah* – was published as early as 1899. Yet to this day, in Egypt at least, the favourite topic among folk singers is the 'honour crime' – the revenge killing of any kinsman of the murderer of a member of your family, and even more commonly the slaughtering by a father or a brother of a woman who has offended against the strictest of sexual codes. The practice seems closer to the standards of the Jāhiliyya (when, as implied in Qur>ān 81:9 some baby daughters were buried alive) than to Islam, but it is perceived as lawful, and the perpetrator is usually shown to be praised by the judge before whom he appears,[35] although in reality the law of the land does not condone the crime but finds it necessary to take a lenient view of it. Perhaps one should keep in mind that although the word *jāhliyya* has been given almost entirely pejorative connotations, the code of manly behaviour it embodied continued to be admired by Muslim society.

It is this that the folk artists retain. Elite writers, on the other hand, seem to be embarrassed by the persistence of such violence. They seldom broach the subject, and when they do it is not to inveigh against the perpetrator, but to approach the occurrence from a different angle, such as stressing the pathos of the victim rather than the machismo of the killer as did men of Ṭāhā Ḥusayn's and Tawfīq al-Ḥakīm's generation, or placing it in a politico-social context as did later authors such as Yūsuf Idrīs.[36]

To sum up: growing out of the same root, the literatures of the elite and that of the common folk have grown not in step with each other, but also not in mutual antagonism. And there is a sense in which they complement and accommodate each other. During the thousand years or so from the eighth century to the eighteenth when the high literature nursed its linguistic aestheticism, it could scarcely have remained so puristic if there had not been an outlet in folk literature for the intrusive realities of daily life. And during the two centuries of radical readjustment since then, it could not have moved at such a vertiginous pace had the humbler folk not had the possibility of keeping their feet on well-trodden paths, enabling them gradually to sense the need not to disown the past but to adapt long-cherished usages and assumptions to new necessities. As Lord Tennyson put it:

> The old order changeth, yielding place to new,
> And God fulfils Himself in many ways
> Lest one *good* custom should corrupt the world.

NOTES

1. See, e.g., <Amr ibn Baḥr al-Jāḥiẓ, *Al-Bayān wa t-Tabyīn*, ed. <Abd as-Salām Muḥammad Hārūn (Cairo, 1948), Pt 3, pp. 27–9.
2. See Manfred Ullmann, *Untersuchungen zur Rağazpoesie* (Wiesbaden, 1966). Several volumes of *rajaz* texts from the Umayyad period, edited by Jaakko Hämeen-Anttila have been published by the Finnish Oriental Society.

3. Ullmann, *Untersuchungen zur Rağazpoesi*, Pt 1, pp. 144–6.
4. 'Le Conflit des Langues Arabes dans la Littérature Egyptienne Moderne', *Actes du XVIIIe Congrès International des Orientalistes* (Leiden, 1932), p. 233.
5. <Abbās Ḥasan, 'ad-da<wa ilā l-<āmmiyya wa tark al->i<rāb intikās fī l-jahāla wa jināya <alā l-qawmiyya', *Risālat al-Islām*, 9 (1957), p. 149.
6. See, *inter alia,* his *Ḥadīṯ al->Arbi<a>* (Cairo, 1937) vol. 1, pp. 5–7; *ibid*., 1957, vol. 3, pp. 12–18; *Mustaqbal aṯ-Ṯaqāfa fī Miṣr* (Cairo, 1938), p. 236; *Xiṣām wa Naqd* (Beirut, 1963), pp. 87–8.
7. As translated by M. Bergé in '*'Abbasid* Belles Lettres', in Julia Ashtiany *et al*. (eds), *The Cambridge History of Arabic Literature* (Cambridge, 1990), p. 119.
8. *Yūsuf aš-Širbīnī's Kitāb Hazz al-Quḥūf bi Šarḥ Qaṣīd >Abī Šādūf*, Arabic text, edited and introduced by Humphrey Davies (Louvain, 2005), vol. I, p. 21.
9. *Ibn Ṭufayl's Ḥayy ibn Yaqẓān: A Philsophical Tale*, trans. with Introduction and Notes by Lenn Evan Goodman (Los Angeles, CA, 1983), pp. 163–4.
10. *The Muqaddimah*, tran. Franz Rosenthal, edited and abridged by N. I. Dawood (Princeton, ninth printing, 1989), pp. 456–9.
11. 'Al->Adab al-<Arabī bayn >Amsih wa X̱adih', *al-Kātib al-Miṣrī*, 1, 1 (October, 1945), pp. 11–13.
12. See <Abd al-X̱anī an-Nābulusī, *Nafaḥāt al-Azhār <alā Nasamāt al-asḥār fī Madḥ an-Nabī al-Muxtār* (Cairo, AH 1299/CE 1882), or my systematisation of it titled *The Arch Rhetorician or the Schemer's Skimmer* (Wiesbaden, 1998).
13. *Ḥadīṯ al->Arbi<ā>* (Cairo, 1937), vol. 1, pp. 217–25.
14. Nabia Abbott, 'A Ninth Century Fragment of the "Thousand Nights"', *Journal of Near Eastern Studies*, 8, 3 (July 1949), pp. 180–1.
15. See Malcolm C. Lyons, *The Arabian Epic*, 3 vols (Cambridge, 1995).
16. Muḥammad ibn Isḥāq ibn an-Nadīm, *The Fihrist of al-Nadīm*, ed. Gustave Fluegel (Leipzig: 1871), tran. B. Dodge (New York, 1970), vol. 2, p. 174.
17. A great deal of relevant information is conveniently brought together by Shmuel Moreh in his *Live Theatre and Dramatic Literature in the Medieval Arab World* (New York, 1992).
18. Enrico Cerulli, *Libro della Scala e la questione delle fonti arabo-spagnole della Divina Commedia* (Vatican, 1949). See also Item 13 in this book.
19. Shmuel Moreh, *Live Theatre and Dramatic Literature*, pp. 141–2.
20. The literature on the subject is too abundant and many-sided to be surveyed here, but a recent exposé of the intricacies involved is in the opening pages of James Monroe's 'Literary Hybridization in the *Zajal*: Ibn Quzmān's *Zajal 88* (The Visit of Sir Gold)', *Journal of Arabic Literature*, 38, 3 (2007), pp. 324–51.
21. In Cynthia Robinson, *Medieval Andalusian Courtly Culture in the Mediterranean* (London and New York, 2007).
22. Translated, with introduction and notes, by James T. Monroe (Berkeley, CA, 1971).
23. *Die Vulgärarabische Poetik – al-Kitāb al-<Āṭil al-Ḥālī wal-Muraḫḫaṣ al-Ğālī*, ed. W. Hoenerbach (Wiesbaden, 1956).
24. See his *Nuzhat an-Nufūs wa Muḍḥik al-<Abūs*, ed. and commented on in Arnoud Vrolijk, *Bringing a Laugh to a Scowling Face* (Leiden, 1998).
25. On the attribution to him of a long stanzaic poem on the Prophet's ascent to the heavens, see Item 13 in this book.
26. al-Ḥillī, *op. cit.*, p. 136.
27. 'Šahrazād', *al->Ahrām*, 13 September 1948.

28. *Funūn al->Adab aš-Ša<bī – al-Ḥalqa al->Ūlā* (Baghdad, 1962).
29. See my *Popular Narrative Ballads of Modern Egypt* (hereafter *'Ballads'*), pp. 92–4.
30. In *al->A<māl al-Kāmila* (Beirut, 1982; vol. 1, pp. 357–8.
31. An-Nābulusī, *op. cit.* (see also note 12), p. 13. His condemnation of the *zahr* is found in his entry on *tawriyah*, 'double entendre' (p. 188) and not the one on the paronomasia.
32. Sung by al-Ḥājj aḍ-Ḍuwī of Qūṣ and taped by the poet <Abd ar-Raḥmān al-Abnūdī. The full text occurs in Item 2 in this book. After the deliberate distortions I add, between square brackets, the words intended.
33. See my 'In a Glass Darkly: The Faintness of Islamic Inspiration in Modern Arabic Literature', *Die Welt des Islams*, 22–4 (1984), pp. 26–44.
34. See <Izz ad-Dīn >Ismā<īl, *at-Tafsīr an-Nafsī li l->Adab* (Cairo, 1963), p. 129; and Kamāl >Abū-Dīb, *Jadaliyyāt al-Xafā> wa t-Tajallī* (Beirut, 1979), pp. 7–8.
35. See *Ballads*, pp. 293–322, especially, p. 284, line 165.
36. See Item 18 in this book.

2

The Egyptian *Mawwāl*: Its Ancestry, its Development, and its Present Forms

One of many tantalising passages in *al-Bayān wa t-Tabyīn* comes in the context of the discussion of the superior eloquence of the Arabs, and proclaims the need to examine 'how the Arabs came to tailor measured tunes to measured verses, combining measured with measured, whereas non-Arabs distort words – now contracting, now stretching them – in order to fit them into the measure of the tune, so that they combine the measured with the unmeasured'.[1] Alas, the ebullient but undisciplined author never gets round to elaborating or illustrating his statement, and one is left with little more than an indication – scarcely surprising in an age of tumultuous racial and cultural contacts – that a multiplicity of artistic traditions was forcing itself on the attention of the intellectuals. Any resulting cross-fertilisation was presumably resisted by Arab and Arabised intellectuals of al-Jāḥiẓ's temper. It may nevertheless have played a part in the multi-rhyme experiments ascribed to Baššar b. Burd, Abū Nuwās and other poets of renown;[2] it may account for the appearance in Umayyad times of the *mutaqārib* metre, soon integrated into 'classical' prosody;[3] it may even have played a part in the emergence of the *x̱azal* genre in poetry.[4] The role of Persians in the development of Arab singing has long been recognised.[5] To what extent the popular literature of Arabic-speaking peoples was an amalgam of different lores and traditions can only be conjectured.

Indeed, almost every aspect of this popular literature – its early development, its distinctive features, its extent, its local sources of inspiration, as well as its reach across the Islamic world – must remain largely a matter of surmise. The attachment of the educated Arab to his language in its classical form has ensured that compositions in the colloquial have seldom been recorded or described. Verse fared even worse than prose in this respect, for whereas tales – like those of the *Arabian Nights* – were sometimes preserved once the language was recast in 'grammatical' form, metrical compositions did not easily lend themselves to such treatment; only now and then do they incidentally break surface in the written sources. The author of *al->Ax̱ānī*, for example, relates with manifest distaste an anecdote about Ibrāhīm al-Mawṣilī (d. 188/804) which includes a couple of lines he was reputed to have sung when in his cups;[6] they conform neither with classical grammar nor with classical scansion. Even if the story is apocryphal, it provides positive evidence that songs in the colloquial and at variance with the classical prosodic system were current in Iraq by the tenth century if not a good deal earlier.

Andalusian *zajal* is the first such form truly to emerge into the full light of literary history. From the twelfth century at least it is sufficiently documented to make a serious study of it possible, and indeed much has been written on its prosody and its possible derivation from either Arab or non-Arab sources. Yet it is by no means unlikely that comparable forms were in use in other regions of the Arabic-speaking world, and that what is distinctive of the Andalusians is not that they were the first to create metrical compositions that diverged from the norms of classical grammar and classical prosody, but that – because a substantial proportion of them were non-Muslims – they were the first to give these non-classical creations literary status, recording some of the texts and bestowing renown on some of the masters.

At all events, the *zajal* – together with its more classically worded cousin, the *muwaššaḥ* – quickly spread to other Arab lands. Furthermore, other non-classical forms were recognised and sometimes systematically studied, and some of these were said to have originated in much earlier days.[7] Together with the mono-rhyme ode and the Andalusian innovations, these came to be known as 'the seven arts' (*al-funūn as-sab<ah*), although it was not always the same seven that were listed.

It is evident that the non-classical 'arts' were practised and enjoyed not only by the masses, but also by the highly literate. A few of these recognised in them distinctive and worthwhile artistic qualities:[8]

> These are the arts in which declension is ungrammatical, chaste diction is barbarous, and mighty utterance is weak … Easy-flowing yet hard to control, accessible [to apprehension] yet beyond the reach [of emulation], in them have the commonalty long reduced the elite to impotence, their fluent compositions outstripping the resources of the eloquent. Let the master of [classical] eloquence attempt one of these arts and he finds that he has been deluded; he gulps but can scarcely make himself swallow.

Most educated Arabs, however, set such store by the classical language that they could not admit to the literary canon anything expressed in a different medium, regarding it rather as entertainment. That eminent men practised these non-classical arts is casually recorded from the twelfth century onward;[9] but the very few who, before modern times, acquired renown solely on such grounds were known as wits rather than men of letters.[10] And although a wide range of compositions in the colloquial has, in the past forty years, been receiving serious attention from a growing number of Arab scholars, the attitude is still encountered even among workers in this field that they are the debased products of centuries of decadence,[11] to which the vulgar may thrill but in which the educated find only an outlet for humour.[12]

These compositions therefore belong to a range of creative activity that is clearly not the same as what the Arabs call *>adab* without qualification; but neither is it entirely co-extensive with folk literature. It may conveniently be called 'popular literature'.

Highly regarded among the 'seven arts' was the *mawāliyā*, which al-Ḥillī calls a connecting link (or isthmus) between classical and colloquial forms, since it is in a classical metre and lends itself to compositions in both inflected and uninflected language. Insofar as one dare make general estimates in a field where much basic research remains to be done, it appears to have remained an extremely popular form in Arab countries from Iraq to North Africa.

Two somewhat legendary accounts are given of the origin of the *mawāliyā* and of its intriguing name. One, given in great detail by al-Ḥillī[13] and repeated by countless other authors, is that it was invented by the inhabitants of Wāsiṭ, who used it with all the magnificence of the classical language to serve the main motifs of classical poetry. Yet, because the songs they composed were short, they were easily picked up by the *mawālī* – the non-Arab Muslims who were also clients of Arab tribes – who sang them as they went about their lowly tasks, concluding them with an apostrophe to their masters: *yā mawālīyā*, hence the name. Then the art passed to the Baghdadis, who brought it to a high pitch of subtlety and refinement, at the same time stripping its language of all inflections, so that it is more commonly associated with them than with the Wāsiṭīs.

No date is given for these developments. The association with the *mawālī*, especially in the role of hewers of wood and drawers of water, suggests early times, for it is in late Umayyad and early Abbasid days that they became a prominent element in Islamic society. On the other hand, some of the *mawālīyās* ascribed to un-named Wāsiṭīs ill accord with an early dating, or even with the assertion of a general progression from the chaste to the commonplace. One of these reads:

أحبابَنا بالطلَبْ   للميَل يرجوني
مديّتُهم بالذّهبْ   أَضحوا يمادوني
منالَهم بالنّصَبْ   بالنّصْبَ يبدوني
مقصودهم بالكثبْ   للمال يعنوني

Our friends, explicitly, request my favour. I supplied them with gold; they now procrastinate. It's an effort to reach them; with trickery they face me. Their goal is at hand – it's for money they trouble me.

Of this al-Ḥillī says that it is distinguished by five artifices: the first is that each word begins and ends with the same letter; the second that each line consists of four words; the third that each line is made up of twenty-four letters; the fourth that in each line there are thirteen dots; and the fifth that each line has an additional 'b' rhyme in the middle.[14] Such verbal jugglery is out of keeping with anything we know of the early Abbasid age, and the language too – for all that it reflects the concerns of the highly literate – has the hallmarks of a late colloquial.

The other oft-quoted tradition[15] also maintains that the *mawālīyā* was born in Wāsiṭ, but goes on to associate it very precisely with the *mawālī* of the Barmecides, for the story is that after the fall of this great family the Caliph Hārūn ar-Rašīd forbade that any poetry be composed to praise or elegise them, yet a slave-girl of Ja<far's circumvented the ban by singing a *mawālīyā*, contending that it did not come within the definition of *ši<r*. Her actual words are recorded:

يا دارَ أين ملوكَ الأَرضَ أين الفُرْسْ
أين الّذين حموها بالقنا والترسْ
قالتْ تراهم رممْ تحت الأَراضي الدرسْ
سكوتَ بعد الفصاحهْ ألسنتهم خرسْ

O mansion! Where are the kings of the earth? Where are the Persians ? Where are those who guarded it with spear and shield? It answered: You'll find them as corpses under the wind-blown earth, Silent, who once were eloquent, and muted their tongues.

Alas for such a pretty story, its credibility is not enhanced when other versions put a different set of words on the songstress's lips, or confidently assert that her name was Mawālī or Mawāliyā, so that it is after her that the entire genre is called.[16]

Taken at face value, the anecdote implies that the *mawāliyā* came into being at some time in the eighth century, for Wāsiṭ was founded between 701 and 705, and the Barmecides met their doom in 803. The sober fact, however, is that the tradition rests on assertions made in much later sources. The earliest known mention of the *mawāliyā* is in a thirteenth-century manuscript,[17] and the earliest convincing attribution of a *mawāliyā* to a known author is to Ibn Nuqṭah, who died 1200–1.[18] The inference, of course, is that by then it was well established, and the silence of earlier authors may reflect no more than the prejudice that has already been shown to exist against popular literature; but another fact argues against a very early beginning. It is that all the references and examples I have come across in written sources, at least as late as the seventeenth century,[19] show the *mawāliyā* to have been metrically strictly uniform, whereas there have been considerable changes since.

A question mark must also remain against the derivation of the word – which incidentally may also be vocalised *mawāliyyā* and *muwālayā*, but such obscurity is shared by other terms in use in popular literature, such as the *>ūmā* and the *wāw.* It is very tempting to seek some connection between it and the *mawālī*, but its metre is a classical Arabic one, and there is nothing except the traditions we have examined to suggest that non-Arabs played a significant part in its development; indeed, the traditions may themselves be born of fanciful musings on a phonetic coincidence. Another conjecture is that – particularly in the form *muwālāyā – the* name is derived from *muwālāh* because of the 'continuity' or 'succession' of rhymes.[20] The collocation is strained and ambiguous, and the rhyming of the early *mawālīyās* seems scarcely distinctive enough to have provided the designation of the entire genre. Also a stab in the dark is the suggestion of some vague association with *walwalah*, 'wailing'.[21]

Another philological curiosity is that in Egypt today the word *mawālīyā* (pl. *mawālīyat*) is still encountered in print, but it is *mawwāl* – which was once used for a composer of the *mawālīyā* – which is more commonly used for the song; the plural is then *mawāwīl.* [22]

One is on firmer ground when examining the metrical form of the *mawālīyā.* The early written sources are unanimous in describing it as two verses of *basīṭ* with all four hemistichs rhyming alike; al-Ḥillī adds that the Wāsiṭīs initially called it a *ṣawt* or *baytayn*.[23] It is evident, however, that what in classical poetry would be a hemistich is here a complete unit, for it is always end-stopped, except in one well-defined position in the five-line *mawālīyā* it is always rhymed, and in later compositions it often occurs in odd numbers. It is this 'hemistich' – called *šaṭr* or *qufl* by al-Ḥillī, *šaṭrah* by modern Egyptian aficionados of the art who have a modicum of education, and sometimes *kilmah* by their humbler brethren – that I refer to throughout this article as 'a line'. All the pre-eighteenth century *mawālīyā* I have encountered are in fact mono-rhyme quatrains in the *basīṭ* metre with the last foot reduced to two long syllables, but the scansion requires such arbitrary vocalisation as has been inserted in the two quatrains already quoted.

Although the *mawālīyā* could accommodate both inflected and uninflected language, theorists such as al-Ḥillī strongly deprecated any mingling of the two idioms, and indeed roundly declared that the less *>i<rāb* was involved the better;[24] and the metrical adjustments deemed desirable or tolerable as a result of the use of the colloquial (alike in the *zajal* and the *mawālīyā*) were set out in some detail.[25] The main difficulty is that the suppression of desinential and other terminal vowels often produces that 'meeting of two quiescent letters' which the classical philologists and prosodists abhor, either in closed syllables containing a long vowel, such as *jār*, or in syllables ending with two consonants, such as *>̃abr*. The solution reached by the scholarly practitioners of the seven arts was a convention whereby – except at the end of a line – a short vowel was inserted after such syllables; but this was always an 'a' and *not* the vowel which classical syntax might have required.

It follows that choice diction and unvocalised script can sometimes combine to conceal most of the differences between an uninflected *mawālīyā* and classical verse. For example al-Ḥillī himself composed this panegyric *mawālīyā*:[26]

يا طاعنَ الخيلَ والأبطالَ قد غارتْ
والمخضبَ الرّبعَ والأمواهَ قد غارت
هواطلَ السّحْب من كفّيك قد غارت
والشّهْبَ من شاهدَتْ طلعتَكَ قد غارت

You who thrust at the horses as the heroes are charging,
Who make the spring encampment blossom when the waters have dried up,
Out of your hands bountiful clouds have brought succour,
And the stars, since they have seen your countenance, are jealous.

The first three lines could all have been vocalised in accordance with classical syntax and the metre would not have been affected; the only indications that the piece is intended to be in uninflected Arabic are in the fourth line, where *ṭal<atka* must be read without a desinential vowel, and where *min* is used instead of *munḏu*, which is explicitly said to be too classical for such compositions.[27] Actually, a modern

scholar has quoted it – with the *min* altered to *muḏ* and *ṭal<atka* to *aḍwāka* – as an example of an anonymous *mawālīyā* in classical Arabic.[28]

No such confusion could arise over Egyptian *mawwāls* in currency today. These appear at first sight to be much more of a folk art. One reason for the apparent change of status may be that the record of the past is distorted, in that it may have been filtered by intellectuals who retained only what they deemed worthy of retention and suppressed some of the more blatantly popular features. Another reason, however, is that in modern times the educated elite, which is largely urban, has assimilated Western European values and norms of literary expression much more quickly and extensively than the masses. Yet on closer examination one finds that some *mawwāls* are indeed composed, sometimes improvised, by village singers; but not a few are by literate town-dwellers. They sometimes appear in cheaply printed booklets before they pass on to itinerant singers, who may or may not be able to name the authors, and who may or may not alter the words. What is significant is that all the literate authors I have been able to trace are products of the traditional Islamic type of education, like the Azhari Šayx Muṣṭafā >Ibrāhīm <Ajāj, who died c. 1936 – an extremely prolific writer of *mawwāls* who appears to have wielded considerable authority in his day and is still remembered with respect by present-day singers. By contrast, the minority of modernists who take an interest in the *mawwāl* do so as researchers, as outsiders looking in. The line of demarcation between elitist and popular literature may no longer be the same as it was when the entire society was unquestioningly Islamic in the values it recognised, and distinctions were based on degrees of learning or sophistication or attachment to the classical language; but it is still not a matter of simple contrast between the literate and the illiterate, or the urban and the rural. Within the ambit of popular literature one does come across texts or features that bespeak now a town and now a countryside background, and there is ample room for even more detailed research into regional characteristics; but at least in so widely diffused a form as the *mawwāl*, internal literary evidence is seldom firm or sharp enough to authenticate the separation theorists would like to make between a 'pure' folk literature of peasant origin and a city-born counterpart of dubious pedigree.

I have never come across a modern Egyptian *mawwāl* in inflected language, although like other popular forms it may be studded with what may be called 'pseudo-classicisms', that is, words or constructions (like *mā>* for *mạyyah*, 'water', or *lam ṭafū* for *mā ṭafūš*, 'they did not extinguish') which differ from the norm of everyday speech but are far from unintelligible even to the illiterate.

Versification is often loose, sometimes even utterly capricious; yet whenever a regular pattern is detected, the metre is always the *basīṭ*.[29] When scanning folk verse, however, one has to take account of the fact that, whereas vowels are precisely regulated in classical Arabic, they are so cavalierly treated in everyday speech that there is little to be gained in recording such haphazard everyday variations. Our concern here, however, is to establish the metrical norms of the *mawwāl*;

so – exceptionally, throughout this article – any vowel that by the rules of classical syntax ought to be long but is shortened will be marked with a tilde.

The scansion is usually smoother if one gives terminal ā and ī full value as long vowels, although they are shortened in everyday speech – as in *<alã* or *<ēnĩ*; but there are hardly any other departures from colloquial pronunciation. The convention encountered earlier whereby an ‘a’ is added to a word that would otherwise have ended in two quiescent letters appears to have died out. Metrical regularity does occasionally seem to call for an additional short vowel to follow a closed syllable containing a long vowel; but this seems to me to happen almost always in contexts where a short pause would be natural; more often than not, a cv̄c syllable is treated metrically exactly like a cvc one. A short vowel is almost invariably inserted after a word ending in two consonants if the next one begins with yet another consonant, but this is a regular feature of everyday speech, as in *taḥtı rigluh*, ‘under his foot’.

Let me illustrate with a *mawwāl* of which I have three versions: one, which I shall call version ‘a’, was recorded for me in October 1972 by the popular one-armed singer nicknamed >Abū Đirā<, who confidently named its author as the late Muḥammad >Abū Sinnah, of aṭ-Ṭal>̃ah in Minūfiyyah; the second, ‘b’, is in an anonymous and undated booklet titled *Ḥadīqatal-<Uššāq*, bought in 1946; and the ‘c’ version is used as the opening of a longer *mawwāl* in another anonymous collection also bought in 1946 and named, after the main entry in the booklet, *Mawwāl l-Adham iš-Šar>̃āwī*. In the ‘a’ version reproduced below, the first line has an irregular ending: lines 2 and 8 have the first syllable of the *mustaf<ilun* foot replaced by two short ones; and line 7 needs a short vowel or pause after the word *šēx* to regularise the metre:

yã tāgir il widdı huwwa l-widdı šagar we >all[30]
You who would trade in affection, is affection [like saleable] trees and timber?

wa llã sawā>̃ĩ l-widād nazaḥit wi mā >hã >̃all[31]
Or have the waterwheels of affection dried, has their water diminished?

iyyām bi-nišrab <asal w iyyām bi-nišrab xall
There are days when we drink honey, and days when we drink vinegar;

w iyyām bi-nilbis ḥarir w iyyām bi-nilbis tall[32]
Days when we wear silk, and days when we wear hemp;

wiyyām ninām <a l-busāṭ w iyyām ninām fĩ ṭ-ṭall[33]
Days when we sleep on a rug, and days when we sleep in the drizzle

w iyyām bi-tīgi <alā wlād il-uṣūl tinzall[34]
And days that turn on the well-born, so they step down.

sa>altı min šēx >̃albuh fĩ l-humūm ṣandal[35]
I enquired of a venerable man whose heart is [as fragrant as] sandalwood even in the midst of cares

sanad il-kitāb min yimīnuh w iltafat >̃āl lĩ
He laid aside the book in his right hand, turned and said to me:

mīn <ašir in nadlı ba<d il x̱andarah yinzall[36]
'He who associates with the vile, though once lordly, will be humbled.'

May one assume that the metrical stringency of a *mawwāl* and the literacy of its author are correlated? The evidence is far from conclusive, if only because it is seldom possible to ascertain the origin of a *mawwāl.* At one extreme, the *mawwāls* printed under the name of a known master like Muṣṭafā >Ibrāhīm <Ajāj scan perfectly; at the other, some recorded from the lips of itinerant singers have no recognisable metre at all. The overlap in the middle, however, is great. In the example just given, it is the version orally transmitted that scans best, and also the only one that names a reputed author; and I have heard improvisations by performers of humble origin that are metrically unexceptionable.[37] An important factor, perhaps the most important, to be considered in an examination of the metre is that the *singing* of the *mawwāl* is essentially an interpretative art. There is no set tune, instead the singer now modulates, now drops almost to a speaking voice to bring out the sense or heighten the emotional impact of the words – as one of them put it, one cannot sing 'I am tired' (*ana ta<bān*) and 'Off to war!' (*yā llāh nḥārib*) in the same way. Performers also differ in the features of their art to which they give prominence, some favouring melody, some stressing the rhyme, some making free with wording and metre to achieve dramatic effect. In his extremely useful anthology of *The Folk Music of Egypt*,[38] Tiberiu Alexandru calls the *mawwāl* 'freesong', and readers who have access to the discs will find it revealing to listen to the third sample recorded, for it is yet another version of the *mawwāl* I have quoted. The words are not distinct throughout, but I transcribe them below as faithfully as I can, showing the length this particular singer gives to the vowels and the pauses he takes:

ya zāri< il wārd/ya zāri< il-ward iyāk il-wardı sagaruh >̃all/wa lla ssawā>̃i l-widād nazaḥit wa lla mā >̃all/wa lla ssawā>̃i l-widād nazaḥit/wa lla mā >̃all >iyyam bi-nišrab<asal/iyyam bi-nišrab <asal/w iyyam bi-nēšrab xall/w iyyam bi-nilbis ḥarīr xāṣṣ w ayyām/bi-nilbis tall w iyyām ninam<al-marāḍi/w iyyam ninam fi ṭ-ṭall w ayyam bi-tuḥkum wi tīrsim /<alā wilād il-mulūk tinzāll/ana ruḥtı li šēx<ālim/ya ma >̃albuh mn il-humūm/ya ma >̃albuh/ya ma >̃albuh min il humūm ṣandāl/rama l-kitāb min yamīnuh/w itlaffat >̃al li/min /<āšir in nadlı ba<d il-x̱andarāh yinzall[39]

The virtual disruption of the verse form may in this instance be partly due to the rather tame rhyming, for this *mawwāl* is atypical in its reliance on an echo effect based on a single consonant – the *rawiyy* of classical prosody. Mere rhyming is rather derogatorily called *tastīf*, 'stacking', and sustaining a single rhyme throughout is also unusual, for quite the most prominent feature of the modern *mawwāl* is the elaboration of rhymes and of rhyme schemes.

The aim in the composition of most *mawwāls* today is to have all lines, usually arranged in threesomes, end in paronomasias – preferably compound ones, in which a single word may be matched by a combination of words. This is usually achieved by a deliberate distortion of the normal pronunciation in ways already encountered in the examples quoted earlier. The liberties most commonly taken are with vowels: they may be dropped, arbitrarily lengthened or shortened, and freely interchanged. Here is an example:

> yã šagrit il-bunnı arḍik wēn fanāgīlik
> yã samrit il-lōn yã ramz il-<izzı fanāgīlik
> mi l-<aṣrı li l-<aṣrı nisma< rannit fanāgīlik.

Only in the third line has *fanāgīlik* the sense of 'your cups'; in the first, it is a distortion of *fēn agī-lik*, and in the second it is made up of *fanā gīlik*, so that the tercet may be translated:

> *O coffee-tree, what is your homeland? Where may I come to you?*
> *O dark one, O symbol of dignity, gone is the generation worthy of you.*
> *From one afternoon to the other we hear the clinking of your cups.*

Diphthongs may also become vowels, and glottal stops elided or inserted:

> yã llī šakēt mi z-zaman huwwa z-zaman bīdu>ēh [*i.e.* bidduh ēh]
> tišbah li <ayyān muš lā>ĩ d-dawã bīdu>ēh [bi-ydãwīh]
> izã mã radši l-karīm yib>ã ṭ-ṭabīb bīdu>ēh (bi īduh ēh)

> *You who moan about Fate, what does Fate want of you?*
> *You are like a sick man who finds no medicine to cure him.*
> *When the Bountiful One wills otherwise, what power is there in the physician's hand?*

Consonants are not amenable to such cavalier treatment except in respect of gemination and, occasionally, the interchange of phonetically related emphatics and non-emphatics:

> bi l-amsı gānã l-xabar b-innuh l-ḥabīb sāfir fī šahrı yũlyũ miwāfi> arba<ah sāfir [Ṣafar]
> za<a>tı w >ultı yã rayyis il-x̱alyūn sāfir [ṣaffar]

> *Yesterday came the news that the loved one had departed In July, corresponding to the 4th of Ṣafar.*
> *I cried out and said: O captain of the ship, blow the whistle!*

Exceptionally, regional differences of pronunciation such as the fact that *j* in Lower Egypt and *q* in Upper Egypt both become *g* may be exploited, as in the paronomasias with which the following *mawwāl* begins and ends, which are all pronounced *yigulēh*:

il-baxtı māyil wi ḥimlĩ lam aḥad yigulēh [yigilluh]
Luck turns away, and my load no one can lessen.

isma< yã <ā>̃il wi šūf ma<nã l-kalām yigulēh [yi>̃ūl ēh]
Listen, O wise man, consider the purport of my words, what they say.

ŧamãnyah li l-mar>ı ḥatman kullı zōl yigulēh [yīgū luh]
Eight things inevitably to every man must come –

kalām min il-<ilmı maktūb bi l->̃alam wafurāq [wi f awrāq]
Words of knowledge written with a pen on paper

il-farḥı wi l-ḥiznı<alã kull il-<ibād mãrrīn
Joy and sorrow by all God's creatures must pass

wa suqman wi <āfyah wa ya>tĩ gtim>ā wa furāq
And illness and health there will be meetings and partings;

wa<usrin wa yusrin wi min ba<dı ḥalã marrīn [murrin]
Constraint and ease; and after sweetness bitterness.

w il->̃albı ma<u>x</u>mūm wa lã yōm inšaraḥ wafurãq [wi fīh rāq]
One's heart is careworn; not for one day is it glad and serene

ḥattã <idānã warānã kullı yōm marrīn [māri>īn]
Even our foes are after us, wrangling every day.

illĩ ma<ăh māl tarã kull ir-rigāl nãsbūh
With him who has money all men seek a marriage alliance;

u yiddi<ũ bi l->̃arābah innihum nasbūh [nās abūh]
They pretend to be related, claiming to be his father's kin.

w in xassı māluh yi>̃ūlũ kulluhum nasbūh [nisībuh]
But if his wealth diminishes, they all say: Let's leave him alone.

tarakūh wi sãbūh wi fi l-ašl il-xisi< yigulēh [yigillū]
They have left him and abandoned him, revering baser birth instead.

It seems almost superfluous to add that differences of accentuation are totally disregarded, for the normal stress would be on the second syllable in *yi>̃īluh* but on the third in *yi>̃ūl ēh*. This *mawwāl* is also almost unique in my experience in that a declension plays an indispensable part in the paronomasia at the end of the seventh line, the nunation being needed to force *murr* into the same mould as *mãrrīn*. It is perhaps to prepare the way for this conceit that *<usrin wa yusrin* occurs at the beginning of the same line incorrectly declined, but faintly echoing a Qur>anic phrase (94:5, 6) familiar even to illiterate peasants.

The rhetorical device for which so much violence is done to the language is usually called *jinās*, 'paronomasia', sometimes *tawriyah*, 'double entendre', by those who have a modicum of education. Among the humbler practitioners of the art, it is more commonly known as *zahr*, 'flower', and the process of explaining the hidden meaning to the uninitiated is called *tazhīr*, by analogy with the opening of a flower.

Explanations are seldom needed by the villagers and inhabitants of the more populous quarters in cities who make up the regular audience of the *mawwāl* singer; they are on the look-out for the floristry, take great delight in spotting it, and when nonplussed are loath to admit it. But the puns are often so ingenious and complicated, not to say tortuous, that the casual observer may be thrown off the scent altogether, and assume that what he is dealing with is mere repetition.[40] A term is in use for a composition devoid of *zahr:* it is called 'white', *mawwāl abyaḍ.* But unlike 'blank' verse, this denotes not so much a recognised variation as a deviation from the norm. I have never known a singer to include in his repertoire a *mawwāl* which he acknowledged to be 'white'. Examples are given if specifically asked for; I have usually found that what they revealed was the informant's failure to detect the *jeux de mots*, but the misapprehension still helps to establish what the native artists understand by the term. Maḥmūd <Abd al-Bā>ī,[41] a devoted disciple of <Ajāj, explicitly declares the following to be a *mawwāl abyaḍ* because *ba<dēn* is used in the same sense at least in the first three lines (although I have other interpretations to offer):

>āḍĩ l-x̱arām gār axxar galsitĩ ba<dēn [ba< <adnĩ]
The judge in the court of love has been unjust: he has postponed my hearing and sent me away,

wi ṣabaḥtı miḥtār min gūr iz-zamān ba<dēn [bīh<adwanah]
I have become perplexed at the tyranny of Fate; there is enmity in it.

w illĩ nkatab <a l-gibīn >ismitĩ ba<dēn [b-a<īd anã]
What is written on my forehead is my portion, I keep saying
min ēn agīb ṣabrı yix̱nīnĩ <alã bu<duh [ba<ḍuh]
Where shall I find the fortitude to avail me against some of it?

anã hagart il-manām šuft il-<aƶab ba<dēn [bi-y<ũdnĩ]
I have forsaken sleep for I found it was torment that visited me.

iz-zād kamã ṭ-ṭabn[42] w il-mā> murrı min ba<duh
Food is like crumbs and water is bitter now he is gone.

lã xillī gānĩ wa lã rtaḥt anã ba<dēn [ba<dı >ann]
My beloved has not come to me, nor have I found rest after moaning.

u firḥũ l-<awaƶil ma< al-axṣām<alã bu<duh [ba<ḍ]
My censurers rejoice, as do my enemies, together.

w aṣbaḥtı ba<d il-ḥabīb a>ūl yã tarã w ba<dēn [bi<id wēn]
After my loved one's departure I keep saying: I wonder where he's gone.

as>alka[43] yā rabbı yã man >amartı bi-bu<duh
I beseech you, O Lord, who have commanded that he be distant,

tiktib lĩ >urbuh wa law sā<ah w >amut ba<dēn
Ordain that he be near, if only for an hour, and then I shall die.

If a *mawwāl* is not 'white', it is termed either 'green', *axḍar*, or 'red', *aḥmar.* The view most commonly asserted on the difference between these two is that the green *mawwāl* is cheerful, dealing with such topics as requited love and the bounty of nature, whereas the red is pessimistic, bewailing the sufferings of the abandoned lover, the plight of the orphan, the harshness of Fate or the disappearance of pristine virtues. Unfortunately, it is not always possible to fit the examples given by singers – who are seldom very articulate on theoretical problems – into the categories so described; and even in printed material one finds in a collection by <Ajāj that a *mawwāl* in praise of Khedive <Abbās Ḥilmī II as well as several others on love, both happy and unhappy, are all labelled 'red'.[44] At all events, the distinction is a matter of content and not of form, and it is essential that both green and red *mawwāls* should be 'flowery'.[45]

A further, but rather rare, embellishment may be an internal rhyme. This may be the same as the end-rhyme. I have come across only two instances of such an arrangement;[46] in both we have not simple rhymes but paronomasias, and the first term occurs not in the middle of the line but immediately after the first foot, that is – assuming the line to be perfectly regular – at the fifth syllable. Here is one:

fãris ramaḥ xal gãyy yubruz ma<ăy fĩ l-xal [*for* xalī *and* xalā]
wi nirkab il-xāl u titfarrag <alēnã l-xāl [xēl *and* xulāh]
w in kãn rāḍĩ xāl ḥ-as>īh il-marār wi l-xal [xill and xall]

A knight running free has come to joust with me in the open;
We mount our horses and are watched by the idle;
If he has a mate he satisfies, I shall make him drink gall and vinegar.

Slightly more frequently, I have encountered lines in which two simple rhymes, independent of the end one, are embedded; but I have never known this to be sustained right through a *mawwāl.* Here is a passage from one of many versions of the story of *Šafĩ>ah w Mitwalli*,[47] describing how the girl brought shame on her family:

Mitwallĩ <ēltuh tizīn il-gam<ı wiblādhum [wi baladhum]
Mitwallī's family was an ornament to the community and their village

wi f wusṭihum bintı lahã axlāq mafsūdah
But in their midst was a girl whose morals were corrupt.

min ṭafrit[48] il-**<arḍı** nāmũ <a l-**>arḍı** wiblādhum [wi balathum]
Making free with her honour levelled them down to the ground;
she brought them misfortune.

wi aṣbaḥū f **<ār** ka-mišlı giw**ār** mafsūdah [mā fīh sōdah]
They dwelt in shame as in a neighbourhood devoid of authority.

wi dam<ihum ṭabbı fōq il-xaddı wiblādhum [wi ballithum]
Their tears fell upon their cheeks, and they were soaked.

amruhum mak**tūb** ṣabax̱ it-**tōb** mafsūdah [mā> fīh sawād]
Their fate was decreed: their clothing was dyed in blackened water.

A line containing an internal rhyme of either variety is said to be *mikarrar*, 'repeated', or more commonly *misa>̃ >̃af*. The latter term is usually taken to mean 'roofed', each rhyme being topped by another; but a derivation from the clapping of hands would also seem to be appropriate.

In both varieties of the *misa>̃ >̃af*, the echo effect of the internal rhyme is achieved within the one line. The 'belted' *mawwāl* (*mumanṭaq*), which is marked by the recurrence of internal rhymes different from the end-rhyme at corresponding points in all lines (and which is exemplified by the first *mawāliyā* quoted in this study),[49] is not – as far as I know – in use in modern Egypt.

The last refinement to be noted in the modern *mawwāl* is the elaboration of rhyme schemes. The mono-rhyme quatrain is now out of favour, but not entirely unknown. Here is one, unusually deft in wording and even more unusual in that it does not trumpet its sentiment but implies it; it may well have been composed by an intellectual, but it has passed into the anonymity of a popular collection:[50]

wi ḥa>̃>̃ı yā badrı tax̱rībak wi tax̱rībī
lā titba< in-nafsı tigrī-bak wi tigrī-bī
xallī l-ma>̃ādir tigrī-bak wi tigrī-bī
wi tunẓur in-nās tagrībak wi tagrībī

It is right, O Moon[-like beauty], that we be banished, you and I.
Be not guided by the heart: it deludes us, you and me.
Let the fates direct our courses, yours and mine,
And let men see how we're tested, you and I.

The rhyme schemes more commonly in honour today all appear to have arisen from the insertion of additional material between the third and fourth lines of the original quatrain, so that no matter how long a *mawwāl* may be its last line almost always rhymes with the first. When so split, each of the first three lines is called a *<atabah*,[51] 'doorstep', the association being with the lowest part of a construction and the first to be laid down; implying a 'topping up' but without regard for consistency in imagery, the last line is then called the *ṭa>̃iyyah*, the 'skull-cap'.

The simplest regular rhyme scheme in use results from the addition of an unrhymed line to the quatrain, giving the arrangement aaaxa; this is called the *a<raj*, 'lame', or *muxammas*, 'fivefold', sometimes also *iskandarāni*, 'Alexandrian':

min ṣux̲rı sinnī w anā ḥādī wiraḥmālī [wi arā ḥimā lī]
fī l-barrı w il-baḥrı mitmaryis wiraḥmālī [warā aḥmālī]
w inṣaḥḥı lī ḍēm min ir-raḥmān wiraḥmālī [wi raḥmah lī]
w il-ḥanḍal il-murrı waṣafū-lī r-rigāl milā kēl
ṣabaḥtı mā lī kēf min id-dunyā wiraḥmālī [wi rāḥ mālī]

Since early days I have gone my own way and deemed me my own guardian.
On land and sea I have busied myself with my own burdens,
And from the Beneficent both hardship and mercy have been my due.
But bitter colocynth has been prescribed for me by men, in full measure.
Now I have no taste for this world, and my wealth is gone.

Not infrequently, the unrhymed line contains some part of the verb *qāla*, 'to say', and the last line is then a proverb or aphorism ascribed to some wise man:

in-nās bihā garḥı sālīhum wi kāyidhum [kayy iddīhum]
w anā ma<ī >alfı wi xṣāmī b-akāyidhum
w a<ūd ma<āhum wa tna>̃ >̃al min waḥāyidhum
mas̃al simi<nāh min illī >̃ablinā >̃ālū
fi l-gaddı xallīk u<and il-hazlı ḥāyidhum

Mankind has a wound: bring it solace – and cautery.
I have a thousand [allies]; my enemies I can outwit,
Then return to my own, and go from each to each.
Here is a saying received from our forebears; they said:
Stick to serious pursuits; stand aside from frivolity.

The first of the modern *mawwāls* quoted here,[52] though it runs to more than five lines, shares this feature, which is reminiscent of the Andalusian *muwaššaḥ*.

Another standard rhyme scheme is produced when instead of the single unrhymed line a tercet with a rhyme of its own is introduced; furthermore, the last line often has somewhere within it an echo – not necessarily a full paronomasia – of the new rhyme. This is called the *nu<mānī* or the *sab<ānī*, 'sevenfold', and may be represented as: aaa zzz (z)a. Here is an example, which incidentally is described as 'red' by the informant:[53]

>̃albī hiwī ẓabyı turkī wimat<aššāš [wi mētā<aššiš]
My heart is fond of a Turkish gazelle – when did she nest [in this land]?

xallā >̃atīl il-hawā mux̲ram wimat<aššāš [wi māt <a š-šāš]
She reduced the victim of passion to infatuation; he died [and was laid out] on the muslin sheet.

mimmā garā-lī abāt abkī wi mā t<aššāš
Because of what happened to me I spend the night weeping and have no supper.

xallã ḍil<ĩ nār u guwwa l-ḥašã xazzah
She has set fire to my ribs, and in my entrails is a thorn.

yã mã x̱iwãyāt fĩ baḥr il-hawã x̱azzah
How many temptations are out on the sea of passion, raiding!

illã l-<azūl fēn ramã fitnah wi rāḥ x̱azzah
But where is the reprover? He has sown dissension and gone off to Gaza.

yiblāh bi-x̱azzah fĩ ganbuh wimat<aššāš [wi mōt<a š-šīš]
May He afflict him with a stitch in his side – and death on a rapier!

Both the *a<raj* and the *nu<mānī* are well-established forms, known even outside Egypt; <Alī l-Xāqānī[54] asserts that they were evolved in the eleventh century AH (seventeenth AD), but he gives no evidence for such precise dating. A further form seems to have come into being in Egypt, probably late in the nineteenth century, for there is no mention of it in *Safīnat al-Mulk*, whose author[55] died in 1857, yet it is a favourite of <Ajāj who flourished early in the twentieth century and who used it in the *mawwāl* already mentioned in praise of <Abbās Ḥilmī II. Its distinguishing feature is the insertion after the third line of at least one sestet with two alternating rhymes, producing the scheme: aaa b cbcbc dede de fgfgfg … zzz (z)a. A *mawwāl* so constructed is called *mardūf*, which may be loosely translated as 'pillioned', for the alternation of rhymes is thought of as comparable with the placing of two riders on one horse. The addition of one sestet to the *nu<mānī* produces a thirteen-line *mawwāl*, that is extremely popular for lyrical purposes:

sã>yah min il-ḥubbı dãyrah wi t-turūs<ayzīn [<a yzinnũ][56]
A waterwheel of love, turning – its cogs are whining

sawwã>hã wād <āl luh kull il-milāḥ <ayzīn
Its driver is an excellent lad, for whom fair maids all invoke protection.

il-mã> zulāl ka l-<asal yirwĩ š-šagar <ayzīn [<a yizīn]
The water is sweet as honey; it irrigates the trees to make them decorative

yiṭraḥ safargal wi samānī wi l-kurūm <annāb [<inab]
They yield quinces and fat dates, and the vines give grapes,

wi l-gōz wi l-lōz min aḥlã ṭ-ṭa<am manãwīš
And walnuts and almonds – most delectable food – form patterns

il-baxšawangĩ āfandĩ yiṣallĩ kullı yōm<annab [<an-nabĩ][57]
The gardener is a gentleman who calls down blessings on the Prophet every day,

amīr min it-turk <alã fi <l il-azã manawīš [mã nãwīš]
A Turkish prince, with no intention of doing evil;

tãb<āh fawāris wi dīmã yišrukum <a n-nāb [<a n-nāb]
He is followed by horsemen constantly grinding their teeth.

il-<iṭrišān intašã x̱aṭṭã d-dūlāb manawīš [minnuh wišš][58]
The aromatic plants have livened, and covered one side of the waterwheel,

il-karmı ṭāyib wi ḥãlīh il->ilāh bi z-zahr [zahar]
The vines are ripening, and God adorns them with brightness.

nifsĩ anūl ma>ṣadĩ w ašrab <asal miz-zahr
I wish I could reach my aim and drink honey from the flowers.

ādi sabab >uṣrı bā <ī wi ḥall iz-zahr
This is the cause of my helplessness and my ill-fortune

yā xsārah iz-zihrı mã b-yiddīšı li l-<ayzīn
A pity – desire ensures no gift to those who want.

The multiplication of sestets in the *mardūf* is particularly well suited to the narrative *mawwāl*,[59] which may run to hundreds of lines; but it is no stranger to the lyrical *mawwāl* either. The sestet may also be extended, and further variations may be brought about by the omission of the zzz tercet immediately before the *ṭã>iyyah*, as in this *mawwāl* which may also be used to illustrate the degree of stability such texts enjoy, for it appeared in one of the many undated booklets published by <Ajāj, *Al-Fann al-<ajīb fī munājāti ṭ-ṭabīb*, and was also recited with very few variations, placed here between round brackets, by Maḥmūd <Abd al-Bā>ī in 1959:

yã ṭabīb mi<ī garḥı f <aḍāyã (ḥašāyã) walamutna [wi lāmĩ ŧŧanã]
Doctor, there is a wound in my organ (entrails)s, and my body writhes;

ma>fūl <alã x̱iššı fī gasadī walamutna [wi lōm atānī]
It has closed over treachery in my body, and a reproach has reached me.

w in ṭibt l-a<ṭīk mīt nā>ah walamutna [walīmitnã]
If I am healed I shall give you a hundred camels for our banquet.

>arrab ta<ãlgāy šūf garḥī halak kēfī
Approach, come near and see how my wound has destroyed my zest.

min >illit in-nōm mã hãn lī (ma hinīš) ṭa<ām wi šurāb
Because of sleeplessness I find no pleasure in food or drink.

wi <dimt il-aḥbāb mã <ād (wi lã <ād) lī kamān kēfi [kuf >ī]
I am now without friends, nor have I a peer [to associate with].

unẓur li-ḥālī tarã (>arrib ta<ālgāy šūf) lōnī n>aṭaf wišurāb [w iššarrab]
Look at my condition, you will see how pale and faint is my colour.

>āl iṭ-ṭabīb mã l-<amal (yã <alil) garḥak yi<ūd kēfī [kayyı fīh]
The doctor said: What is to be done O patient? Your wound needs further cauterisation,

lākin <alã šarṭı limm ahlak ḥidāk wišurāb [wi šūr abb]
But on condition you gather your kinsfolk about you and consult your father,

ḥattã li >̃arāyib il-balad (l-ḥabāyib il-bu<ād) ib<aŧ yīgũ fĩ l-ḥāl
Even your relatives at home (loved ones far away) send for that they come at once,

l-agl in garã šē> ab>̃ã min is-su>āl xalĩ
So if anything befalls you I shall not be answerable.

anã >̃ultı yã ṭabīb haddēt il-gawã filḥāl [fĩ l-ḥall]
I said, Doctor, you have appeased my passion by this solution.

i<mil xalāṣak mã fĩš lī ṣḥāb (mã līš ahl) wa lã xāli [xill]
Do what will satisfy you, for I have no associate (kinfolk) or friend.

sim< iṭ-ṭabīb il-kalām mana< (simi< il-kalām iṭ-ṭabīb ṣana<) id-dawã filḥāl [fĩ l-ḥallah]
The doctor listened to my words then withheld (made up) the potion in the vessel.

atarīh mixāwiz ramã s-summı wa lã xāli [xāl luh]
He proved a traitor who threw in poison – nor did it trouble him.

za<a>̃tı min <azmı mā bĩ (mimmã garā-lĩ) yã ṭabīb filḥāl [fallı ḥēlĩ]
The violence of what I endured (what happened to me) made me cry out: Doctor, my strength has unravelled.

ahõ zād <ayãya wa lã l>̃īt <ammĩ (wa lã gā-lĩ abb) wa lã xālĩ
My illness is worse. (No father has come.) I see neither paternal nor maternal uncle [by my side].

wa lã fĩš dawã ṣaḥḥı lã ṭibnã wa lã mutnã
There is no true cure: I am neither healed nor dead.

Indeed not all *mawwāl*-makers feel bound to adhere to a strictly regular rhyme scheme or to coin multiple paronomasias, as this green *mawwāl* shows:[60]

il-ḥilwı >̃āl lĩ ēš bi tākul >̃ultı lu>̃mah ḥāf
The fair one asked: 'What are you eating?' I said, 'A dry morsel';

w aṭḥan iṭ-ṭabnı fĩ kaffĩ w atiffuh ḥāf [ḥēf]
I crush the crumbs in my palm then spit them out – a waste!

>̃ālit ēš balāk bi l-maḥabbah >̃ultı naẓar yišāf [yišiff]
She asked: 'What has afflicted you with love?' I said: 'A glance that emaciates.'

šāyif wāḥdah gamīlah wi dãxlah <a l-balad di lissa [liṣṣah]
I see a beautiful girl entering this village like a thief.

mišīt warāhã w >̃ultı-lhã wi n-nabĩ <alafēn [<illah fĩnã]
I followed her and said to her: 'By the Prophet, we are afflicted.'

il-bintı ḥilwah >̃awĩ wi l-<a>̃lı labisha [il-lubbı sahã]
The girl was very pretty and my mind, my heart was distracted.

fiḍiltı miḥtār wi muš <ārif arūḥ <alafēn [<a l-laffı fēn]
I was left perplexed, and did not know where to go circling.

mišīt warāhã wi kãn biddĩ agãlishã
I followed her, wishing to sit in her company,

fĩmã >̃ālit il-bintı yã <āši>̃ tirūḥ <alafēn [<alã llĩ finĩ]
Whereupon the girl said, 'Lover, you will join those who have perished.'

>̃ālit yã x̱arīr dannak nāši> fĩ l-x̱arām lissa
She said, 'You greenhorn, you are still a novice in love.'

>̃ultı-lhã yã bint anã amatta< wi simtĩ alfēn [il-fann]
I said, 'Girl, I give pleasure. My way is that of art.'

mišīt ma<āhã wi biddĩ agalisha [agĩ li s-sahwah]
I went with her, wishing to get to the bedroom,

fĩmã >̃ālit il-bintı <iddı min id-dahab alfēn
Whereupon the girl said: 'Count out two thousand [pieces] of gold,

x̱ēr mã ti>̃la< hudūmak ill inta lãbishã
Besides taking off the clothes which you are wearing.'

>̃lĩ ṭafaš rāḥ muš <ārif hu rāḥ <alafēn [<ilĩ fēn]
My mind flew off, it went – I do not know where it has soared.

il-bintı ṭal>̃it bi-<ēnhã >̃umt anã ḥabbēt
The girl let her eye rove, and I fell in love,

wi >̃ult anaẓẓim <alēhã min kullı mawwāl bēt
And I said: 'I shall compose about her a verse of every [kind of] mawwāl.'

wi ḥliftı yamīnēn bi l-k<abah wi rabb il-bēt
And I swore two oaths – by the K<abah and the Lord of the House –

l-āxuđ wiṣālĩ min ḥabībĩ w il-<azūl lam šāf
That I should achieve union with my beloved while the reprover cannot see us.

A liberty hardly ever taken is the omission of a *ṭã>̃iyyah* rhyming with the opening line. The following *mawwāl*, which is also metrically very irregular, may be a fragment, but it was sung by a highly regarded singer as complete:[61]

mã dãm ma<āk māl yizhar lak kullı yōm ṣāḥib [sāḥib]
As long as you have money, even the cloudy day will brighten for you.

w il-jēb <amrān yitḥawaṭūk mīt ṣāḥib [sāḥib]
While your pocket is loaded, a hundred will surround you to draw [your money out].

ahō l-māl fara<u>x</u> rāḥ mã tlammĕtišwa lã <alã ṣāḥib
Now my money is emptied out, gone, and I meet not a single friend.

ṭabīb yã xālĩ ta<alā-lĩ w sallimnĩ
Physician, O dear one, come to me and make me whole.

lamã kān m<āy māl kānit kull in-nās tikallimni [tākul minnĩ]
When I had money, all people used to eat off me.

andah a>̃ul yā walad miyyah tisallimnĩ
I used to call out: Boy, hand me a hundred [pieces of gold].

lammã xaffı gēbĩ andah <alã xūya bnı wāldĩ
Now that my pocket is light I call my brother, my father's son,

<imil aṭraš mã riḍīšyikallimnĩ
He pretended to be deaf and would not speak to me.

ra>̃adtı <ayyān lammã l-faršı kallimnī [kall ı minnĩ]
I lay down, ill, until my bed wearied of me.

Needless to say, popular literature does not concern it self with problems of copyright, and the structure of the *mawwāl* is such that one man may not only adapt another man's work – and the same paronomasias do turn up in different contexts – but also expand it. In an undated booklet already old when bought in 1947, I came across the following lame *mawwāl:*

iṣ-ṣōt wi n-nāy wi l-ālāt ma<a l-<īdān
ya<milũ >ēh fĩ gismĩ ba>̃ã <īdān [<ayy ḍanĩ]
in-nās lahã <īd w anã lĩ fĩ l-li>̃ã <īdān [<īdēn]
yã akḥal il-<ēn itraffa>̃ bi-ḥālātĩ
xallēt gismĩ >̃afaṣ mabnĩ <alã <īdān

The tune, the flute, the various instruments with the lutes,
What can they do for my body? It is weak and emaciated.
People celebrate one feast [a year]; in love trysts I have two.
O dark-eyed one, take pity on my condition:
You have reduced my body to a cage made of dry sticks.

I remembered then that some six years earlier I had taken down from the lips of an itinerant singer this version, revealingly, if rather drearily, eked out:

il-<ūd wi n-nāy wi n-na<u>x</u>am wi ṣ-ṣōt wi ṣ-ṣalṭīn[62] wi l-<īdān
The lute, the flute, the melody, the tune, the psaltery, the lutes,

ḥa-y<amilũ ēh f illĩ gismuh ṣabaḥ <īdān [<ayy ḍanĩ]
What can they do for one whose body is weak and emaciated?

in-nās lahã <īd w anã lĩ fĩ l-li>̃ã <īdān [<īdēn]
People celebrate one feast [a year]; in love trysts I have two.

u fēn ḥabībĩ llĩ kunt ašrab kãsāt il-hanã wiyyāh
Where is my loved one, with whom I once drank cups of delight?

sāfir wi fãtnĩ wi dam<ĩ <alã l-xudūd >̃a<dīn [>̃ã<id dannuh]
He has gone and left me, and my tears are still on my cheeks.

anã kuntı <ašmān yihannīnĩ z-zamān wiyyāh [>aza> min nawãyāh]
I hoped that he would gladden me, but he turned back from his intentions.

xãyif a>̃ūl āh šãyif lammitĩ >̃a<dīn [>̃u<diyyīn]
I dare not say 'Ah!' for I find my kinsmen irresolute.

iḥtãrt arūḥ fēn wi balānĩ zzamānwiyyāh [z-zamān wayyuh]
I know not where to turn, and Fate has afflicted me – woe to it!

in gã ḥabībĩ l-ađbaḥ li ṣ-ṣafã >̃ã<dīn [>̃ã<ũdēn]
If my loved one returns, I shall slaughter two young camels to celebrate our union.

yã llĩ tilawwim <alayyã >̃arrab wi šũf ḥālĩ [ḥall]
You who reprove me, come close and find a solution.

iḥtārt arūh fēn w aškĩ li-mĭn <alã ḥālĩ [ḥu>ūlĩ]
I know not where to turn, to whom to complain of the change in me.

wa lã fĩšrafĩq zēn yīgĩ yšūf illĩ garã l-ḥālĩ [ḥōlĩ]
And I have no good friend who comes to see what has happened to my strength.

irḥam li-ḥālĩ ṣabaḥtı zayy il->̃afaṣ mirakkab <alã l-<īdān
Pity my condition: I am now like a crate made of dry sticks.

Insofar as an art form limits, directs or challenges the artist, the *mawwāl* does seem to channel much of his creativity into verbal games. But it is no straitjacket, and even its rigid rhyme-schemes have a stimulation of their own; the thirteen-line *mawwāl*, for example, has something of the balance and cohesion, the musicality and subtlety of the rondeau. With all its variations, the *mawwāl* offers much room for the interplay of words, images and perceptions.

Notes

1. al-Jāḥiẓ, *al-Bayān wa t-Tabyīn*, ed. <Abd as-Salām Muḥammad Hārūn (Cairo, 1948), vol. 1, p. 385.
2. See Johann Fück, *<Arabiya*, trans. C. Denizeau (Paris, 1955), pp. 82–5. Also >Ibrāhīm <Alī >Abū Xašab, *Tārīx al->Adab al-<Arabī fī l->Andalus* (Cairo, 1966), pp. 271–8.

3. L. P. Elwell-Sutton, 'The Foundations of Persian Prosody and Metrics', *Iran*, 13 (1975), p. 86.
4. Elwell-Sutton, 'The Foundations of Persian Prosody and Metrics', p. 92.
5. Ibn Xaldūn, *Muqaddima* (Cairo, n.d.), ch. 5, section 32, pp. 423–8.
6. Abū l-Faraj al->Iṣfahānī, *Kitāb al->Axānī* (Cairo, 1963) (reprint of 1927 Dār al-Kutub edn), vol. 5, pp. 156–7.
7. Ṣafiyy ad-Dīn al-Ḥillī, *Die Vulgärarabische Poetik – al-Kitāb al-'Āṭil al-Ḥālī wal-Muraḫḫaṣ al-Ġālī*, ed. W. Hoenerbach (Wiesbaden, 1956), p. 7.
8. al-Ḥillī, *Die Vulgärarabische Poetik*, p. 6.
9. See, e.g., mention of Šihāb ad-Dīn Aḥmad b. Muhammad b. Aḥmad, known as al-Fār, in Ibn Taxrī Bardī, *an-Nujūm az-Zāhirah* (Cairo, reprinted 1963), vol. 11, p. 106.
10. Such a man was Ibn Nuqṭah (d. 597/1200–1), mentioned in Ismā<il b. <Umar b. Kaṯīr, *al-Bidāyah wa n-Nihāyah* (Cairo, 1932–8), vol. 13, pp. 31–2.
11. <Alī l-Xāqānī, *Funūn al->Adab aš-Ša<bī, al-Ḥalqa l->Ūlā* (Baghdad, 1962).
12. >Ibrāhīm >Abū l-Xašab, *Tārīx al->Adab al-<Arabī fī l->Andalus* (Cairo, 1966), p. 299.
13. >Abū l-Xašab, *Tārīx al->Adab*, pp. 132–4.
14. >Abū l-Xašab, *Tārīx al->Adab*, pp. 133–4. The printed text has كسب for كثب in the last line. This reflects colloquial pronunciation, but leaves the line three dots short: as the Arabic 'ṯ' ث has three dots and the 's' س has none, the substitution destroys the boasted artifice of having the same number of dots in each line. The vocalisation of this *mawāliyā* and the next will be discussed below, beginning with note 24.
15. As-Sayyid Muḥammad b. >Ismā<Il b. <Umar Šihāb ad-Dīn, *Safīnat al-Mulk wa Nafīsat al-Fulk* (Cairo, 1309/1891-2), p. 380. The story is given there on the authority of as-Suyūṭī in *Šarḥ al-Muwaššaḥ an-Naḥwī.*
16. Buṭrus al-Bustānī, *Muḥīṭ al-Muḥīṭ* (Beirut, 1870), vol. 2, p. 2289.
17. *Majmū< Mawāliyāt wa Muwaššaḥāt*, Aya Sofia 4874, compiled at the behest of the Caliph al-Mustanṣir, d. 640/1242–3. For this and other pre-modern sources on the *mawāliyā*, see W. Hoenerbach's introduction to his edition of al-Ḥillī, *Die Vulgärarabische Poetik*, p. 24. Also >Aḥmad Taymūr, *Mu<jam Taymūr al-Kabīr*, ed. Ḥusayn Naṣṣār (Cairo, 1971), vol. 1, pp. 191–2.
18. See note 10.
19. E.g., the anthology compiled in 912/1506 by Muḥammad b. >Aḥmad b. >Ilyās al-Ḥanafī, *ad-Durr al-Maknūn fī s-Saba< Funūn*, B.M. MS Add. 9570 fols 104v–108r. Also the brief exposition of the 'seven arts' which forms part of biographical notice of >Abū Bakr b. Manṣūr b. Barakāt b. Ḥasan b. <Ali l-<Umarī (d. 1048/1638) in Muḥammad al->Amīn Faḍl Allāh, also called b. Muḥibb ad-Dīn or Amīn Šalabī, *Xulāṣat al->Aṯar fī >A<yān al-qarn al-ḥādī <ašar* (Cairo, 1868), vol. 1, pp. 108–9. The latter is the source of von Hammer Purgstall's information in 'Notice sur dix formes de versification arabe dont une couple à peine était connues jusqu'à présent des orientalistes européens', *Journal Asiatique*, 3rd series, 8 (August 1839), pp. 162–71.
20. <Abd al-Karīm al-<Allāf, *al-Mawwāl al-Baxdādī* (Baghdad, 1964), p. 8.
21. Reported, without indication of the source, by >Aḥmad Mursī in *al->Uxniya š-Ša<biyya* (Cairo, 1970), p. 27.
22. See entry in *an-Nujūm az-Zāhirah* referred to in note 9.
23. *an-Nujūm az-Zāhirah*, p. 132.
24. *an-Nujūm az-Zāhirah*, p. 136.
25. *an-Nujūm az-Zāhirah*, pp. 30–97, 135.
26. *an-Nujūm az-Zāhirah*, p. 137.

27. *an-Nujūm az-Zāhirah*, p. 80.
28. <Alī l-Xaqanī, *Funūn al->Adab aš-Ša<bī*, p. 18.
29. The irregularities led Nada Tomiche – in 'Le Mawwal Égyptien', *Mélanges Marcel Cohen* (The Hague: Mouton, 1970), pp. 429–38 – to confuse it with a somewhat similar metre, the *rajaz.*
30. *>all* is a deliberate mispronunciation, for rhyming purposes, of *>āla.* In version 'b' the line ends with *šajarit >all*, a mispronunciation of *>alla*, 'a mountain-top tree', 'c' has *šajarit fall*, for either *fill*, 'a cork-tree', or *full*, 'an Arabian jasmine tree'. There are, in the colloquial, variations in vocalisation and gemination, in transcribing texts that have reached me by word of mouth I have followed my informant's pronunciation.
31. Versions 'b' and 'c' have *widd* for *widād*, and 'c' ends *with fall*, for *falā* 'and their water has turned to desert'.
32. *Tall* stands for *tīl* 'hemp', or possibly *tull* 'tulle', 'b' and 'c' replace it by *fall*, of which I cannot make sense unless it is an extreme distortion *oi fanilla*, 'flannel'.
33. Line omitted from 'b' and 'c'.
34. The rhyme word lends itself to two interpretations. It may be a colloquial pronunciation of the Standard Arabic *tindall*, 'they are humbled', or it may be *tinzal*, with the final letter doubled, meaning 'they come down'. Version 'b' ends: *<alā >awlād il-mulūk tindall*, for *tindilī* 'on the sons of kings, so they are let down', 'c' also has *tindall* for the rhyme word.
35. Version 'b' reads: *sa>altı <an šēx <ālim >albuh fi l-humūm tandall*, for *tannuh dall*, 'I enquired about a venerable and learned man, whose heart in the midst of cares still guides aright', 'c' reads: *sa>alt ı min šēx <ālim fa>īh min il-humūm ṣandal*, 'I enquired of a venerable and learned man, versed in the Law, [fragrant as] sandalwood as a result of cares.'
36. Both 'b' and 'c' add *yōm*, 'for a single day', after *nadl*, in 'c' the rhyme word is *yindall*, perhaps for *yindilī* as in note 34.
37. One such was asked by a member of the audience to pay a compliment to a girl called Sūsu, after a brief pause he composed a punning tercet of which I remember the last line: *>aḥia min il->aṣab illi y ixla min sūsub*, 'sweeter than sugar cane that is free of weevils'.
38. Two discs and an accompanying booklet in four languages, issued by the Ministry of Culture of the United Arab Republic some time between 1967 and 1972.
39. Translation, ignoring repetitions: You who plant roses, is it that rose-trees have become rare? Or have the waterwheels of affection dried up, and has water become scarce? There are days when we drink honey and days when we drink vinegar, and days when we wear special silk and days when we wear hemp, and days when we sleep in amity and days when we sleep in the drizzle, and days that rule and ordain that the sons of kings step down. I went to a venerable and learned man – o how like sandalwood was his heart as a result of cares! He threw the book out of his right hand, turned and said to me: 'He who associates with the vile, though lordly once, will be humbled.'
40. Nada Tomiche, 'Le Mawwal Égyptien', spotted one paronomasia among the *mawwāls* that she examined, but took all others to be mere reduplication.
41. In a long interview recorded in 1959 by <Abd al-Malik al-Xamīsī, of the Folk Arts Centre in Cairo, who gave me much help in tracing and transcribing material.
42. The first three words are indistinct on the tape, but the third unmistakably starts with an emphatic consonant, and is not the *tibn*, 'straw', one expects, the word I hear, *tabn*, is unknown to me, but I take it to be a variant of *tibn.* It occurs again in line 2 of the *mawwāl* to which reference is made in note 60.
43. The classical form used here in preference to the colloquial *as>alak* fits the metre better, but is also not inappropriate in an invocation.

44. *Ḥusn al-maqāl*, pp. 8 and 9.
45. See also Hoenerbach's introduction of al-Ḥillī, *Die Vulgärarabische Poetik*, p. 35.
46. One instance was given to me by Mr Ḥusnī Luṭfī, director of the Folk Arts Centre in Cairo, who placed the resources of the Centre and his own considerable knowledge at my disposal, the one reproduced here was recorded for me by Abu Đirā< in October 1972.
47. Based on the notorious honour crime of *Šafī>a w Mitwalli* amply covered in my *Popular Narrative Ballads of Modern Egypt* and often mentioned in this book. The extract given here is from the version recorded for me by Abu Đrā< in 1972 and attributed by him to aš-Šišnāwī Xāṭir of al-Maḥalla l-Kubrā.
48. *Ṭafrah*, 'a leap', does not fit the context, unless possibly in the secondary sense of an outbreak of pustules. There appears to be a metathetic connection with the root f-r-ṭ, cf. *tafrīṭ*, 'dissipation'.
49. See first passage in Arabic script, at note 14. See also Hoenerbach, *Die Vulgärarabische Poetik*, p. 34.
50. *Bustān al-Jamīl fī Muṭrib al-Mawāwīl*, compiled by >Amīn <Abd al-Wāḥid az-Zayyāt.
51. I have also heard the word applied to any line of a *mawwāl.* May there be a link here with the Lebanese *<atābā*, which is also in the *basīṭ* metre?
52. The one rhyming in *-all*, beginning with note 30.
53. Maḥmūd <Abd al-Bā>ī, see note 41.
54. Maḥmūd <Abd al-Bā>ī, pp. 25–7.
55. See note 15.
56. *<a* is an abbreviation of *<ammāl*, 'active, doing', and in Upper Egyptian usage is prefixed to the aorist verb to denote continuity in the present, it is the equivalent of Lower Egyptian *bi-*, which is believed to stand for *dā>ib*, 'persistently active, assiduous'. As occurs two lines below, *<a* may also be short for *<alā šān* or *<ašān*, meaning 'in order that' or 'for the sake of'.
57. This line scans perfectly if *>afandī* is omitted, if this may be presumed to be a late addition, it illustrates the difference in the priorities of composer and performer.
58. Colloquial form of *wajh.*
59. This is why Nada Tomiche's informant described the longer compositions he recited as *mawwāl xazalī šabīh bi l->īṣṣah*, 'an amatory *mawwāl* is similar to a narrative''Le Mawwal Égyptien', p. 429.
60. Recited by Maḥmūd <Abd al-Bā>ī (note 41) and attributed by him to a confectioner of Ḥilwān called Sayyid <Afīfī l-Ḥalawānī.
61. Al-Ḥājj aḍ-Ḍuwī of Qūṣ, recorded by the poet <Abd ar-Raḥmān al->Abnūdī.
62. Colloquial form of *santūr.*

3

The Nahḍa's First Stirrings of Interest in *Alf Layla*

On 3 September 1948, Ṭāhā Ḥusayn (1889–1973) published in *al-Ahrām* an article titled 'Šahrazād'. It was one of the regular pieces he contributed to the newspaper even while vacationing in France. It seems to have been occasioned by accounts in the French press of two plays sharing that title.[1] But it is his broader observations which reveal, by what is said or by what is implied, the cultural climate in which he and his contemporaries reacted to *Alf Layla*. So let me give you the gist of the article in Ṭāhā Ḥusayn's own words:

> Was I on a tryst with Šahrazād? I do not know, but when embarking on my summer trip I asked my companion [i.e., his amanuensis] to include *Alf Layla wa Layla* in his luggage, I made this request with some embarrassment, for it is clear that *Alf Layla wa Layla* is a book that it is improper for older men who put on an appearance of venerability to read. I recall that I read this book with some of my brothers when I was twenty or a little older. And I remember the unforgettable, shameful day when our aged father discovered that his sons were poring over the booklore neither of the [State] schools nor of the Azhar, but over this hateful, ill-starred book that never enters a house without bringing it adversity, and that engages the attention only of idlers who are of no avail to others or to themselves.
>
> No sooner had I dealt with matters that awaited me in Paris … than I asked my companion to bring the book out of his bags. I turned to it, delving into it and scarcely leaving it except to read the newspapers very quickly before returning to it.
>
> Thinking about Šahrazād has been constant in the West since the sixteenth century when *Kitāb Alf Layla wa Layla* was first translated. Interest in Šahrazād grew from the early eighteenth century when Galland's magnificent translation was published, extensively and deeply affecting all European literatures.
>
> While the Europeans' interest in Šahrazād was growing, that of the Easterners was steadily waning. There is no doubt that what eclipsed Šahrazād in the East was the printing press, for the storytellers used to treasure manuscripts of *Alf Layla wa Layla*, passing them on by inheritance or gift, reading them to the multitudes who came to listen at nightfall, adding, subtracting, or altering as occasion demanded, seeking in all this to please the listeners and rouse their simple, immediate emotions. Once the printing press was established in the East and this book among others was printed, many got hold of it. Reading it substituted for listening, and one version of it became standard.
>
> The printing press's offence to Šahrazād did not stop there. It made available to Easterners other books than Šahrazād's. It published translations of modern European narratives that did not conform with older Oriental storytelling.

> Attention to *Alf Layla* was not renewed in the East until Easterners found out that Westerners were interested in this text, and they followed their lead.
>
> But the West, I believe, has grossly misunderstood Šahrazād and her book. For to Westerners, Šahrazād symbolises the Oriental woman, sumptuous, elusive, mysterious; and her book stands for sumptuousness carried to its utmost extravagance. It may perhaps be said that some European poets and writers have overstepped the mark in their depiction of Šahrazād, taking lines of which the least that can be said is that they befit a thoroughly corrupt civilisation.
>
> So Šahrazād is being unfairly treated both in the East and in the West. She is full of kindness towards the weak, mercy towards the wretched, charity towards the deprived. She diverts them from their worries, offers them solace from their travails, helps them to hope and function and live. She lifts from them during the night the heavy, the excessive burdens they have carried during the day. She is none but the eternal spirit of the common people that musters hope against pain, dreams against wakefulness, and sweet imagination against bitter reality. If people knew Šahrazād as she ought to be known they would love and esteem her differently. They would take hold of this magnificent, eternal book of hers and attune it to the way people live in this modern age.

The article usefully identifies the main features of the Arab elite's response to *Alf Layla* in Ṭāhā Ḥusayn's generation: its initial diffidence towards folk values, its immense admiration of things Western, and its high sense of responsibility and service.

A somewhat cynical definition of literary classics is that they are texts more often cited than read. To the educated Arab, *Alf Layla* was the exact opposite. Its component tales (and many others of the same ilk) were common knowledge, but they were seen as at best 'idle stories' that fell under Qur>anic condemnation (31:6), to say nothing of raunchy and unedifying passages which caused some of my Egyptian schoolmates in the 1930s to get severely beaten if caught reading them. Besides, although when written down the material was put into at least minimally correct classical Arabic, it was not in the high style which Ṭāhā Ḥusayn himself once declared a *sine qua non* of the literary canon. It is in keeping with this that the oldest manuscript of *Alf Layla* did not command scholarly attention until Harvard Professor Muḥsin Mahdī (1936–2007) edited it in 1984. But what animated the pioneers of the Nahḍa was the example of Europe. It was, of course, the technological achievements of Britain and France, forcefully demonstrated in their military successes, that foisted themselves on the attention of the forward-looking Arabs, eager not to submit to foreigners, but by emulating them to acquire the means of reasserting themselves. The validity of Western cultural norms was not disputed but taken for granted in countless contributions to the journals that gained currency in the last quarter of the nineteenth century, with reservations only about religion and the role of women in society, and even this citadel was being gradually dismantled, for the first feminist book, *Taḥrīr al-Mar>ah*, 'The Emancipation of Woman', by Qāsim >Amīn (1865–1908) appeared in 1899. The effect of ready-made models on literary production was neither immediate nor uniform. But >Ibrāhīm <Abd-al-Qādir al-Māzinī (1890–1949) realised late in his career that he and other stalwarts of the Nahḍa had been deluded when they thought they were drawing on their own experiences:[2] it was natural that this civilisation should sweep them along. It was as if they were living in a whirlpool of dreams and blinding lights. Their thinking was based on imagining an ideal society whose values were not drawn from the actual but from Western civilisation, in comparison with which their own society was to be discarded as backward.

Most of the 1930s and 1940s were the heyday of a tearful romanticism openly imitative of mainly French nineteenth-century models and welcomed by Muḥammad Ḥusayn Haykal (1888–1956) as answering the human need to weep, long denied by the aridity of classical literature.[3] Far from needing to disguise or deny European inspiration, it became an advantage to a writer to display his familiarity with things Western, no matter how relevant or irrelevant. The most pretentious literary journal of the period flaunted *Apollo* as its name, and contributors to it were known as the *Apollo group*. This did not proclaim a rising interest in classicism: what mattered was that things Hellenic were part of Europe. Even in contexts far removed from the literary, it became prestigious to invoke Greek deities: during a visit to a provincial town in the late 1930s I witnessed the local photographer change the name of his establishment to *Studio Venus*, and his example was soon followed by the neighbouring draper, then even less appropriately by the butcher. I have been told by people in the know that young men with literary ambitions found it easier to break into print if they submitted their effusions vaguely labelled 'a free translation' (*mutarjama bi-taṣarruf*) rather than as an original piece. And a short story by someone who did not subsequently make a name for himself as a literary figure tells of a youth whose wedding night starts in high exaltation until his bride suddenly and for no reason given dies in is arms; it contains such gems as:[4]

> wa hunāka bayna akālīli z-zuhūr … jalasat wa <alā ra>sihā tājun min zuhūri l->uqḥuwāni muḥallan bi l-jirānyūm wa muraṣṣa<un bi l-fiyūlīd … wa kānati l-ḥayātu ḥulman rā>i<an raqaṣat fīhi l-malā>ikatu <alā >anx̱āmi l-jāzband.

It is no wonder, then, that because it was highly prized by Europeans, *Alf Layla* now began to command attention from Arab intellectuals. But the use to which it was to be put was informed by the Nahḍa's high sense of purpose and responsibility. I have pointed out elsewhere[5] that literary genres of mainly entertainment value – such as detective novels, translations of which were popular – have been scantily served in Arabic. Leading writers assumed that they were reformers shaping the future of their society. The 1930s and early 1940s coincided with my own school and undergraduate days, when cultural moods and events impacted on my life, and I can bear witness that my schoolmates, at an age when their Western counterparts would dream at best of saving their school team from defeat on the playing field, took it for granted that the mere fact that they were vouchsafed valuable knowledge inaccessible to the majority marked them out – if not as future leaders – at least as members of their nation's vanguard. And I have read of one Moroccan youth who solemnly got his friends together and asked them whether he would serve his country better as a poet – with all the lax self-discipline that he anticipated such an occupation to entail – or as a strict man of learning.[6] And yet another[7] wrote:

> Now past fifteen, shall I still play,
> Dabble in the pleasures of life, rejoice?
> Mine is a lofty outlook, a spirit proud
> That seeks a station higher than the Milky Way.
> Mine are hopes I am determined to attain
> That would vanish and be gone if with my days I trifle.
> Mine also is an ill-starred nation that has not found
> Its way to the kind of life it seeks.

I daresay that most of these high-minded youths ended up pushing a pen in some dusty office, but once in a while green corn does bear the promise of a golden crop, and this last teenage versifier was none other than Morocco's nationalist leader, <Allāl al-Fāsī (1906–73).

Ṭāhạ Ḥusayn's nod of recognition for *Alf Layla* is significant, for he had not been well disposed towards folk literature, and it is now the orally transmitted rather than the printed version of the text that he favoured, although he once considered the vernacular incapable of expressing refined perceptions or lofty sentiment. To what extent was his new receptivity shared by his fellow pioneers of the Nahḍa?[8]

In the inner sanctum of poetry, Šahrazād was given an early but unsustained welcome: in 1916, <Abbās Maḥmūd al-<Aqqād (1889–1964) composed a poem titled *Šahrazād aw Siḥr al-Ḥadīṯh*,[9] 'Šahrazād or the Magic of Words'. The power that al-<Aqqād invokes is dual:

> Of two wonders is magic made. To master both
> Is mastery that reduces monarchs to slaves.
> Words captivate enchanting beauties,
> And beauties captivate the wielder of fine words:
> Two wondrous signs of enchantment, hunting and hunted –
> Now predator and now prey.
> Muster these two and you have mastered prodigies
> Of the magicians' art. So you attain the utmost.

And he credits Šahrazād with subtlety in dealing with the king:

> In malice he harboured evil towards women,
> And malice refuses to discriminate.
> But Šahrazād perceived how to doctor his disease,
> Calling him 'happy' in his wretchedness.

Gross was his heart, closed was his soul,
    Secretive, implacable, obdurate.
She softened him with words. He listened
    For there are words that soften iron.

But al-<Aqqād's lead was not followed by any of the major literary figures of his time. It was poets of a different temper who next sought in *Alf Layla* material to animate a more probing and purposeful Muse, one of whose spokesmen was <Abd al-Wahhāb al-Bayyātī (1926–99) who, in *>Abārīq Muhaššama*, 'Shattered Pitchers' – one of the earliest collections of Arabic free verse – included a poem carrying the heavily charged title of *al-ḥarīm* , 'the harem'.[10] Its opening lines read:

Your lips are a wound with blood still flowing
    Upon our pillow the whole night long, O sparrow mine,
        A running wound.
And under her balcony her knight keeps singing
    All through the night. Thousands of women
Are born and die at dawn, excepting you, my beautiful dream,
    Upon our pillow, all through the night, my beautiful dream!

Given tongue here are perceptions and priorities that do not comfortably mesh with those either of the common folk or of preceding generations of the elite.

Strikingly, the popular live theatre, itself an activity of no recognised status, followed a very different course. Its pioneer,[11] Mārūn an-Naqqāš (1817–1855), found a formula for his first and third plays in Molière's comedies, but his second was *>Abū l-Ḥasan al-Muxaffal* (1849), which embroidered the theme of 'the Caliph for a Day' drawn from *Alf Layla.* Later in the nineteenth century, >Aḥmad >Abū-Xalīl al-Qabbānī (1841–1902) put on no fewer than three plays derived from the same source: *Hārūn ar-Rašīd ma< al->Amīr X̱ānim ibn->Ayyūb*; *Hārūn ar-Rašīd ma<a Uns al-Julīs*; and *al->Amīr Maḥmūd Najl Šāh al-<Ajam.* One Maḥmūd Wāṣif is also credited with a play titled *Hārūn ar-Rašīd ma<a Qūt al-Qulūb wa Xalīfa ṣ-Ṣayyād.* But this early crop must be weighed against the fact that all through the nineteenth century and into the early twentieth, the live theatre – like *Alf Layla* itself – was viewed as an entertainment, not as an artistic endeavour. Their linkage was a rapprochement between two pariahs. Serious plays were translated and written, but they were seldom staged, and none of them was drawn from folk literature. The main attraction was the singing. The text of the play was seldom published at the time, and its authorship was usually unacknowledged – it was the property of the acting company.

On the state of the live theatre as late as the 1920s, we have the witness of an insider: Tawfīq al-Ḥakīm (1898–1987).[12] There was a lively market for melodramas, comedies and musical plays, often termed operettas – on record is one such, with the suggestive title of *Šahwa-zād*, the wordplay no doubt intended to rouse the appetites. Like many others, al-Ḥakīm supplied this market, usually by adapting the plot of foreign plays, mostly French. The indebtedness was not always acknowledged, and indeed the adaptation could amount to re-invention, for the plot had to be brought into line with what was considered proper at the time; for example, male and female characters could not appear in the same scene unless they were shown to be related. The practice grew of labelling the text 'from the pen of So-and-So', a formula which blurred the distinction between what was translated, what was adapted and what was created. The playwright then had to sell his script to an acting company, usually for a lump sum. Tawfīq al-Ḥakīm repeatedly served the <Ukāša brothers in this manner; for one play of which he was the sole author and which contained no songs, he was paid Egyptian £20. Also noteworthy is that two of the plays he wrote then drew on *Alf Layla* themes: *<Alī Bāba* and *Xātim Sulaymān*, the latter staged in 1922.

Tawfīq al-Ḥakīm, however, all but disowned his early works. Actual creative writing, he was to assert later 'did not begin seriously for me until after I had been to Europe and drunk at the true springs of culture'.[13] He returned from Paris in 1928, without the doctorate in law his father had sent him to obtain, but resolved to create a dramatic literature with a high intellectual content even if the public was not ready for it. One of his early efforts was *Šahrazād* (1934). In it, Šahriyār recognises in Šahrazād a great heart and a beautiful body, but he has outgrown delight in these and is now hankering for something else: for knowledge, for a truth that goes beyond myth, for the secret of who Šahrazād is, of what Nature ultimately is. Šahrazād has no answer to his questions, and even though she tests him by bringing the black slave into her apartments, she has to let him go on his endless quest.

This is not the best of al-Ḥakīm's plays. There is little development in the theme, the interpretation of which he was content to leave to the reader. There are none of the piquant situations that his experience of the live theatre had taught him to invent. The comic relief he brings in mainly on the tongue of the unemployed executioner is not very comical. But Šahriyār's unfocused quest is in line with the thesis he has put forward more than once and in which one may find an expression of the playwright's vague deism, but also some kinship with Ṭāhā Ḥusayn's identification of Šahrazād with Egypt's abiding spirit:[14]

> Tragedy generally gives expression to a struggle between Man and other forces … To the Greeks, the struggle was between Man and his gods. To Europeans like Corneille and Racine, it was between Man and his emotions. I perceived that in the Arab or Egyptian tragedy, the struggle had to be … between Man and Time, with the resulting concept of resurrection, resorting to the material defences of embalming and monumental construction by the Ancient Egyptians and to the spiritual defence of faith in an eternal Paradise in Islam and Christianity. I believe that sediments of the millennia are always to be found in our depths. Egypt has fought Time from the beginning of Creation, and she always triumphs over Time thanks to her ever-renewed spirit.
>
> The true basis of tragedy in my view is Man's sense that he is not alone in the Universe … There is not one thinker in the Western world today who genuinely believes in a god other than Man himself … This is a matter which – though I may apprehend it with my mind, which is abreast of mankind's intellectual development – my Oriental religious heart does not believe in.

Al-Ḥakīm returned to the same characters in a short piece in dialogue titled >*Alf Layla wa Laylatan*[15] in which Šahrazād, having exhausted her stock of stories, places herself at Šahriyār's mercy, but he tells her that it is his viziers who are more deserving of death for having concealed from him his own nature and the temper of his people. Now that she has held a true mirror up to him, he has the bright vision that he could let the people elect their viziers, and the only burden left to him would be to look down benignly upon them all.

Of the same generation, although later in rising to notoriety, <Alī>Aḥmad Bā-Kaṯīr (1910–69) improved on al-<Aqqād's interpretation by turning to psychology in his *Sirr Šahrazād*, 'Šahrazād's Secret' (1952). The secret is actually Šahriyār's, for he is impotent, and it is both to hide his infirmity and to vent his rage that he puts women to the sword, and he is equally sanguinary with soldiers who lose battles. Šahrazād is percipient enough both to diagnose and to solve his problem by pleading night after night that she is not strong enough to cope with his ardour, and she persists in this flattering pretence until the knot is undone on the seventy-first night, to the relief of many.

A somewhat similar but more abrupt course is followed in *Šahriyār* (1955) a verse play written by >Aḥmad Šawqī's disciple <Azīz >Abāẓa (1898–1969), with the collaboration of <Abd-Allāh al-Bašīr. Here Šahriyār is indeed – as in the original story – infuriated by his wife's betrayal. He gives full scope to his vengeful rage and shows nothing but contempt for Šahrazād's stories of gentle characters and pitiable situations, but it has to be assumed that some redemptive force is at work in him for at the end, haunted by disturbing visions, he finds faith, abandons his kingdom, and sets off on the *ḥajj* to atone for his sins.

To prose narratives, the genre closest to *Alf Layla*, Ṭāhā Ḥusayn was himself the main contributor. He had reviewed Tawfīq al-Ḥakīm's *Šahrazād* in terms to which al-Ḥakīm took offence, but they soon resumed their friendship and in 1936 while they were both holidaying in the Alps they celebrated their reconciliation by joining forces in writing *al-Qaṣr al-Masḥūr*, 'The Enchanted Castle'. It starts with Šahrazād, who has a castle nearby, revealing to a sympathetic Ṭāhā Ḥusayn that she is determined to punish al-Ḥakīm for misrepresenting her and the other characters in his play. Thereafter the two authors each in turn write a chapter in which he places his friend in a ludicrously awkward situation. From this the other has to escape and then turn the table on his co-author. Eventually, al-Ḥakīm is brought to trial before that very 'Time' whom he considered an essential item in his tragedies, and he successfully defends himself by proclaiming the unrestricted freedom of the artist to make what he will of his characters, at the same time admitting that in the search for beauty he is pursuing perfection but does not claim that he has reached it. In their separate introductions, Ṭāhā Ḥusayn admits that the piece is no more than a pleasantry between friends, al-Ḥakīm concurring but adding – perhaps with his plea for artistic freedom in mind – that sometimes true words are spoken in jest.

Much more substantial than this parlour game is Ṭāhā Ḥusayn's novel >*Aḥlām*

Šahrazād, 'The Dreams of Šahrazād' (1943). In it, the dream is of Fātina, the wise and beautiful daughter of the king of the jinns in Ḥaḍramawt. She is courted by other kings of jinn, but she scorns them all. As her father approaches death, both anticipate that the rejected suitors will join forces against her. She asks him to proclaim that she will marry whichever takes the city by force. When the crisis comes, Fātina uses her powerful magic to immobilise all the enemy forces, and she gives the tyrannical kings the choice between death and the admission of their guilt, to be followed by a trial before their own subjects. Instalments of the dream are interspersed with accounts of Šahrazād in her waking hours completing the healing of Šahriyār, and the two strands are tied together when she tells him that it is time to turn to affairs of state.

It is easy to identify Fātina with Šahrazād and with the abiding spirit of Egypt. And the paternalism that shaped the political commitment of Ṭāhā Ḥusayn and many of his contemporaries is most explicit when Fātina's father asks rhetorically whether it is not the duty of kings to stir their subjects from their apathy, whether this is engendered by Nature or induced by conditioning.[16]

What, then, are we to infer from this survey?

If we set aside the activities of the acting companies before the 1930s, the most striking feature is that only the frame story of *Alf Layla* was tapped by the literary elite. It commended itself to the early leaders of the Nahḍa mainly because it had commended itself to their European models, and they used it as a vehicle for the ideas and perceptions generated by contact with European culture. So far as I have been able to ascertain, no interest was shown in the narrative techniques that are so engaging a feature *of Alf Layla.* Nor was the door opened wide enough to let in other forms of folk literature, least of all its contemporary manifestations. The elite that had set out not to be elitist continued to dedicate itself to serving the masses without seeking an input from them.

These results have to be gauged against the enormity of the task undertaken by the fathers of the Nahḍa, which was nothing less than a cultural reorientation, occasioned by contacts that were not always friendly and not entirely congenial. Within this turbulence, the impetus provided by a native text backed by a foreign commendation came late, and by the middle of the twentieth century – which is when the present survey closes and a new generation emerges – it had not made an eminently distinctive mark.

More was to come.

Notes

1. Of the first, a three-act comedy by Jules Supervielle, he says only that it was being staged in the provinces before opening in Paris. The second, by Henri de Régnier, he roundly condemns for portraying Šahrazād 'as a woman who had wearied of the love of men and strayed from it to another, repulsive and damaging'; but in a tailpiece he admits that he has read only a second-hand partial account of it, and wishes his judgement not to be taken as final.

2. From *Qiṣṣat Ḥayāh*, quoted in <Abd al-Muḥsin Ṭāhā Badr in *Taṭawwur ar-Riwāya al-<Arabiyyā al-Ḥadīṯa* (Cairo, 1963), pp. 285, 287.
3. *Jān Jāk Rūsū* (Cairo, 1965), p. 210.
4. >Aḥmad Šafīq Ḥilmī, 'al-Wafā> al-Maḏbūḥ', *ar-Risāla*, XVII, 854 (14 November 1949), pp. 1611–13. Foreign words transliterated into Arabic are italicised in this translation: 'There among bouquets of flowers … she sat, crowned with *camomiles* adored with *geraniums* and decorated with *violets* … The night was a magnificent dream in which angels danced to the music of the *jazz band.*'
5. 'Unwritten Arabic fiction and drama', *An Overview of Modern Arabic Literature* (Edinburgh, 1990), ch. 10, pp. 171–8.
6. Muḥummad al-Makkī an-Nāṣirī's autobiographical entry dated 20 February 1929 in Sa<d Mīxā>īl, *Ādāb al-<Aṣr* (Cairo, n.d.), vol. 1, pp. 78–82.
7. Muḥammad <Allāl al-Fāsī, in Sa<d Mīxā>īl, *op. cit.*, vol. 2, pp. 2–3.
8. A title that may conveniently be restricted to those who were born before 1926 or had acquired a literary reputation by 1940.
9. *Dīwān*, Pt.1 (1918), pp. 103, 115.
10. Reprinted in his *Dīwān* (Beirut, 1972), pp. 266–7.
11. Much of the factual information that follows is to be found in Muḥammad Yūsuf Najm, *al-Masraḥiyya fī l->Adab al-<Arabī al-Ḥadīṯ 1847–1914* (Beirut, 1999), and in Fārūq Sa<d, *Min Waḥy >Alf Layla* (Beirut, 1962), vol. 1.
12. Notably in his autobiographical *Sijn al-<Umr* (1964), which I translated as *The Prison of Life* (Cairo, 1992), esp. chs 10, 13–15.
13. *The Prison of Life*, p. 156.
14. In this composite passage, the first paragraph is drawn from <Abd al-Fattāḥ ad-Dīdī, 'Fi Dār al-Kutub', *Majallat aṯ-Ṯaqāfa* (3 December 1951), reprinted as *>Aḥādīṯ ma<a Tawfīq al-Hakīm* (Cairo, 1971), pp. 7, 8. The second paragraph is from Tawfīq al-Ḥakīm's introduction to his *al-Malik >Ūdīb* in several updated printings, pp. 34, 37, 48–9.
15. *>Āxir Sā<a*, No. 695 (18 February 1948).
16. Ṭāhā Ḥusayn, *al-Majmu<a al-Kāmila* (Beirut, 1974), vol. 14, Pt 2, p. 547.

4

The Career of Muṣṭafā ›Ibrāhīm ‹Ajāj: A Giant of Egyptian Popular Literature

For about a thousand years, perhaps even longer, Arab creativity has found outlets not only in lofty compositions retaining the syntax (if not always the vocabulary) of the language in which the Qur>ān was revealed, but also in the coining of proverbs, the singing of songs, the recitation of poems, the telling of tales and the presentation of rather rudimentary playlets and puppet shows, all in the local dialects. Yet the immensely powerful and constant attachment of Arab intellectuals to their 'classical' language was such that only texts couched in this idiom were deemed worthy of serious attention, and it is these alone that Arab scholars and Orientalists alike habitually call 'Arabic literature' without further qualification. Anything expressed in the colloquial, when not openly scorned, was looked upon as mere entertainment; more often than not the text went unrecorded, the artistry unrecognised, the author unremembered. Modern Arabs have altered their attitude to the language quite substantially in some respects, but – perhaps for the very reason that they are caught up in momentous social and intellectual changes – only a handful of scholars among them have begun to give serious attention to this 'popular literature', which they are used to treating with more familiarity than respect.

The character of this literature, and above all the lines of demarcation between it and the literature of the educated elite, are not as easy to determine as may seem at first sight. Its reliance on the colloquial as the medium of expression is probably its most distinctive trait, but it cannot be identified by this alone since the colloquial has also come to be used in some plays, novels and poems which are undoubtedly elite. It has some of the features associated with European folk literature in that the bulk of it is orally transmitted by rural artists of little or no formal education, addressing crowds at religious festivals; but that it excludes neither city dwellers nor pen-and-paper compositions is obvious from the career of Muṣṭafā >Ibrāhīm <Ajāj.[1]

About the man we have only scraps of information. His full name was Muṣṭafā ibn >Ibrāhīm ibn Muṣṭafā ibn as-Sayyid aš-Šarīf al-Xaššāb, but he was known as aš-Šayx Muṣṭafā >Ibrāhīm <Ajāj, and in at least one of his publications he claimed to be descended from the Prophet through al-Ḥusayn. He appears to have been of Upper Egyptian stock, and to have started his career late in the nineteenth century, for he has several verse compositions in praise of Khedive <Abbās Ḥilmī II, who ruled Egypt from 1892 to 1914, and another celebrating the war in the Sudan, which ended in 1898.[2] By singers who still remember him, <Ajāj is said to have died in or about 1936.

It is clear that he had a fairly substantial education of a traditional Islamic type; but the claim made for him by some present-day singers that he studied at the Azhar for fifteen years and had the title of *<ālim* is probably exaggerated, for he appears to have commanded only modest employment: in most of his booklets he describes himself as a *kātib* – that is, a clerk, or probably a letter-writer – in Būlāq, and in one as an employee of the railway yards in Būlāq. It is not impossible, however, that he was content to hold a humdrum job that ensured his material needs while he sought an outlet for his creativity and ambitions in popular literature.

Such artistic devotion is not unparalleled in a field that offers few glittering prizes. As has already been noted, the intellectuals seldom take these popular arts seriously. Even in rural communities, villagers with a stock of good songs or good stories naturally enjoy the admiration and approbation of their fellows and may make some extra money by performing at local festive occasions; but to earn a living as full-time performers they generally need to take to the road, going from one local saint's day celebration to another, and being then regarded as little better than vagrants, so that not a few of the 'full-timers' are either gypsies or men who started by running away from home early in life and serving a long apprenticeship with some itinerant singer before branching out on their own.

Either because he was not endowed with a good singing voice, or because he was entitled to a higher social status, <Ajāj was never a professional performer, but he was a prolific pen-and-paper versifier. He did occasionally compose in classical Arabic and in accordance with the conventions of classical Arabic poetry; but his efforts then were confined to a few lines laden with the rhetorical artifices with which, by the late nineteenth century, the new modernistic elite was already becoming impatient. Below, for example, is a couplet in the *basīṭ* metre,[3] which combines a pun on the word *xāl* (which may mean either a beauty spot or a maternal uncle) with a fanciful reference to the canonical law of inheritance:

li-llāhi xālun <alā xaddi l-ḥabībi lahū
bi l-<āšiqīna kamā šā>a l-hawā <abaṯū
warraṯtuhū ḥabbata l-qalbi l-qatīli bihī
wa-kāna <ahdī >anna l-xāla lā yariṯū

Ah for a beauty-spot on the cheek of the beloved which
Plays havoc with lovers, as passions will!
To it I have bequeathed the core of a heart that has died for it
Although I knew that a maternal uncle has no right to inherit.

He was much more prolific, however, in the colloquial, using a variety of post-classical metrical forms, in most of which what is a hemistich in classical poetry forms a complete unit, and in this paper will be called 'a line'. One of these was the *zajal*, which is generally held to have been invented in Andalusia in about the eleventh century and which is not restricted to any one rhythm or rhyme scheme but maintains a strictly regular stanzaic pattern within the one poem, the stanzas being further bound together by having the same closing rhyme. Thus, in an exhortatory poem abounding in Qur>anic echoes <Ajāj apostrophises his own soul in a series of stanzas each consisting of a sestet of alternating rhymes followed by a couplet ending in -īm; one of them reads:

yā nafsı di d-dunyā matā< il-x̱urūr
O soul, this world is of the stuff of delusion

ma tbaddilīš fīha l-malīḥ bi l->asā
Do not barter what is good in it for sorrow.

xōfī <alēki min <azāb il->̃ubūr
How I fear for you the punishment of the grave

wi tutrakī yā nafsı mitnakkasa
Lest you should end, O soul, hanging your head in shame.

yā nafsı di l-a>̃wām nahār il-ḥarūr
O soul, the nations on the day of the burning sun

yitḥāsbu fīha r-rigāl wi n-nisā
Shall be called to account, both men and women.

yā nafsı lēh fi<lik dawāman ẕamīm
O soul, why are your actions always open to rebuke?

muš xā>ifah min yōm ḥisābuh <aẓīm
Do you not fear a day of mighty reckoning?

Another form used by <Ajāj is the *murabba<* or *wāw.* The metre is basically

⏑- -/⏑- -/⏑- -

and the lines are arranged in quatrains with alternating rhymes; but the rhymes are occasionally elaborated into paronomasias achieved by deliberate distortion of the normal pronunciation. The liberties most commonly taken are with the quality and length of vowels and the gemination of consonants; advantage may even be taken of dialectal variations, for both the ‘j’ and the ‘q’ of classical Arabic may be used in punning as they both may be pronounced ‘g’, although only in different regions. The result is often a succession of riddles which audiences brought up on such mental gymnastics delight in solving, but which outsiders miss completely, assuming that the native artists are indulging in mere repetition. In the following example – part of a long poem by <Ajāj praising God and warning man of his accountability – the correct form of the words used in the paronomasias is added, between square brackets, at the end of each line:

yā <abdı >in kān ḥisābāk [ḥisābak]
O man, if your account

xafīf rīš <addēt nājī
Is feather-light, you will be let in, saved.

wi rabb il-xalāyi>̃ ḥisābāk [ḥāss bīk]
The Lord of Creation is aware of you.

illi >āmin bīh nājī
The believer communes with Him.

w in kān ẓunūbak kēf ijbāl [jibāl]
But if your sins are like mountains,

maskīn yā ṭūl <aẓabak
Poor man, how long will be your torment!

mālik yiĝūl lak[4] kēf ijbāl
An angel will ask: 'What are your propensities?

šūf fī jahannam <aẓabak [<aẓā> bīk]
Go seek in Hell some solace in you!'

It is in the *mawwāl* or *mawāliyā*, however, that <Ajāj displayed the greatest verve. This is a type of metrical composition,[5] usually sung, known to have existed at least since the twelfth century AD. Initially, it consisted of a mono-rhyme quatrain of *basīṭ*,[3] but over the centuries it has been expanded so as to produce fixed-form poems with the following rhyme schemes: aaaxa, aaazzza or aaabcbcbczzza, the last line in the thirteen-line *mawwāl* often having an internal 'z' rhyme as well. Furthermore, the elaboration of all rhyme-words into the paronomasias that we have already encountered in the *murabba<* has become the rule rather than the exception.

<Ajāj has composed innumerable *mawwāls*, especially of the thirteen-line variety, his favourite themes being the praise of God and of the Prophet, somewhat hackneyed reflections on the wickedness of man, the corruption of society, and the vanity of worldly ambitions, as well as love-songs more often than not in the form of appeals to the physician to alleviate the pangs of unrequited passion. He is unique in that he has also used both the seven-line and the thirteen-line *mawwāl* as stanzas in long narratives, mostly recounting stories of the prophets. He was fond of producing strings of *mawwāls* related in some formal way, as by having each *mawwāl* start with a successive letter of the alphabet. The following, which has a rather rare touch of humour, is one of a series of *mawwāls* each of which incorporates a popular proverb in its last line:

yā ḥilw[6] anā xillı ṣādi>̃ fi l-widād garbān [garribnī]
O *fair one, I am a true lover*; *in affection try me.*

xuđnī ḥabībak >anā šāyif ḥadāk garbān [ğurb bāyyin]
Make me your beloved, for I see in you a clear [disposition to] intimacy.

alfat wi >̃āl li l-<awāzil fī l-waṭan garbān [ğarrū bēn]
He turned round and said: 'Trouble-makers at home have caused a rift.'

fa-ğultı luh yā ḥabīb kuff il-malām w inẓur
I told him: 'Beloved, refrain from reproaching, and consider:

min il-<awāzil wi lā tixšā hasūd wi ğarīb
From among trouble-makers, fear not the envious or the watchers;

w iskun fī bustān xālī mn il-<idā winẓur [w inzār]
Dwell in a garden void of enemies, where you may be visited.

w aṣrif <alēk māl min <ibbī kiŧīr wiragīb [warā gēbī]
I shall spend on you much wealth – out of my bunched shirt, when my pocket has been emptied!

w illī yi <ārḍak >aḍāy>̃uh fi l-ma<āš w inẓur [wi >anziruh]
Should anyone oppose you, I shall make life difficult for him, threaten him.

w armīh <ala tallı <ālī fī gabal wiragīb [warā gubb]
Cast him on a high hill, on a mountain beyond a chasm.'

alfat wi ğāl lī maniš <āwiz gudud wa lā barr [burr]
He turned round and said: 'I want neither coins nor grain;

la̱ <udt ağāblak wa lā <andī buḥūr wa lā barr
I shall no longer meet you, nor have I sea or shore [for you to visit]'

fa-ğultı luh rūḥ mā fīkšī lā xēr wi lā barr [birr]
So I said: 'Go, then! There is in you no goodness or generosity

<umr id-dihān <al-wabar lam yinfa< il-garbān
Ointment over fur never cured the mangy!'

For the diffusion of these compositions, <Ajāj resorted to the printing press. Still in circulation are cheaply printed and undated booklets each consisting of between forty and fifty pages, all issued by a printer in the vicinity of al->Azhar, called Sa<īd <Alī l-Xuṣūṣī; in my collection are six such booklets, into which are squeezed over 13,000 lines. According to one present-day professional singer, all that the author would get for one such booklet would be an initial payment by the printer of Egyptian £5 to £15.

<Ajāj seems also to have taught his art to others. It is indeed by word of mouth that many popular songs are transmitted, the learner paying a few piastres for each addition to his stock-in-trade, whether or not his informant is also the originator of the song. I have not been able to ascertain whether <Ajāj retailed his compositions

in this way, but he did have devoted disciples. One Maḥmūd <Abd al-Bāqī related[7] that he had run away from home at the age of eleven and attached himself to <Ajāj for three years – presumably paying his way by serving him – then remained in close association with him to the end of his days. He claimed to have memorised the contents of thirty-nine quires, each holding more than 200 *mawwāls* by the master; and that after satisfying himself that his pupil was also able to compose, <Ajāj gave him in 1934 a written certificate declaring him a master of the art and appointing him his deputy 'from Imbabih to Jirjā>', a stretch of territory spanning six of Upper Egypt's eight provinces.

Such reminiscences by Maḥmūd <Abd al-Bāqi tally with those of others active in popular literature to this day. Are we to infer from <Ajāj's own standing, the certificates he delivered, the appointments he made, that he was at the head of some nationwide hierarchy, perhaps a guild-like organisation? If any such existed once, there is no trace of it today. But even if the titles he bestowed had prestige value only, they imply that his own reputation was solid and widespread.

The question arises, however, whether the compositions of this literate, city-based man who reached his widest public through the printed word are genuinely 'popular'. The fact is that – his own background notwithstanding – he addressed himself not to the Western-educated modernistic elite, but to a humbler public comprising not only the rural illiterate masses but also many who had a modicum of education but remained attached to the traditional values of an Islamic society. He wrote in the language this public understood and remained within the artistic conventions it recognised; he even pandered to its prejudices. For example, whereas the trend in modern elitist literature has been to play down religious loyalties that might prove divisive of the nation,[8] <Ajāj in his version of the story of Abraham persistently calls the idolatrous opponents of the patriarch 'Nazarenes', although he must have known that the term was as anachronistic as it was provocative. In the face of the prestige he had in his lifetime and the fact that he is still remembered with respect by itinerant singers a generation after his death, it would be sheer dogmatism to exclude him from the canon of popular literature.

What is even clearer is that he has no place in the ranks of elitist writers. And it is an indication of the gulf that still separates the two literatures that he figures in no study or anthology purporting to deal with the whole of modern Arabic literature.

Notes

1. The fact that <Ajāj's creative work is known mainly through the printed word has the disadvantage that the Arabic script does not distinguish between regional pronunciations, yet the differences are exploited in rhyming and punning. The distinction is made in the transcription used in this book, but the reader who turns to the original booklets has to use his own acumen to detect the wordplay.
2. My information has been culled from obscure itinerant singers, and from six undated booklets published by <Ajāj, titled: *al-Fann al-<ajīb fī munājāt aṭ-ṭabīb*; *Ḥusn al-maqāl*

al-kabīr fī l-mawāwīl wa l->azjāl; *Murawwiq al-mizāj fī l-mawāwīl l-ibn <Ajāj*; *Mun<iš al-<alīl fī l-azjāl wa l-mawāwīl*; *Nūr aḍ-ḍiyā wa l-ibtihāj fī fann al-mawāliyā l-ibn <Ajāj*; and *an-Nūr al-waḍḍāḥ fī l-mawāwīl al-milāḥ*. These are so inaccessible to most readers that I see no merit in pinpointing the derivation of each statement or quotation in the pages that follow.

3. A combination of short and long syllables which gives the following pattern for each hemistich:
 -̮-̬- / -̬̌- / -̌-̬- / ̬-̬-
4. A reference to the belief that the dead will be interrogated and punished in the grave, by two angels called Munkar and Nakīr, during the night immediately following burial.
5. A fuller exposition of the development of the Egyptian *mawwāl* can be found in Item 2 of this book.
6. It is a convention in Arabic poetry, both classical and popular, to use the masculine gender in references to the beloved.
7. In an interview recorded in 1959 by the Folk Arts Centre in Cairo; I am indebted to the Centre and to its Director Mr Ḥusnī Luṭfī for supplying me with much valuable information.
8. See M. Badawi, 'Islam in Modern Egyptian Literature', and P. Cachia, 'Themes related to Christianity and Judaism in Modern Egyptian Drama and Fiction', *Journal of Arabic Literature*, 2 (1971), pp. 154–94.

PART 2

Single or Related Items

5

The Prophet's Shirt: Three Versions of an Egyptian Narrative Ballad

I. Introduction

Long neglected and indeed despised by the Arabs themselves, literary compositions in colloquial idioms are now beginning to receive serious attention from Arab scholars. Not surprisingly, for the field is vast, so specific a genre as the narrative ballad has been touched on only in the context of broader studies.

The subject is both hedged and criss-crossed with theoretical and technical questions. How distinctively 'folk' are these compositions? How do they relate to the better known recorded literature that has so far been called 'Arabic' without further qualification? How ancient, how 'pure' a tradition do they perpetuate? Into what metrical and musical forms do they fall, and where do these derive from? To what extent do intellectuals contribute to them, or interfere with them? How stable are the texts? How are they composed and transmitted? How reliant are the practitioners on the techniques of oral composition? How local is their art? What conventions do they observe?

There is no scope here to do more than state that I have come across such a variety of forms and techniques as can be fitted into only the most elastic of theories. I have also been impressed by a number of linguistic features: the extent of the vocabulary; the inconsistencies in vocalisation and even in gemination; and the fact that the same performer will sometimes combine features of what are generally held to be different regional dialects.

I can do no better service here than present – as raw material for the folklorist, the literary critic or historian, and the linguist – and therefore with a minimum of comment, a meticulous collation of three versions of the same ballad. The sample is particularly suitable for such treatment, but it must not be regarded as typical of the entire genre where contemporary themes abound and where much in honour is a kind of interpretative freesong which makes light of regularity of metre or rhyme. Here the theme is traditional but so far untraced to a specific source. The authorship is unknown, but the arrangement in quatrains with a rhyme scheme similar to that of Andalusian *zajal* and the overall similarity in wording bespeak both a common origin to the text and no small reliance on memory for its transmission. Yet there is also – in differences of substance and of wording, in irregularities of patterning, in strains to maintain the rhythm, in the transposition of formulae of praise applicable to the Prophet – evidence both of intentional variation and of improvisation, perhaps coming to the rescue of faltering memory.

Of particular interest in this instance is the difference in the immediate provenance of the three versions.

Version A (see Figure 5.1) is sung by Rašīd >Abū Sarī<, an illiterate gypsy in his forties, born in the governorate of Banī Swef. It was recorded in 1974, in Fayyum, by <Abd al-Ḥamīd Ḥawwās and <Abd al-Malik al-Xamīsī, members of the Centre for the Study of Folk Arts, which is part of the Egyptian Academy of the Arts. Another very active and knowledgeable member of the Centre, Muhammad <Imrān, kindly copied the tape for me and provided me with a rough transcription of the material. Each quatrain is sung to much the same tune, with a chorus either singing the last line of the quatrain twice, or else repeating the rhyme word enough times to fill up the line and then singing the whole line once.

Figure 5.1 Male singer: gypsy from Fayyum

A remarkable feature of the language is that, in a much more haphazard fashion than I have encountered elsewhere, this performer pronounces ق now as a glottal stop, now as a hard g, but ج always as g.

Version B (see Figure 5.2) is on a cassette produced and marketed by a firm called Nefertiti. I was able to trace the singer and interview her on 29 July 1979. She is Fāṭima Sirḥān, aged about forty, born of peasant stock in Basyūn al-X̱arbiyya near Ṭanṭā. She is completely illiterate. Her career began when, in the teeth of fierce family opposition, she married a professional itinerant singer. Since 1960, she has performed only in Cairo theatres. It was at Nefertiti's invitation and in return for a lump sum that she recorded the song. Although she had long been vaguely familiar with it, she had to learn it specially for the occasion. The version used had been obtained by the producer 'from an old man', and she was aware that it had been edited, mainly to fit it into a forty minute recording. There is no chorus, but the soloist sings the first two lines of each quatrain twice, sometimes with variations

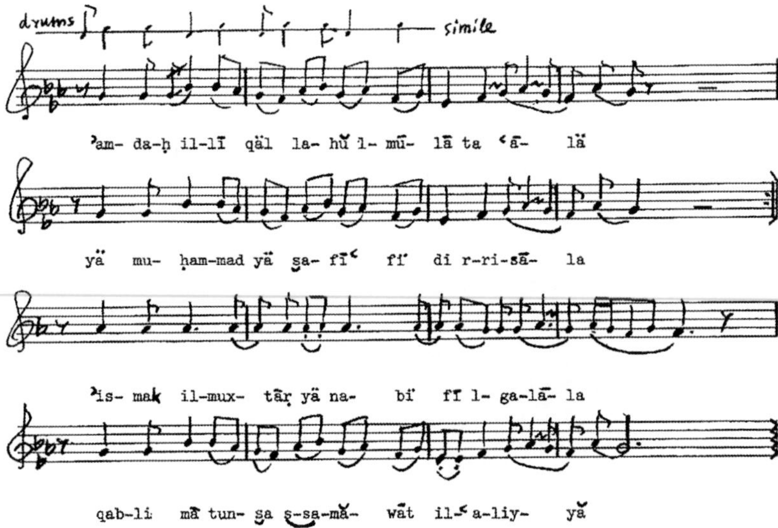

Figure 5.2 Female singer: Fāṭima Sirḥān

that are clearly corrections or improvements made on the spur of the moment (see section III. Variants and Linguistic Comments).

Version C is taken from an anonymous and undated booklet with no other title than that of the song and of two other compositions of the same type. It bears the imprint of Maktabat aš-Šamarlī, Alexandria, and was bought in Cairo in 1965. I have corrected obvious misprints and transpositions without burdening the text with additional notes, but in the very few instances in which I have filled in lacunae, I have used square brackets.

The transcription of A and B reproduces as faithfully as possible the pronunciation of the performers, even when they arbitrarily lengthen or shorten vowels to fit the rhythm. Differences in pronunciation alone, however, have not been noted. In C, I have attempted to follow standard Cairene usage in prose, without regard for metrical patterns.

Because version A squares up best with the assumption – by no means unchallengeable – that the art is most genuine when practised by the unlettered in a rural setting, it is made the basis of the transcription below.

II. The Texts

>̃amīṣ in-nabi

1. >amdaḥ illi >̃al lahū l-mūlā ta<āla
[yā rasūl allāh >ana ddīk ir-risāla[1]
>ismak il-muxtār [ya nābi[2] fi l-galālā
>̃ablı mā [tinša s-sāma wayya l-<ulayyā[3]

I praise him to whom the Lord, may He be exalted, said:
'O Apostle of God, to you I entrust Apostleship.'
Your name, O Prophet, is the one chosen in majesty
Before the firmament, together with highest heaven, was founded.

2. >̃ablı ma tinša [s-samā w ayya l->arāḍi[4]
[ṣawwar in-nābi[5] wi kān il-mulkı fāḍi
[min x̱arāmak yā nābi >ana ṣirt anādī[6]
>inkawēt [bi š-šōḡ ya bu ṭ-ṭal<a l-bahiyyā[7]

Before the firmament, together with the lands, was founded,
He formed the Prophet; till then the Kingdom had been empty.
With love of you, O Prophet, I now cry out.
I am branded with yearning, you whose countenance is resplendent.

3. <inkawēt [bi š-šōḡ[8] wi fik zād imtidāḥi
[min ḍiya xadd ēn-nābi ḥabīb iṣ-ṣabāḥī[9]
[kullı ma mdaḥ fi n-nabi[10] tibrā gurāḥi
[>̃al in-nabi >ana ḥēbb min ṣallā <alayyā[11]

I am branded with yearning, and my praise of you waxes.
Thanks to the splendour of the cheek of the Prophet, beloved of the morning,
Whenever I praise the Prophet, my wounds are healed.
Says the Prophet: 'I love him who invokes blessings upon me.

4. titmiḥī[12] <annū z-zinub kull il-xaṭiyya
>isma<ū ya hl ēl-kamāl <ala di l->̃aḍiyyā
>̃amīṣ il-muṣṭafa xayr il-bariyya

His misdeeds are wiped out, all of his sin.'
Now listen, O men of perfection, to this matter:
The shirt of the favoured one, the best of creation.

5. fī[13] >̃amīṣ il-muṣṭafā w isma< gawābi
[<ala rāgil wi kān yisma l-<urabi[14]
[<andu māl kiŧīr wa lā yi>̃bal yirābi[15]
lu xadām [we <abīd wi ṣāḥib mamlakiyyā[16]

Concerning the shirt of the favoured one, hear my response,
About a man of means who was called il-<Urābi.
He owned much property, yet would not stoop to usury
He had servants and slaves, and possessed a kingdom.

6. lu xadām we <abīd wi kān lu >̃adrı <āli [ya <ālī[17]
yikrim [iḍ-ḍēyuf ya nās min x̱ēr muḥāli[18]
mal[19] <alēh id-dahrı yā >ahl il-kamāli
[maddı >īdu li s-su>āl ba<d il-<aṭiyyā[20]

He had servants and slaves and exalted status, O exalted one.
He honoured guests, good people, without hypocrisy.
Then Time inclined against him, O men of perfection,
And he stretched out his hand in begging instead of bestowing.

7. [maddı >īdu li s-su>āl ba<d il-x̱anāwa[21]
[>as>̃atu d-dinyā l-marār ba<d il-ḥalāwa[22]
[māl <alēh id-dahr ma ddahšı hanāwa[23]
yiltag̃i <yālu min ēg-gū< fī baliyya

He stretched out his hand in begging after having been rich.
To him the world poured bitterness after sweetness.
Time inclined against him and gave him no bliss.
He found his children much afflicted by hunger.

8. yiltag̃i <yālu [bi >amr allāh ḥazāna[24]
>̃ā<idīn[25] yibkū wa lā yiddūš[26] hawāna
ṣār yiḥallaf bintē <ammu[27] bi l->amāna
>uṣburī [lamma tāgīna yyām haniyyā[28]

He found his children, by God's command, grieving,
They sat weeping, showing no alleviation,
By the trust [between them] he adjured his cousin:
'Be patient till we come to days of ease.

9. >uṣburī lammā[29] tāgīna yyām malīḥa
[yistarīḥ il->̃albı ḥammāl il-faḍīḥa[30]
ya bnı <ammī dōl[31] ŧalaŧŧ iyyām ṣaḥīḥa
lam >akalna zād [sawa šurb il-miwạyya[32]

Be patient till we come to pleasant days
When the heart now laden with shame shall find rest.'
'O cousin, it is now three whole days
That we have had no food – only water to drink.

10. lam >akalna [zād <iyālna ma yiṣburūši][33]
[šuf linā ya bnı <ammi[34] gayyid[35] ma<ūšī
>̃al laha bass[36] in-nābi[37] ma ruḥtı lūši
dōl yi>̃ūlu <a n-nābi kinz il-<aṭiyyā

We have had no food; this our children cannot endure.
Find us, cousin, some generous man who sustains [the poor]'.
He said: 'There remains only the Prophet whom I have not sought
People say of the Prophet he is a treasure of liberality.

11. dōl yi>̃ūlu <a n-nābi kinz il-<aṭāya
[>amm arūḥ w as>al in-nābi <ala di l-ḥikāya[38]
[raḥ il-<urābi li n-nābi xēr il-barāya[39]
[yiltag̃īh g̃ā<id bi >anwāru l-bahiyya[40]

People say of the Prophet he is a treasure of bounties.
Let me go and consult the Prophet in this matter.'
Il-<Urābī went to the Prophet, the best of creation,
And found him sitting with all his resplendent lights.

12. [yiltag̃īh g̃ā<id][41] <alā xaddu <alāma
[salam minnī li >aḥmad ibnı rāma[42]
[sa<ēt wi gītak ya <arūs al->̃iyāma[43]
ya miwaṣṣi <a l-x̱arīb [waṣṣī <alayyā[44]

He found him sitting, with a mark on his cheek.
'A greeting from me, O >Aḥmad son of Rāma.
I have sought and reached you, O bridegroom of the Resurrection.
You who enjoin care of the stranger, do so for me

13. ya miwaṣṣi <ā l-x̱arīb min[45] kullı šidda
[>̃atalt il->̃ōm ya nabi bi s-sēf wi ll-i<dā
ya rasūl allāh >anā gītak fi šidda[46]
[lam la>̃ēt rāgil karīm[47] ḥannin[48] <alayya

You who enjoin shielding the stranger from all hardship,
With the sword, O Prophet, you have killed the tribe – all enemies.
O Messenger of God, I come to you in hardship:
I have found no generous man who showed me compassion.

14. [lam la>̃ēt rāgil karīm[47] [ya zēn[49] <aṭāni
[>il->̃ašal ya muṣṭafā x̱ayyar bi ḥālī[50]
[šuf liḥāga ya zēn >an a>̃awwit <iyālī[51]
[g̃al lahu l-muxtār[52] yikūn ṣabrak šiwayyā

I have found no generous man, O fair one, who gave me alms.
Penury, O favoured one, has altered my condition.
Find me something, O fair one, to feed my children.'
To him the chosen one said: 'Be patient for a little.'

15. g̃al lahu l-muxtār nabīna kinz il->̃abāyil
>inzilī ya faṭim <ala babna sā>il
nizilit fāṭma wi d-dam<ı<a l-xaddı sāyĭl
>amāyil il-<ēn kama tayyār miwạyya[53]

To him [sic] *the chosen one said – our Prophet, the treasure of the tribes:*
'Come down, O Fāṭima, there is a beggar at our door.'
Down came Fāṭima, her tears running on her cheeks
From the corners of her eyes, like a torrent of water.

16. >̃alit lu ya būya l-yōm <ala bābna gamā<a
ṭālibīn iḥsān ya ṣaḥb iš-šifā<a
rāgil fa>̃īr il-ḥāl <iyālu gawā<ā
>̃a<idīn ya zēn fī ḥāla radiyya[53]

She said: 'O Father, at our door today is a whole group
Asking for alms, O Master of intercession;
And one man of poor condition , whose children are hungry –
They sit there, O fair one, in sorry condition.'

17. >̃al lahā ya fāṭim d ana zāyid hanāya
m il->̃ašal ya binti >ana m aḥkum x̱adāya
ma ḥīlitīš >illa l->̃amīṣ w ādi l-<abāya
>iddi lu l->̃āmīṣ ya bu ṭ-ṭal<a l-bahiyya[53]

He said: 'O Fāṭima, I am extremely gratified [sic].
Such is my penury, daughter, I am not sure of my own meal.
My sole resources are my shirt and this cloak of mine.'
'Give him the shirt, man of resplendent countenance!

18. [>iddi lu l->̃amīṣ ya būya[54] mā mi<ūši
raḥ warā l-manbar wi xala<ū[55] ma biṭīši
ya fa>̃īr il-ḥāl [ṭab adīk[56] >̃amīṣī
[<asa llah burdati tisbil <alayya[57]

Give him the shirt, O Father, he has nothing'
He went behind the pulpit, took it off without delay.
'O man in need, here now is my shirt.
Please God, my cloak should prove ample for me.'

19. [quatrain missing[58]; chorus reads:]
yib>̃a lak ya šēx bi r-raddı <alayya
It remains for you, old man, to respond to me.

20. yib>̃ā lak [yā šēx[59] [l aglı[60] ma tāxuđ wi tiddi
[>in ḥaddı kallāmak ya šēx[61] hatū li<andi
[kullı m amdaḥ fi n-nabi yizūli karbī
kaŧŧar allah xēr >abu l-yadd is-saxiyyā[62]

You shall have the right, Sheikh – so you may give and take,
Should anyone question you, Sheikh – to bring him to me.'
'Whenever I praise the Prophet, my cares fall away from me.
May God prosper the liberal-handed one

21. kaŧŧar allah xēr[63] >abu l-<ēn il-kaḥīla
[da y>̃aḍḍi <aylitī gum<a ṭawīla
xađ il-<urābi ŧ-ŧōb mišī yamm il-midīna
yiltaği l-<ašrā l-kurām galsīn sawiyyā[64]

May God prosper the one with kohl-coloured eyes
This will suffice my family for a whole long week.'
il-<Urābī took the garment and made for Medina
To meet the noble ten sitting together.

22. yiltaği[65] l-<ašrā l-kurām >aḥbāb[66] nabīna
>̃a<dīn[67] yitagru[68] [fī ṣalāt[69] nabīnā
[>̃al luhum ya bawādi šūrum <alēna
fēni dāllāl il-midīna l-mamlakiyya[70]

To meet the noble ten, beloved of our Prophet,
Sitting and trading blessings on our Prophet.
He said: 'O (?) eminent men, advise us –
Where is the auctioneer of this regal city?

23. fēni dāllāl il-midīna[71] ya bawādi
>abī<[72] ŧōb in-nābi [w ablu<u>x</u> murādī[73]
[ruḥ li wāḥid fi ṣ-ṣifūf[74] <ammāl yinādī
[>ismu <ammār[75] ta<rafu kull ir-ra<iyyā

Where is the auctioneer of this city, (?) eminent ones,
That I may sell the Prophet's garment and achieve my purpose?'
'Go to one in the ranks who is shouting out;
His name is <Ammār – he is known to all the subjects.'

24. [šayya<ū yā nās li <ammār gābūlu[76]
[<irif il -kālām ya nās >̃ablı >in yigūlu[77]
[misik ŧōb in-nabi wi b īdu sallamūlu[78]
>̃al[79] iftaḥum[80] bābu tēbān fīh il-<aṭiyyā

Good people, they sent for <Ammār and had him brought to him.
He knew what was afoot, good people, even before they reached him.
He took the Prophet's garment and with his own hand entrusted it to him,
Saying: 'Open the door [to bidding] and [the value of] the gift shall be made clear.'

25. >awwil fitūḥ il-bāb <ašar ṣalawāt <aṭātu[81]
>̃al il-<urābi yiftaḥ allah fī širātu[81]
da >̃amīṣ [ṭāhā n-nabī zīdū f [82] ṣalātu
fazz abū bakr iṣ-ṣaddī>̃ dam<u miwạyyā

As soon as the door was opened, ten blessings he was offered.
Said il-<Urābī: 'God open [wider doors] in the sale of it.
This is Ṭāhā the Prophet's shirt – call down more blessings upon him.'
Up got >Abū Bakr the Truthful, his tears [a stream of] water.

26. [>abū bakrı g̃al wi g̃al ya ḥasūdi
hāƶa ŧ-ŧōb da malbūs ḥabībi
>iƶ kān ya dallāl ḥa yib>̃a min naṣībi[83]
nādi yā dallāl wi >̃ūl iŧ-ŧōb[84] bi-miyyā

>Abū Bakr spoke; he said: 'You who envy me,
This garment is what my loved one has worn.
If it is, auctioneer, to be my portion
Then call out, auctioneer, that the garment is worth a hundred.

27. miyya li d-dallāl min iđ-đahab iṣ-ṣalāyib[85]
kurma li n-nābi bi yzīḥ il-x̱aḍāyib
g̃al il->amīr ḥamza fi <yūnu rax̱āyib
>̃al <alayya ŧōb ḥabībi b-ŧulŧimiyya

A hundred pieces for the auctioneer, of solid gold
In honour of the Prophet who wipes anger away.'
Prince Ḥamza spoke up, with desire in his eyes,
Saying: 'I will have my beloved's garment for three hundred.

28. >̃ul ŧulŧimiyya min iđ-đahab iṣ-ṣaḥīḥa[85]
kurma li n-nābi b rī>̃u šāfa s-saṭīḥa
>̃al il->amīr <ušmān b->anātu l-malīḥa
>̃al <alayya ŧōb ḥabībi b-xumsimiyyā

Call out "Three hundred sound pieces of gold"
In honour of the Prophet whose saliva cures the bedridden.'
Prince <Ušmān spoke up, with his fair self-possession,
Saying: 'I will have my beloved's garment for five hundred.

29. xumsimiyya ya dallāl min iđ-đahab it-tigāra[85]
kurma li n-nābi tisir yammu l->amāra
g̃al il->amīr <abbās wi g̃a<id fī dāra
>̃al <alayya ŧōb ḥabībi b sub<imiyyā

Five hundred pieces, auctioneer, of gold as used in trade
In honour of the Prophet towards whom authority advances [to make submission]'
Prince <Abbās, sitting in his home, spoke up
Saying: 'I will have my beloved's garment for seven hundred.

30. sub<imiyya yā dallāl mi đ-đahab iṣ-ṣaḥīḥa[85]
kurma li n-nābi b >anātu l-malīḥa
>̃al il->amīr ḥamza kan >̃ā<id fi rīḥa
<alayya ŧōb ḥabībi b tus<imiyyā

Seven hundred, auctioneer, sound pieces of gold
In honour of the Prophet with his fair self-possession.'
Said Prince Ḥamza, who was sitting by him:
'I will have my beloved's garment for nine hundred.

31. tus<imiyya yā dallāl min iđ-đahab it-tigāra[85]
kurma li n-nābi bi <iyūn il->amāra
>̃al il->amīr <ālī u g̃ā<id fī dāra
<alayya ŧōb ibni <ammi b <uširimiyyā

Nine hundred pieces, auctioneer, of gold as used in trade
In honour of the Prophet, with eyes full of authority.'
Then said Prince <Ālī who was sitting in his home:
'I will have my cousin's garment for ten hundred.

32. <uširimiyya yā dallāl min iđ-đahab il-miwag̃g̃ad[85]
kullı min šaf il->̃āmīṣ lāzim yizawwad
>̃amiṣ in-nabi >ahu muluk li l->alfı w azwad
w il-<urābi fi l-<aṭā bi yg̃ūl šiwayyā[86]

Ten hundred pieces, auctioneer, of glowing gold.'
Whoever saw the shirt had to increase the bid,
So now the Prophet's shirt commands a thousand and more,
Yet to all offers il-<Urābi says: 'Too little'

33. yirga< kalāmi fī l-midīna tāgir yahūdi[87]
<andu <abdı lahu msammīh is-si<ūdi
...
>̃al lu ya sīdi ra>ēt fi s-sū>̃ >̃aḍiyya

Let me hark back: In Medina was a Jewish merchant
Who had a slave whom he called is-Si<ūdī.
He asked him: 'What detained you from me, slave?'
He said: 'Master, I have seen a strange matter in the market.'

34. >̃al [lu ya sīdi ra>ēt >̃amīṣ fi l-midīna[89] dāyir
[ŧamanu ya sīdi[90] x̱ilib ŧaman il-gawāhir
>̃al lu [yā <bēdi[91] fi ṣalāt iṣ-ṣubḥı[92] bākir
>in wiṣil >alfēn ŧalāŧa >̃ūl <alayyā[93]

He said: 'Master, I have seen a shirt taken round Medina
The cost of which, O Master, exceeds the price of gems.'
Said he: 'Tomorrow, slave, at the time of morning prayer,
Though it reach two or three thousand, call out: "I will have it."'

35. ṣabaḥ iṣ-ṣabāḥ wi l-<abdı miši yāmm il-madīna
yilta>̃i l-<ašrā l-kurām >aḥbāb nabīna
<amaltū >ēh ma tšūru <alēna
<amalna mn ēl-gawāhir <ušrimiyyā[94]

Morning came and the slave made for Medina
To meet the noble ten, beloved of our Prophet.
'What have you done? Will you not advise us?'
'We have assigned ten hundred gems.'

36. [<ušrimiyya w <ušrimiyya w <ušrimiyya[95]
[w intā ya dallāl <ašar sanayim g̃abālak
>inta ya dallāl <ašar gimāl g̃abālak[96]
[>̃al lu yā <bēdi bi<ti lak[97] bi ṣafwı niyyā

'Ten hundred and ten hundred and ten hundred –
And for you, auctioneer, ten (?) big-humped camels before you;
For you, auctioneer, ten camels here before you.'
He said: 'I sell it to you, slave, in good faith!'

37. [<alī bnı <amm in-nābi >̃al izzāy[98] ya ḥasūdi
[tibī< ŧōb[99] ibnı <ammi li l-yahūdi
l a>̃aṭṭa<ak āna[100] bi s-sēf wi ḥyāt gidūdi
[<ēbitak fi l-muslimīn tiṣ<ab <alayyā[101]

<Alī, the Prophet's cousin, said: 'How dare you, envious one,
Sell my cousin's garment to the Jew ?
I shall cut you to pieces with my sword, by my forefathers!
The shame you bring on Muslims is hard for me to bear.

38. <ēbitak[102] fī l-muslimīn ya ma hī xusāra
l ašḥatak ana w awaddīk l ibnı rāma
sa<u li n-nabi raḥu humma ŧ-ŧalāta
>̃al lu sību ya >māmi di ḍ-ḍamāna <alayyā

The shame you bring on Muslims is such a loss
I shall drive you out myself and take you to the son of Rāma.'
And so they went, all three, seeking the Prophet.
He said: 'Let go of him, Imam, I guarantee [the outcome].'

39. [xađ il->̃amīṣ il-<abd u rāḥ li sīdu
kān il-<ama ya nās lāṭiš fi <uyūnu
misik >̃amīṣ in-nābi mallas bu gibīnu[103]
fattaḥēt <ēneh[104] min ir-rīḥa z-zakiyya

The slave then took the shirt and went on to his master.
Now blindness, good people, had afflicted his eyes.
He got hold of the Prophet's shirt and with it stroked his forehead;
His eyes were opened thanks to the fine fragrance.

40. fattaḥit[105] <ēnēh wi šāf l-iswid wi l-abyaḍ
kurma li n-nābi wi >ašhad wa la >agḥad
x̱er dīn in-nabi >ana lam <udtı >a<bid
iṣ-ṣanam w ayya l-habal ḥurum <alayyā

His eyes were opened, he could see white and black.
'In honour of the Prophet, I declare and shall not deny:
Other than the Prophet's faith I no longer worship.
The idol and all folly are forbidden me.'

41. xađ[105] il->̃amīṣ wi s-sēf wi rikib il-hagīna
silimit wara l->̃amīṣ wi tis<īn midīna
raḥ il-yahūdi w itfaḍḍal li nabīna
ya rasūl allāh >i>̃bal minnil-hidiyyā

He took the shirt and sword and mounted his camel.
Beside the shirt, ninety cities were surrendered.
The Jew went forward and presented himself to the Prophet:
'O Apostle of God, accept from me this present.'

III. Variants and Linguistic Comments

1. B: ya muḥammad ya šafī< fi di r-risāla *O Muhammad, intercessor in [connection with] this Apostleship.*
   C: >inta ḥabībi >a<ṭīk ir-risāla *You are my beloved I grant you Apostleship.*
2. C: <andi *by me.*
3. B, C: tunša s-samāwāt il-<aliyyā *the high heavens were founded.*
4. B: s-samāwāt wi l->arāḍi *the heavens and the lands.*
5. B, C: ṣawwarak y aḥmad *He formed you, >Aḥmad.*
6. B: >ismak yā nābi mināwwar <a l->arāḍi *Your name, O Prophet, shines over the lands.*
   C: min x̱arāmak ya kaḥīl b anādi
   With love of you, you [whose eyes are] kohl-coloured, I cry out.
7. B: bi n-nār wē tib>̃a yyām haniyyā *with fire, and there will be happy days.*
8. B: bi n-nār *with fire.*
9. B: Min ḍiya xadd in-nābi kama fagrı lāḥi *Thanks to the splendour of the Prophet's cheek, like looming dawn.*
   C: min ḍiya xaddak yi>̃ūl il-fagrı lāḥi *Thanks to the splendour of your cheek, which proclaims that dawn is looming.*
10. B: ḥīn >azūr il-muṣṭafā *Whenever I visit the favoured one,*
    C: ḥīn >azūrak ya nabi *Whenever I visit you, O Prophet,*
11. B: tinṭifi n-nīrān w ašūf il-bahga gayyā *The fires are put out and I see joy approaching.*
    C: tinṭifi n-nīrān wi tib>̃a yyām haniyya *The fires are put out, and happy days follow.*
12. Instead of this stanza, B has – with C variations in parentheses:
    tinṭifi n-nīrān ḥa>̃ī>̃ [ba lā (min x̱ēr) muḥāla
    ḥin (lammā) >azūr illi >atāna bi r-risāla
    >isma<ū sabab (>aṣl) il->̃aḍiyya wi d-dilālā
    [line missing from printed version]

    The fires are put out, truly, without pretence
    When I visit him who brought us the message.
    Listen to what caused (was the root of) the matter, and its significance
    Concerning the shirt of the favoured one, the best of creation.
13. B: <an *Regarding*
14. B: <an ragil šārīf wi kān ismu l-<urābi *Regarding a noble man whose name was il-<Urābī.*
    C differs from A only in having '<an' for '<ala'.
15. B: <andu m il->amwāl kiŧīr wa lā yurābi *He had ample possessions and did not practice usury.*
    C: qad malak >amwāl wi <umru lam yirābi *He had possessions and never in his life had practised usury*

16. B: yā ma wi <andu mamlakiyyā – *how many! – and he possessed a kingdom.* C: wi <yāl wi >amlāk >aliyya *and children and exalted possessions*. In the next line, C again has '<iyāl' instead of '<abīd'.
17. B and C omit.
18. B, with C variations in parentheses: iḍ-ḍīyūf (iḍ-ḍīfān) ḥa>ī> [ba lā (min x̱ēr) muḥāli *guests truly, without hypocrisy.*
19. C: gār *oppressed*
20. B: >am ṭili< min ēl-balad zāyid >asiyya *So he left town in excessive grief.* Both here and in the next line, C differs from A in having 'bi s-su>āl' instead of 'li s-su>āl'.
21 B: >am ṭili< min ēl-balad wa la tawāni *So he left town without weakening.*
22. B: yišḥat [for classical 'yašḥaḏ'] il->ut li l-<iyāl wa la tawāni *Begging sustenance for his children without weakening.*

    C has 'marār' without the article; it also reverses the order of the second and third lines.
23. B: rigi< fi saww il-ḥāl bi la tawāni *He fell back into an evil condition, without respite.*

    C: mīn yikīdu d-dahrı lam yūrīh hanāwa *When Time vents its malice on someone, it shows him no bliss*. Then, making the fourth line part of a different quatrain, C interposes:

    dār <a l->agawīd gam<an bi s-sawiyya *He went round men of liberality, all alike.*

    dār <a l->agawīd ba>um yiṭṭili<ūlu
    bassı bi l->a<yān wi >iḥsān lam <aṭūlu
    lamma šammat fīh <azūlu
    farrı hārib min il-balad w izdād >asiyya

    He went round men of liberality, and they turned to him
    With their eyes only; alms they did not give.
    When he saw that Time made his censurer gloat over him,
    He ran away, escaping from the town, and his grief increased.

    farrı hārib min il-balad bi x̱ēr tawāni
    yišḥat [for cl. 'yašḥaḏ'] il->ūt li l-<iyāl ya >ahl il-kamāli
    ma >aḥad <aṭāh rigi< [fi] sawwi ḥāli

    He ran away, escaping from the town without weakening
    Begging sustenance for his children, O men of perfection.
    No one gave him, and he fell back into an evil condition
24. B: min guwwa l-bēt ga<āna *inside the house, hungry.*

    C: wi >ahlı bētu ḥazāna *and his household grieving*
25. B: dayirīn *going round*
26. C: yi<ṭūš, a synonym.

27. Since by custom a man has first claim on his cousin's hand, the word 'cousin' is sometimes used for 'spouse'.
28. C: >iyyāk tigīna maziyya *in the hope that something special will come our way.*
29. C: >iyyāk *in the hope that*
30. B: wa ḥyāt in-nābi >illi >āmir fiṣīḥā *by the life of the Prophet who gives commands, eloquently.*
    C: yistarīḥ il->̃albı min gūr il-fiḍīḥa *the heart will find rest from the oppression of shame.*
31. C: >ādi *it is now*
32. B: wa la šribna miwạyya *nor drunk water*
33. B, with C variation in parentheses: w ēl-<iyāl ma [b yi<zurūši (yiṣburūši) *and the children brook no excuse* (*cannot endure*).
34. B inverts: ya bnı <ammi šuf lina
35. C: xayyir *virtuous*. The next word in all versions, ma<ūši, appears to be an irregular formation from the root <-y-š, *to live*, ostensibly with the sense of *ensuring survival.*
36. B, C: fāḍil *there remains*
37. B adds: >illi *to whom*
38. B: lamm aruḥ lu w as>alu fi di l-ḥikāya *Let me go to him and consult him in this matter*. C differs from B in omitting 'lu' *to him*
39. B: raḥ wi >̃āl lu ya mubaššir bi l-hadāya *He went and said to him: 'You who give good tidings of guidance*
    C: wi fatha rāḥ li n-nabi ṣāḥib il-hidạya *He left her and went to the Prophet, the master of guidance*
41. C: >akḥal il-<enēn *with kohl-coloured eyes*
42. C: >̃al salāmi <ala l-miẓallal bi l-x̱amāma *He said: 'My greetings to the one shaded by the cloud* – a reference to the legend found in classical sources that a cloud moved over the Prophet to protect him from the sun.
43. C: minni s-salām <alēk y aḥmad ibnı rāma *A greeting from me to you, O >Aḥmad son of Rāma.*
44. C: kull il-waṣiyya *a full injunction*
45. C: fi *in*
46. B: ya lli bi sēfak yā nābi >̃aṭṭa<t il-a<da
    >āna gētak ya nabi min ba<dı mudda

    You who with your sword, O Prophet, have cut down the enemies,
    I have come to you, O Prophet, after much delay

    C: ya mīn bi sēfak >̃aṭṭa<t il yahūd wi n-naṣraniyya
    >adīni >atētak ya nabi fi wa>̃tı šidda

    You who with your sword have cut down Jews and Christendom,
    Here have I come to you, O Prophet, in time of hardship.

47. B: lam la>̃ēt wāḥid kărīm *I have found no generous person.*
C: ma ra>yak wāḥid karīm *What do you say of a generous person?*
48. B: <aṭaf *who showed kindness*
C: >ašfa>̃ *who showed pity*
49. B, C: y aḥmad *O >Aḥmad*
50. B, with C variation in parentheses: >illa l-gū< (il->̃atl) ya muṣṭafā lli ḍarrı ḥāli *Except hunger (death), O favoured one, that has damaged my condition.*
51. B, with C variation – presumably a misprint – in parentheses [line missing from printed version] *The chosen one bowed his head over his palm (the infidels) and said*
52. B, C: ya fa>̃īr il-ḥāl *you who are in poverty*
53. In both the other versions, quatrains 15–17 are reduced to one.
B:
>aṭra>̃ il-muxtār w ahō badr il-budūra
kinzi l il->islām lawi ṣabha ḍarūra
rabbinā >arsal lu gēbrīlibi nūrā
>iddilu l->̃amīṣ ya bu ṭ-ṭal<a l-bahiyyā

The chosen one bowed his head, who is the full moon of full moons,
The treasure of Islam should it be afflicted with need.
Our Lord sent him Gabriel with His light:
'Give him the shirt,you whose countenance is resplendent!
C:
>aṭra>̃ il-muxtār wi huwwa badr il-budūra
kan yirayyaḥ in-nās >iza gatha ḍarūra
>allah >arsal lu gibrīl bi šūra
>a<ṭāh il->̃amīṣ ya bu ṭ-ṭal<a l-bahiyya
The chosen one bowed his heaḍ, who is the full moon of full moons.

He used to relieve people when they were afflicted by need.
God sent him Gabriel, conveying advice
He gave him the shirt, O you whose countenance is resplendent.

The word 'raḍiyya' at the end of quatrain 16 in version A evidently does not mean 'content' as it would in classical Arabic, but corresponds to classical 'radī>a' – a rare change from 'd' to 'ḍ' producing virtually an antonym. Also suspect is 'hanāya' at the end of the next line; some irregular derivation from h-w-n, with the sense of 'being humbled' or 'reduced', would fit the context better.
54. C: >a<ṭah il->̃amīṣ ya zēn da *He gave him the shirt, O fair one, for ...*
55. C: >̃ala<u, a synonym.
56. C: ta<āla xuđ *come and take*
57. C: bass ana lli burditi tifḍal <alayya *Only I will be left with my cloak upon me.* In B, the entire quatrain is as follows, the first two lines being sung twice with variations indicated in parentheses:

>iddilu l->̃amīṣ [ya nābi(da fa>̃īr wi) ma m<ahūši
da fa>̃īr il-māl (il-ḥāl) gā lak wa la ḥiltihūši
>̃am rasūl allāh wi >̃āla< ma biṭīši
xuđ il->̃amīṣi w burdēti tifḍal <alayya

Give him the shirt [O Prophet (he is poor and) he has nothing.
He is poor in wealth (in condition); he has come to you resourceless.
The Apostle of God rose and stripped, did not tarry:
'Take the shirt my mantle will be left to me.'

58. In B, with C variations in parentheses:
[burditī ya šēx w āho ŧawbi >̃ubālak
(bass ana >albis burditi wi ŧōbi >̃ubālak)
rūḥ (ya fa>̃īr) bī< il->̃amīṣ wi >̃awwit bih (C omits) <iyālak
[w in (>in) garā lak ḍēm w alla ḥaddı sālak
yib>̃ā lak ya šēx bi r-rag<a (r-raddı) <alayya

[My mantle, O Sheikh – and here is my garment before you.
(Enough that I should wear my mantle – here is my garment before you.)
Go (Poor man), sell the shirt and feed your children.
Should harm befall you, or anyone question you,
It shall be your right, Sheikh, that I answer for you.

59. C omits.
60. B: >̃abli; C: min >̃abl *before*
61. B and (C): >in ḥaddı sa>alak <a (<ala) l->̃amīṣ *Should anyone question you about the shirt*
62. B:
>̃al ya nābi >ana rētı zād rušdī
bass arūḥ bu li l-<iyāl sā>līn <alayya

He said: 'O Prophet I see that my wisdom increases. Only with it I must go to the children: they are asking for me.'

C:
>̃āl ra>ēt ya muḥammad zād rušdi
>̃āl xuđ ya šēx <aṭāk rabb il-bariyya

He said: 'I see, Muḥammad, that my wisdom increases.'
He said: 'Take it, Sheikh, may the Lord of Creation give you [more]'

B then adds:
bassı >axđu li l-<iyāl yistabrakū bu
w alla >axđu s-sū>̃ w izā ma nba<š agību
w alla ra>yak >ēh >iza ma rḍitš asību
>aškur allah ya nābi <ala di l-<aṭiyya

'Only let me take it to the children that they may find a blessing in it,
Or take it to the market, and if it is not sold, bring it back;

Or what would you say if I refuse to part with it,
Thanking God, O Prophet, for this gift?'
C adds:
>̃al lu xuđu <aṭāk rabb il-<ibād
il->̃amīṣ bī<u w infi>̃ <ala l-wilād
xađ il->̃amīṣ wi xaṭṭa ya bawād
>̃al >arūḥ li l-<iyāl <ayṭīn 'alayya

(It is evident from a comparison of the three versions of quatrain 22 that 'bawād' is a complimentary term, perhaps an irregular formation from b-d-w in the sense of 'evident' or 'prominent' it could also mean 'nomads,' or – from b-y-d – 'mortals'.)

He said: 'Take it, may the Lord of Mankind give you.
Sell the shirt, and provide for the children.'
He took the shirt and stepped out, O (?) eminent ones,
Saying: 'Let me go to the children, who are crying for me.'

>̃al >arūḥ <ala l-<iyāl >ēš ya<milū bu
lamm aruḥ bu s-sū>̃ w in ma nba<š agību
w alla >awaddīh li l-<iyāl yitbarrakū bu
wi kaŧŧar allah x̱ēr >abu l-yadd is-saxiyya

He said: 'If I take it to the children, what will they do with it?
Let me take it to the market, and if it is not sold, bring it back.
Or shall I send it to the children that they may seek a blessing in it?
May God prosper the one with the liberal hand'

63. B: xērak ya, ... *prosper you, O*

64. B:
da yi>̃aḍḍi >awlādi (repeated as: <iyāli >̃ūl) mudda ṭawīla
>āxađ il->̃amīṣ wi mā bi l-yaddı ḥīla
bi l-madīna šaf kurām >̃a<dīn šiwayya

It will suffice my children a long time.'
He took the shirt, having no resource [of his own] in hand.
In Medina he saw some noble men resting awhile.
C:
>abu t-tāg wi l-mi<rāg wi l-wasīla
xađ il->̃amīṣ minnu wi rāḥ yamm il-madīna
li>̃i l-<ašra l-kirām >̃a<dīn sawiyya

He of the crown and the journey to Heaven and the means [of intercession].'
He took the shirt from him and went towards Medina.
He found the noble ten sitting together.

65. B: yēla>̃i, and, on repeating the whole quatrain, yilti>̃i;
C: li>̃i – all variants of the same verb.

66. B, C: >aṣḥāb *companions*

67. B: dāyirīn *going round*

68. C: yitraḥḥamu *seeking mercy*
69. B: ya ṣalāt *ah, what blessings*
70. B:

yi>̃ul li-hōm ya >̃ṭāb ta<ālu šūru <alēna
>̃uṭbı minhum šāfi dam< il-<ēn miwạyya

Saying to them: 'Great leaders, come and advise us!'
One of them saw the tears in his eyes [running like] water.

C:
>̃al luhum ya giwād ta<ā [*for*: ta<ālu] šūru <alayya
fēn dallāl il-balad yi>ti >ilayya

He said to them: 'O liberal ones, come and advise me:
Where is the town's auctioneer? Let him come to me.'

On changing over to the second side of the cassette, B repeats quatrains 1, 2 (three times) and 22, then adds:
>̃am il->̃uṭbı >̃al lu >̃ul li ya <urābi
fēni dallāl il-bālad yiḥḍar li bābi
hađa ŧ-ŧōb yisāwi kam malbūs ḥabībī
ya <urābi >ēh ḥikaytak samma< <alayya

The leader rose and said: 'Tell me, <Urābī,
Where is the town's auctioneer that he may come to my door?
This garment, my beloved's raiment, what is it worth?
What is your story, <Urābī? Recount it to me'

71. B: il-bālad di *this town*
72. B, C: lamm abī< *That I may sell*
73. B, C: w a>̃awwit wilādi *and feed my children*
74. B and (C): >̃ām (fazz) waḥēd min iṣ-ṣifūf *One rose* (*sprang up*) *from the ranks.* C also omits the next word, <ammāl.
75. B and (C: ruḥ li <āmir (<ammār) *Go to <Āmir* (*<Ammār*)
76. B and (C): šayya<ū >iŧnēn lē [repeated as: l aglı] <āmir (<ammār) yindahūlu (nadūlu) *They sent two to <Āmir* (*<Ammār*) *to call him* (*and they called him*)
77. B: wāṣal il-xābar min >̃abl in ya <ēn yigūlu, repeated as: waṣal il-xabar ya <ēn min >̃abl in yigūlu *The news reached him – ah, me! – before they came to him.* C: il-fa>̃īr kan ya<rafu >̃abl in yigīlu *The poor man knew him before coming to him.*
78. B and (C): ḥaṭṭı >īdu <a (fi) l->̃amīṣ wi yislamhūlu (sallimhūlu) *He placed his hand on* (*inside*) *the shirt, entrusting* (*and entrusted*) *it to him.*
79. B and C omit.
80. B, C: >iftaḥu *open*
81. The first two lines of quatrain 25 are missing from C. B condenses quatrains 25–32 into one:

fataḥu bābu <ašar ṣalawāt <alēk ya >aḥmad

kullı min misik il->̃āmīṣ miyya yizawwid
lamma wāṣal >alf wē n-nāsē tizawwid
wi l-<urābi fi l-<aṭa bi y>̃ūl šiwayya

They opened the door – ten blessings upon you, >Aḥmad!
Whoever touched the shirt bid another hundred
Until it reached a thousand, people still bidding,
And to all offers il-<Urābī said: 'Too little!'

82. C: il-muṣṭafa zīd *of the favoured one – added*
83. C:
fazz >abū bakr iṣ-ṣaddī>̃ >̃al ya <urābi
lēh tibī< il->̃amīṣ malbūs ḥabībi
mu>nis[i] fil-x̱ār wi ṭabībi

>Abū Bakr the Truthful sprang up and said: 'O <Urābī ,
Why will you sell the shirt that is the raiment of my beloved,
My comforting companion in the cave, my physician?

The last line alludes to the classical account of the Prophet's flight from Mecca, with >Abū Bakr as his sole companion; at one point, they hid in a cave at the entrance of which a dove then laid her eggs, so that their pursuers were convinced the cave was untenanted.

84. C: >i<milūh *make it*
85. In C, quatrains 27–32 read:
>̃ūl bi mīt maḥbūb min iđ-đahab iṣ-ṣalāyib
mištiri>>abū bakrı kān šāri wi rāx̱ib
lamma diri <ušmān <alēh radd il-ḥisāb [? read 'ḥasāyib']
>̃al <alayya di l->̃amīṣ bi ŧulŧimiyya

Say: 'For a hundred pieces of solid gold'
A [prospective] buyer was >Abū Bakr – bidding and eager.
When <Ušmān heard of this, he revised his expectations.
He said: 'I will have this shirt for three hundred.

ŧulŧimīt maḥbūb đahab miṣaffi
ŧulŧimīt ḥamra min kaffak li kaffi
<umar ibn il-xaṭṭāb kān >̃ādir wi y<affi
>̃āl >̃amīṣ iz-zēn <alayya b xumsimiyya

Three hundred pieces of refined gold,
Three hundred red ones [passing] from your palm to mine [sic]*'*
<Umar ibn al-Xaṭṭāb had means and (?) *increasing strength.*
He said: 'Let the fair one's shirt be mine for five hundred.'

...
>il->imām <ali bi hay>itu l-malīḥa
>̃āl <alayya da l->̃amīṣ bi sub<imiyya

Imam <Alī with his fine appearance
Said: 'I will have this shirt for seven hundred –

sub<imīt maḥbūb ma<dūda tamām
li >aglı Ṭāhā <alēh >azka s-salām
ḥīn diri l-ḥamza >̃āl >isma< kalāmi
bī< wi sāmiḥ ya <urābi b tus<imiyya

Seven hundred pieces counted out in full
For Ṭāhā's sake – upon him be the purest greeting'
When Ḥamza heard, he said: 'Listen to my words:
Sell – and be accommodating, <Urābī – for nine hundred.

tus<imīt maḥbūb đahab minawwar
li->aglı ṭāhā l-muṣṭafa >a>̃dar w adawwar
lamma diri l-<abbās wi kān lu waghı mnawwar
>̃āl <alayya l->̃amīṣ bi <ušrimiyya

Nine hundred pieces of shining gold.
For the sake of Ṭāhā the favoured one, I will find [the means] and go seeking.'
When <Abbas heard of this – he had a shining face –
He said: 'I will have the shirt for ten hundred.'

dār <ala l-kirām >aṣḥāb muḥammad
kullı min >axađ il->̃amīṣ ṣār yizawwad
ḥaṣṣalu l->̃amīṣ li l->alfi w azyad
wi l-<urābi fi l-<aṭa yi>̃ūl šiwayya

It was taken round the noble ones, Muḥammad's companions.
Whoever held the shirt kept raising the bid.
They took [the price of] the shirt up to a thousand and more,
Yet to all offers il-<Urābī said: 'Too little!'

86. B and C add three quatrains here. The C variations are in parentheses, except for the second quatrain where both versions are reproduced in full:
>il-<urābi fi l-<aṭa bi (C omits) y>̃ūl m asību
kulli wāḥid (minna) yā kurām [yirḍa b (yāxuđ) naṣību
il-kubār (it-tuggār) w ahl il-madīna (il-balad) istamta<ū bu
[kullihum <araḍu l->̃amīṣ <ala <ušrimiyya
(yilti>̃u l->̃amīṣ wā>̃if bi <ušrimiyya)

To all offers il-<Urābi said: 'I will not part with it.
Let each one (*of us*), *O noble ones, [be content with* (*accept*) *his lot.'*
[The high-placed ones (*The merchants*) *and the people of Medina* (*the town*) *were delighted with it.*
[Each of them hiked the shirt up to ten hundred.
(*They found the bidding for the shirt settling at ten hundred.*)

B:
ma ḥaddı zawwid <an xēlāf hazihi l<aṭāya
>̃ālit in-nās il-kurām >ahl ir-riwāya
il->̃amīṣ da lu ḥikāya m il-bidāya
>alfı maḥbūb fī >̃amīṣ iz-zēn šiwayya

No one bid more against these offers.
Noble people, transmitters of lore, then said:
'There has been something about this shirt right from the start.
A thousand gold pieces for the fair one's shirt is not enough'
C:
la>̃u l->̃amīṣ wā>̃if <ala l-<ušrimiyya
ma ḥaddı zawwid xilāf hāzihi l-<aṭāya
>̃ālit in-nās il kubār >ahl iz-zawāya
>alfı maḥbūb fi l->̃amīṣ šwayya

They found [the bidding for] the shirt settling at ten hundred.
No one bid more against these offers.
The leading people, those in the places of prayer, said:
'A thousand pieces for the shirt is not enough.'

>alfı maḥbūb [ya >̃amīṣ (fil->̃amīṣ) ma ḥaddı zādak
bi< wi sāmiḥ ya <urābi l->̃albı rādak (C omits)
xuđ [<ašar miyyāt wi rūḥ (<ašar dananīr) >̃awwit wilādak (<iyālak)
[l-aglı yirtaḥ >̃albak ḥammāl il->asiyya
(yistarīḥ il->̃albı min gūr il-baliyya

A thousand pieces, O shirt (for the shirt) – no one bid more.
'Sell and be accommodating, <Urābī ; your heart [mis]leads you.
Take [ten hundred, go (ten dinars) and feed your children,
[That your heart, laden with sorrow, may find rest.
(That your heart may find rest from the oppression of misfortunes.)

87. In the other versions, this quatrain is expanded in different ways:
B:
yirtaḥ il->̃albı ya <ēn ḥamil [repeated as: 'min'] il->asāwi
yirtigi< >̃ōli<alā tāgir mi>̃āwi
>̃al lu >alfı maḥbūbi da >akŧar yisāwī
>aṣlu tāgir fi l-mādīna l-aḥmadiyyā

That the heart – ah, me – laden with sorrows may find rest.
'Now let me hark back to an aggressive merchant
Who said: '"A thousand pieces? It is worth more"'
He was, in fact, a merchant in >Aḥmad's city.

>aṣlu tāgir fil-mādīna kan sa<īdi
kan mirabbi <abdı w msammīh <ibēdi

>̃al lu >ēš abṭak <alayya ya <ibēdi
>̃al ya sīdi >ana ra>ēt fi s-sū>̃ >̃aḍiyya

He was, in fact, a merchant in Medina; he was fortunate.
He had brought up a slave whom he called <Ibēdi.
He asked him: 'What kept you back from me, <Ibēdi?'
He said: 'Master, I have seen a strange thing in the market.'
C:
yirtāḥ il->̃albı min gūr il-balāwi
li >aglı Ṭāhā z-zēn illi xaddu ḍāwi
yirtigi< il->̃ōl li kāfir kān mi>̃āwi
>aṣlu fāgir fi l-madīna l-misammiyya

The heart would rest from the oppression of calamities
For the sake of Ṭāhā, the fair one with the luminous cheek.'
My words hark back to an aggressive unbeliever
He was, in fact, a gross sinner in the city named [after the Prophet].

>aṣlu tāgir fi l-madīna yahūdi
mirabbi <abdı wi msammīh sa<ūdi
>̃al >ēš >abtāk ya <ibēdi
>̃āl ra>ēt >̃amīṣ ma yigīš wi>̃iyya

He was in fact a merchant in Medina, a Jew
Who had brought up a slave he called Sa<ūdī.
He asked him: 'What kept you back, slave?'
He answered: 'I have seen a shirt that weighs scarcely an ounce.'

88. A line is missing here.
89. B: ya sīdi >anā ra>ēt >̃amīṣ wi *'Master, I have seen a shirt*
C: ra>ēt >̃amīṣ fis-sū>̃ *'I have seen a shirt in the market*
90. B: si<ru <āli >̃am *The price of which is high, so*
C: si<ru ya sīdi *The price of which, Master*
91. B, C: sīdu *his master*
92. B: il-fagrı *dawn*
93. C adds:
>in waṣal >alfēn ŧalāŧa m asību
da >̃amīṣ il-muṣṭafa nitbarkū bu
>̃al lu l-<abdı >ana bākir >agību
da >̃amīṣ il-muṣṭafa yib>̃a hidiyya

Though it reach two or three thousand, I shall not part with it.
It is the shirt of the favoured one; we shall draw a blessing from it.'
The slave said: 'I shall fetch it tomorrow.
The shirt of the favoured one is a gift indeed!'

94. In B and (C), the quatrain is expanded to:
[>̃al lu ḥāḍir l aglı sīdi >alfı ṭā<a

(ṣibiḥ yimši <ali l-<abdı ma bēn il-gamā<a)
iṣ-ṣalā wagabit <āla ṣāḥib iš-šafā<a
>̃al <aṭētu kām (lu) yā rbāb iš-šagā<a
[>̃al <aṭēna mn id-darāhim <ušrimiyyā
(>̃ālu <aṭenāh maḥabīb <ušrimiyya)

[*He said: 'It shall be done. A thousand acts of obedience for my master's sake.'*
(*Next morning <Alī* [sic] *the slave went ambling in the crowd.*)
It is a duty to call down blessings on him who has the right of intercession.
He asked: 'How much (*What*) *did you offer* (*offer him*), *O men of valour?'*
They said: 'We offered (*offered him*) *ten hundred pieces.'*

>̃ālu <ăṭāna (<aṭenāh) [<išrīn u (<ušrimiyya) ma rtaḍāši
>̃al m abī<ūši wa law (C omits) >arga< ba lā ši
[fī ma >̃āl (>̃al lihum) il-<abd bāṭṭalū na>̃āši (l-x̱awāšī)
[da >̃amīṣ iz-zēn bi ŧalaŧŧ alāf <alayyā
(ŧalaŧŧ alāf da l->̃amīṣ <alayya)

They said: 'We offered him twenty (*ten hundred*) *but he was not satisfied.*
He said: "I shall not sell it [even if I (*but*) *go back empty-handed."'*
To them the slave said: 'Stop arguing (*dissimulation*)*!*
[I will have the fair one's shirt for three thousand.
(*For three thousand I shall have this shirt.*)*'*

95. B, C: w inta yā dallāl tēhāwid fī su>ālak *And you auctioneer, moderate your demand.*
96. B:

xuđ <ašar galālīb wē guxtēnı >̃ubālak
w inta tāxuđ ḥimlēnı tamrı li <iyālak

Take ten robes and two broadcloth [mantles] here before you
And you shall have two loads of dates for your children.'
C:
xuđ <ašar ikyās wi >̃awwit <iyālak
x̱ēr ḥimlēn tamrı dōl minnī >̃ubālak

Take ten sackfuls and feed your children,
Besides two loads of dates – these I lay before you.'

97. B and (C): >̃al >anā (C omits) bi<t il->̃āmīṣ *He said: 'I sell the shirt*
98. B omits quatrains 37 and 38. In C this line begins: >̃al il->imām tigza min allah *The Imam [<Alī] said: 'May God requite you*
99. C: lēh tibī< >̃amīṣ *'Why do you sell the shirt of*
100. C omits the pronoun
101. C: ba<dı m astafti <alēk fidi l->̃aḍiyya *After seeking an authoritative pronouncement concerning you in this matter.*
102. B omits this quatrain. C expands it as follows:

ba<dı m astafti <alēk di l-wa>̃ti ḥāṣil
li >aglı ṭāhā lli tisīr lu l-maḥāmil
>axađu ll-iṯnēn >ila zēn il->̃abāyil
yilta>̃ūh gālis wi lu >anwār zahiyya

After seeking a pronouncement concerning you – this right away,
For Ṭāhā's sake, towards whom laden processions travel.'
They took them both to the fairest among tribes,
And found him seated, emitting bright lights.

yilta>̃ūh gālis wi lu <a l-xaddı šāma
>il-ḥaṣa sabbiḥ wi f kaffu <alāma
>̃ālu s-salām <ala l-miẓallal bi l-x̱amāma
>abṭaḥi makka xēr il-bariyya

They found him seated, with a mole upon his cheek –
The very pebbles chanting praises – and with a mark on his palm.
They said: 'Greeting to him who is shaded by the cloud,
The dweller in Mecca's plain, the best of creation.

>abṭaḥi makka nabi <arabi <arūs il->̃iyāma
rabbina xtārak wi xaṣṣak bi l-karāma
<an >̃amīṣak ya nabi ma<na <alāma
ma<a rāgil širīf wi lu šēba na>̃iyya

Dweller in Mecca's plain, Arab prophet, bridegroom of the Resurrection, Our Lord has chosen you and singled you for dignity [or: for wonders].
Concerning your shirt, O Prophet, we have a sign
Involving a man of eminence with pure white hair

ma<a rāgil širīf lu šēba malīḥa
<ēbtu fil-muslimīn ba>̃it fiḍīḥa
waṣṣalnā lu >alfı maḥbūb [ṣaḥīḥa]
zād fi >̃ōlu yiftaḥ il-mawla <alayya

Involving a man of eminence with fine white hair
Whose shaming of the Muslims has become a scandal.
We raised our bids to fully a thousand pieces,
Yet he kept saying: 'The Lord open to me [doors to greater gain]!'

zād fi>̃ōlu yiftaḥ allah fī dalāla
rabbina xtārak wi xaṣṣak bi l-karāma
sabna w rakan <ala >̃ōm ḍalāla
wi bā< >̃amīṣak ṣu<ub <alayya

Yet he kept saying: 'May God open an indication!'.
Our Lord has chosen you and singled you for dignity.

He has abandoned us, relied on an erring nation,
And sold your shirt – I find this hard to bear!'

>̃āl in-nabi l->̃amịṣ xarag minni lu
>in kān yibī<u li l-yahūdi w alla yišīlu
>in kān yibī<u li l-yahūdi w alla yiṣirru
>̃abbiḍu ya <abdı wi ḍamānak <alayya

Said the Prophet: 'The shirt has passed from me to him.
Whether he sells it to the Jew or carries it,
Whether he sells it to the Jew or bundles it –
Pay him, slave, and I shall be your surety'

>̃abbaḍu l-<abdı ḥa>̃>̃ iŧ-ŧōb kulla
allāh >ax̱nāh min ba<dı ẕilla
xađ il->̃amīṣ il-<abdı w rawwaḥ bīh maḥalla
wi >̃āl xuđ >ādi sabab il->̃aḍiyya

The slave paid him the full price of the garment,
And God enriched him after his abasement.
The slave took the shirt, and went back home with it,
And said: 'Take. This is the cause of the whole matter.'

>̃āl xuđ ya sīdi >ana ll izād >̃adri
>̃al lu sīdu rīḥak zāyid wi <iṭri
>̃al >̃amīṣ ṭāhā >in kuntı tidri
>̃am xađu minnu w >̃āl w allah hidiyya

He said: 'Take, Master as for me, my standing is enhanced.'
His master said: 'Your breath is sweeter; it is perfumed.'
He said: 'It is Ṭāhā's shirt, if you but knew'
So he took it from him saying: 'A gift, by God'

This last quatrain is matched in B as follows:
xađ il->̃amīṣ il-<abdı w rāḥ li sīdu yēgri
>̃al lu sīdu >inta šāyil miskı <iṭri
>̃al lu rēḥt il->̃āmīṣ >iza kuntı tidri
xađ il->̃amīṣ wi >̃āl w allahi >aḥsan hidiyyā

The slave took the shirt and went running to his master.
His master said: 'You are carrying fragrant musk.'
He said: 'It is the smell of the shirt, if you but knew.'
So he took the shirt saying: 'By God, the best of gifts'

103. B:
xađ il->̃amīṣ yā <ēni minnu bi yamīnu
kan il-<amā ṭāmis <enēh min fō>̃ gibīnu
ba<dı mā kān il-<ama dāyim fi<ēnu
[missing line]

He took the shirt – ah, me – from him in his right hand.
Blindness overlaid his eyes upon his forehead.
And whereas blindness had been permanent in his eye,
[missing line]
C:
>̃am xađu minnu wi šālu b yimīnu
>istabārak bīh wi mallas bīh gibīnu
ba<dı ma kān il-<ama ṭāmis fi <ēnu
He took it from him and carried it in his right hand.
He sought a blessing from it and stroked his forehead with it,
After blindness had overlaid his eye,

104. C uses the singular <ēnu
105. The closing quatrains differ in all three versions.
B:
fattaḥit <ēnu wi šāf l-abyaḍ wi l-iswid
>ašhad bi >annak ya rasūl allāh muḥammad
x̱ērı dīnak ya nabi lam <udtı >a<bud
>aslam il-kāfir wi gēšu l-<ušrimiyya

His eyes opened, discerning white and black.
'I witness that you are, O Apostle of God, the highly praised one.
Other than your faith, O Prophet, I no longer worship.'
The infidel became a Muslim with his army of ten hundred.

>̃āl ta<ā [for: ta<āla] ya <abd ana f zāmānihēntak
bukra bākir >ākūn li n-nābi ba<aŧtak
[repeated as: bukra li n-nābi >anā >akūn ba<aŧtak]
l aglı ma n>̃ul lu >ana xalāṣ <ata>̃tak
wa la >arḍa ykūnı <andi <abdı liyya

He said: 'Come, slave. I did in my time abase you.
Early (By) tomorrow I shall have sent you to the Prophet
So we may tell him: "It is settled, I have freed you,
And will not brook that I should have a slave."'

xađ il->̃amīṣ wē >̃al ya >arbāb il-finūni
>ab<aŧ salāmi li n-nābi >̃urrit <iyūni
>amdaḥ nabīna z-zēn wē n-nās yisma<ūni
>in kān xilaf kiđā ḥayāti muntahiyya

He took the shirt and said, 'O men of the arts:
I send my greeting to the Prophet, in whom my eye finds rest.
I praise our fair Prophet in the hearing of the people.
Should it be otherwise, let my life be ended'

B then twice repeats the first two quatrains of the song
C is close to B:

fattaḥ wi šāf l-abyaḍ min ill-iswid
>̃āl >ašhad inn allāh karīm w inta muḥammad
x̱ēr dīnak ya nabi lam <udtı >a<bid
>aslam il-kāfir wi gēšu bi s-sawiyya

He opened his eyes, discerning white and black.
He said: 'I witness that God is generous and you the highly praised.
Other than your faith, O Prophet, I no longer worship,'
The infidel became a Muslim, together with his army.

>̃āl ta<āla ya <abd ana lli zamāni hintak
iṣ-ṣubḥı badri li n-nabi bākir taba<tak
in >̃ibil minnak il->̃amīṣ li llāh <ata>̃tak
wi xidmitak ya <abdı tiḥram <alayya

He said: 'Come, slave it is I who in my time abased you.
To-morrow, early in the morning, I shall follow you to the Prophet.
If he accepts the shirt from you, for God's sake I shall free you.
No longer will it be lawful that I be served by you.'

>axađ il->̃amīṣ ya >ahl il-funūni
>̃āl salāmi <ala n-nabi >̃urrit <uyūni
[law] >̃ibilt iŧ-ŧōb >asyādi yi<ta>̃ūni
habaṭ gibrīl min id-daraga l-<ulayyā

He took the shirt, O men of the arts,
And said: 'My greeting to the Prophet, in whom my eyes find rest.
If you accept the garment, my masters will manumit me.'
Then Gabriel came down from the highest degree.

>̃am habaṭ gibrīl <ala n-nabi wi >̃al lu
>aslam iƶ-ƶimmi ya hādi w gēšu kullu
>ādi >̃amīṣ in-nabi rawwaḥ maḥallu
da l-ḥābīb >̃al lu >in-nabi >̃ibil il-hidiyya

So Gabriel came down to the Prophet and told him:
The believer in non-Muslim Scriptures has become a Muslim,
with all his army.'
And here the Prophet's shirt has come back to its home.
The beloved told him: 'The Prophet accepts the gift.'

The research for this article was made possible mainly by a generous grant from the Translations Program of the US National Endowment for the Humanities.

An Uncommon Use of Nonsense Verse in Colloquial Arabic

In 1893, M. Urbain Bouriant, then Director of the French Archaeological Mission in Cairo, published a volume entitled *Chansons Populaires Arabes en dialecte du Caire d'après les manuscrits d'un chanteur des rues*.[1] The book consists of 160 pages of carefully edited and very well printed texts, with no comment or study of any kind. A note from the publisher, however, refers to the 'stroke of good fortune' that brought the manuscripts into M. Bouriant's hands and announces that the selection presented then was only a forerunner of a translation and study to appear later. Sadly, M. Bouriant was struck down by ill-health in 1895,[2] and as far as I have been able to ascertain never fulfilled his intention of following up on a very promising beginning.

More recently, Muḥammad Qandīl al-Baqlī has published a volume[3] which, though he makes reference in it to a 'booklet' by Bouriant, he claims to be the result of painstaking independent research and a careful confrontation of texts. The truth is, however, that al-Baqlī has drawn solely on Bouriant's material, which he reproduces almost in its entirety, even to incorporating the Frenchman's conjectural emendations. And without mentioning that this material came from the hands of a street singer (indeed, he speaks vaguely of sources accessible only to the well-informed), he builds round it what he claims is a survey of 'dervish' literature. In assigning such a label to these twice-published texts, al-Baqlī seems to have relied heavily on his intuition; his discreditable methods ought not, however, to turn us away from the possibility that, despite their immediate provenance, some of the texts may indeed reflect the once pervasive influence of the Sufi brotherhoods in Arab life, although, of course, the issue will have to be decided on the strength of internal evidence and for each piece on its own merits.

Bouriant's collection will indeed repay close examination, and it is a reflection of the lack of regard for compositions in the colloquial at the time it was published that it went virtually unnoticed by Arab scholars and by Arabists alike.

All but six of its thirty-four pieces follow the most common pattern for the *zajal*: first, an introductory couplet setting what will be the binding (AA) rhyme of the entire song; then, a variable number of stanzas almost always rhyming bbbaa, cccaa, etc., sometimes incorporating the introductory couplet or part of it (e.g., bbbaaA, or cccaAA), and the final stanza virtually always ending with the initial couplet (zzzAA). Furthermore, the penultimate stanza usually consists of praise of the Prophet, and in the last one the poet often names himself amid expressions of piety and humility. Each of the songs so patterned is called a *ḥiml*,[4] literally 'a load'.

A wide range of themes is covered, many being devotional or gnomic, and one at least bears directly on the discipline of a Sufi brotherhood. There are also three narrative songs, two on miracles performed by the intervention of a saint, and one stretching to 250 lines which tells in detail of the Prophet's night journey to the heavens (see Item 13 in this book). Rather difficult to connect with 'dervish' literature are two facetious 'debates': one between watermelons and dates, the other between cream and molasses. There are also love songs. Not the least intriguing are two songs, apparently by the same author, although he names himself in only one of them, in which stanzas proclaiming that the poet is demented by love alternate with others which illustrate his mental derangement.

The inclusion of a stanza in praise of the Prophet is so standard that it carries no implication about the character of the composition. On the other hand, the poet describes himself as a *maddāḥ*, and if the term is used in a technical sense, it may indicate that he made his living mainly by singing at religious gatherings; and the repetition of the initial amatory couplet at the end may be no more than a formality, or it may give some ground for identifying the beloved with the Prophet. Whether the love that is expressed is therefore mystic and the nonsense verse that follows reflects the ecstatic states reached at brotherhood ceremonies, or whether indeed there is method in the madness, it is beyond my competence to establish. But even as a literary device devoid of religious overtones, this alternation of nonsense verse (in itself, no more uncommon in the Arabic than in other literary traditions) with love poetry is new to me and seems worth bringing to the attention of others, especially as I find the 'mad' stanzas full of animation and the 'serious' ones, although laden with the conventional images and conceits of love poetry, not without some deft and delicate touches.

Because the texts are fairly easily accessible, I transcribe and translate below only enough to convey the flavour of one of these compositions, with the stanzas numbered as they would be in the entire song.

ḤMLI ZAGAL <Ā>̃IL WI MAGNŪN

min kalām Aḥmad ill-A<rag:[5]

A LOAD OF VERSE, RATIONAL AND INSANE

by Ahmad the Lame

>̃albī tawalla< bi l-x̱arām il-x̱arīm
My heart is ablaze with contentious passion
fī ẓabyı xađ <a>̃ūt bi laḥẓuh wi māl
For a fawn who stole my reason by his glances, then went his way.
sabnī[6] *hawāh magnūn wi zāyid gunūn*
Desire has left me mad, with madness to spare:
>askar w ax̱īb w aḥḍar bi ḥubb il-gamāl
I get drunk, lose or recover senses, by dint of love of beauty.

(1) *DŌR HAZL* – JESTING STANZA
kasartı baṭṭīxah ra>ēt il-<agab
I split a watermelon and saw something wonderful:
fī >̃albihā >arba< madāyin kubār
It had four large cities within it.
wi fī l-madāyin xal>̃ı mis̃l il-ba>̃ar
In the cities were creatures like cattle,
fī kullı waḥda rba< >̃ilā<āt ḥiṣār
And in each were four fortresses [proof against] siege.
wi fī l->̃ilā< >a>̃wām ṭiwāl id-đi>̃ūn
There were in the fortresses long-bearded people
wi dam<ihum gārī šabīh il-biḥār
Whose tears were flowing as if they were rivers.
min dam<ihum tizra< nigūm is-samā
With these tears you could grow the stars of the heavens
fī xil>̃it il-mišmiš <adīm il-mis̃āl
In the form of unmatchable apricots
wi mīn >akal minnuh nahār il-xamīs
And whoever shall eat of these on a Thursday
yib>̃ā šabīh il-fīl <alā kullı ḥāl
Shall be like an elephant in any case.

(2) *DŌR GADD* – A SERIOUS STANZA
>amrad salab <a>̃lī bi ward il-xidūd
A beardless one has stolen my mind with the roses of his cheeks
>ahyaf rašī>̃ il->̃addı zēn il-milāḥ
Slender, of elegant stature, the best of the fair.
rī>̃uh yifūq iš-šahdı w is-salsabīl
The freshness of his mouth surpasses honey and Eden's river.

yikillı <an waṣfuh labīb il-fuṣāḥ
The sharpest in eloquence fall short of describing him.
law laḥẓı min laḥzuh sabā l-<āši>īn
Should one of his glances take lovers captive,
fīh il-ḥayā w il-mōt bi sur<ah mubāḥ
Then life and death immediately become licit for him.
wi kam >atīl min xamzı xangu l-kaḥīl
How many are slain by a wink from his kohl-painted coquetry,
ka>annı >atl il->ōm bi sur<ah ḥalāl
As if causing quick death was allowed in [God's] law!
huwwā sabab su>mī wi ṭūl[7] *il-<anā*
It is he who has caused my illness and long-suffering
ḥattā <tarānī min hawāh il-xabal
So that I am crack-brained with desire for him.

(3) *DŌR HAZL* – JESTING STANZA
yōm šuftı nāmūsah bi tixzil >aṣab
I once saw a mosquito spinning sugar cane
yiṭraḥ marākib wišā>hum min <asal
The fruit yielded was boats that were tied up with honey.
wi mīn nizil fīhum bi >aṣd is-safar
And those who embarked intending to travel
yiṭla< min il-fayyūm li burg il-ḥamal
Set off from Fayyum to the constellation of Aries.
min fō> ṣawārīhum bi tigri l-biḥār
Above their masts were rivers flowing;
fīhā madāfi< naxlı tiṭraḥ baṣal
Within them were torrents of palm-trees yielding onions.
fī kullı waḥdah xal>ı mišl il-garād
In each there were creatures like locusts
fī xil>it il-gāmūs bi riglēn ṭiwāl
In the form of long-legged water-buffaloes.
w in >ultı da minnuh yigūz il-fidā
If you say it is right to be ransomed from this,
tiṣda> li >inn il->ōl yināfī l-fi<āl
You are truthful, for words are at variance with deeds.

(4) *DŌR GADD* – A SERIOUS STANZA
zēnī >iwāmuh zayyı <ūd ir-rudēn
My fair one's figure is like the shaft of a spear
min i<tidāl >add ista<ārū l-xuṣūn
From such straightness of torso the branches have borrowed!
min fō> xudūduh mā> wi gamr il-lahab
On his cheeks are both water and embers of fire.

mufrad ra>ī> iṭ-ṭab<ı ḥilw il-<iyūn
He is peerless; fine is his nature and sweet are his eyes.
xiṣru n-naḥīl yiški rtigāg il-kafal
His slender waist complains of the shaking of his buttocks.
wi s-sā> sa>ā l-<uššā> li kās il-manūn
His leg pours out to lovers the cup of death.
xāb mīn yi>īs far>uh bi nūr iṣ-ṣabāḥ
He fails who likens the spacing [of his teeth] to the light of morning,
wa llā yi>ūl waghuh yifū> il-hilāl
Or says that his face surpasses the crescent:
min ṭab<ı l-itnēn il-x̱iyāb w il-ḥudūr
The nature of both is to go and to come,
w anā ḥabībī lam yazal fī kamāl
Whereas my beloved e'er a full moon.

(9) *DŌR HAZL* – JESTING STANZA
rikb il-kabīs min fō> ḥuṣānu l-<asal
The date has mounted its honey-made horse
xāḍ il-<Ajāj fī ḥarbı [x̱azl il-banāt[8]
And waded through dust-clouds in the battle of candy floss.
xaffa> bayāri> min mišabbak <u>ad
It made pennants flutter, these being honeyed doughnuts in knots.
garrad ḥusām min šahdı sukkar nabāt
It drew out a sword of honey-like sugar candy.
gā lu l-mixayyaṭ fō> sabāyiṭ balaḥ
The sebesten-plums got there on clusters of dates,
w il-kaḥkı yir>uṣ luh <ala ṣ-ṣāfināt
And for it the cakes danced upon table covers.
šuft il-ḥumār ṭāyir wi xāṭif gamal
I saw the donkey fly, having snatched a camel.
maddū marākib rāxiyīn id-dilāl[9]
They stretched out boats with tresses hanging loose.
l il-ḥarbı tinfa< fī qitāl il-yahūd
In war they would serve for fighting the Jews –
alfēn ḥumārah li s-safar fi l-gibāl
Two thousand she-asses for travel in mountains.

(10) *DŌR GADD – SERIOUS STANZA*
xamrī ngalā min nūr šu<ā< il->amar
My wine has come off the light of a moonbeam.
dār il-ḥabīb fi l-kās li-galb is-surūr
The beloved went round in the cup, to bring joy.
yiḥkī l-mudām l-aḥmar bi lōn il-<a>ī>
He matches the red wine with his ruby-like colour.

min zahruhu l->abyaḍ wugūh il-budūr
Of his dazzling brightness are the full moons' faces made.
lāḥit šumūs burg id-dinān fi l->̃adaḥ
The suns of the constellation of wine-jars loomed in the bowl.
dār in-nadīm mis̃l il-falak mā ydūr
The boon companion went round as does the heavenly sphere.
wi s-sa<dı lī >aqbal >u wāfa l-ḥabīb
To me good fortune turned, and the beloved came;
>̃abbiltı ša̱xruh w iḥtaḍēt bi l-wiṣāl
I kissed him on the mouth and was favoured with union.
ša>̃>̃ il-ḥugub wi n-naḥsı <anna ḥtagab
He ripped the veils, and from us ill-fortune was veiled
x̱āb ir-ra>̃īb lammā wafānī l-hilāl
The watcher departed when the crescent moon joined me.

(12) *DŌR IL-MADĪḤ* – A STANZA OF PRAISE
>̃al lī ḥabībī mdaḥ šafī< il->umam
My beloved told me: Praise the intercessor of nations!
bi l-madḥı fī ṭahā tināl il->̃ubūl
By praise of Ṭāhā you shall gain acceptance.
fa >̃ultı luh kinzī wi zaxrī x̱adā
I said: My treasure, my precious store has become
x̱ošī šafī<ī fī nahār il-wuṣūl
My salvation, my intercessor on the Day of Arrival.
huwwāh muḥammad bal >imām ir-ruṣūl[10]
He is Muḥammad, indeed the leader of apostles,
>aḥmad >abu l->̃āsim >aṣīl il->uṣūl
Aḥmad, Abū l-Qāsim, he of true lineage.
yā rabbinā ṣallī <ala l-muṣṭafā
O Lord, call down blessings upon the favoured one,
wi l->ālı w il->aṣḥāb kirām il->aṣāl
And his kin and companions of noble descent
<add il-ḥaṣā w il-mōg wi >̃aṭr il-maṭar
To the number of pebbles, and waves, and drops of rain
min mubtada d-dunyā li yōm il-ma>āl
From the start of the world to the Day of Return.

(13) *DŌR L-ISTISHHĀD* – STANZA OF CONFESSION
>ana l-fa>̃īr >aḥmad <arī>̃ in-nasab
I am Aḥmad, needful [of His mercy], of an ancient line,
<āgiz <an iṭ-ṭā<ah kitīr iz-zunūb
Short on obedience, and long on sins.
hal ti>̃balūnī <abd ya >ahl il->adab
Will you have me as a slave, O men of letters,

tābi< likum maddāḥ ḥabīb il->ulūb
A follower of yours, a singer of the praises of the beloved of our hearts?
mā lī wasīlah x̱ēr madiḥ in-nabī
I have no resources but the praise of the Prophet
>argu š-šifā<ah fī nahār il-kurūb
I plead for intercession on the Day of Sorrows.
>albī tawalla< bi l-x̱arām il-x̱arīm
My heart is ablaze with contentious passion
fī ẓabyı xađ<a>lī bi laḥẓuh wi māl
For a fawn who stole my reason with his glances, then went his way.
sabnī hawāh magnūn wi zāyid gunūn
Desire has left me mad, with madness to spare:
>askar w ax̱īb w aḥḍar bi ḥubb il-gamāl
I get drunk, lose or recover senses, by dint of love of beauty.

Notes

1. Paris, Ernest Leroux.
2. See his obituary at the end of *Bulletin de l'Institut Français d'Archéologie Orientale*, 3 (1903). He is more fully discussed in the opening pages of Item 13 in this book.
3. *>Adab ad-Darāwīš* (Cairo, 1970).
4. The term invites linkage with the word *ḥimalī*, 'carrier', which I have heard applied to an itinerant singer who does not compose his own songs, but memorises those of others.
5. In Bouriant, pp. 8–11; in al-Baqlī, pp. 188–91. In vocalising the Arabic, I have been guided by the metre which is *sarī<*. The composition is generally so regular that the few breakdowns in the scansion are likely to be due to a copyist's errors.
6. The manuscript is apparently corrupt at this point, but where the hemistich is repeated at the end of the song, it reads: *taraknī* etc. As this does not fit the metre, Bouriant recasts the entire hemistich as *hawāk tarak <a>lī ṣibiḥ fī gunūn*, and is slavishly followed by al-Baqlī. The emendation I propose, *sabnī* instead of *taraknī*, restores the scansion without altering the sense.
7. An emendation proposed by Bouriant; the MS has *su>mı ḥālī*.
8. Literally: 'girls' spinning'.
9. I have found *dilāl* in dictionaries only in the sense of 'brass pot'; however, *rāxya d-dilāl* occurs in other songs in contexts that suggest the present rendering.
10. The use of *rasūl* as a plural is attested in Lisān al-<Arab.

An Early Example of Narrative Verse in Colloquial Arabic

>Abū l-Maḥāsin <Abd al-<Azīz ibn Sarāyā l-Ḥillī ṭ-Ṭā>ī s-Sinbisī, known as Ṣafiyy ad-Dīn al-Ḥillī, who was born in Ḥilla in 677/1278 and died in Baghdad probably in 750/1349, is notable for his ventures in the highways and byways of verse composition. He not only had a solid reputation as a poet in the late classical manner, but also initiated the *badī<iyya* genre with a poem in praise of the Prophet which illustrated every rhetorical device known in his day; he composed a *qaṣīda sāsāniyya*, which expounds the ways, and uses the jargon, of the underworld of vagabonds, beggars and thieves;[1] and he is the author of one of the earliest and fullest treatises on the so-called 'Seven Arts', that is, non-classical verse compositions,[2] mostly in the colloquial.

It is to this last work that we turn our attention here. In it, al-Ḥillī – like many of the scholars of his and of later times – repeatedly displays his admiration for the subtleties of which the non-classical genres are capable; yet he is mildly defensive about his involvement with them, for after a long exposition of the features of *zajal* based on a meticulous scrutiny of the practice of its pioneers, he prefaces his description of the other varieties with the statement that he had indulged in them a great deal 'in his youth' without lending his compositions great weight or troubling to record them, and had retained of them only enough to illustrate the book he had been 'charged' to write.[3]

Of particular interest to those eager to trace back the development of Arabic colloquial narrative verse is the genre known as *kān wa kān*.[4] Of its form, al-Ḥillī says only that it is always a mono-rhyme with a long vowel preceding the rhyming consonant, and that it has a distinctive metre with the second hemistich shorter than the first. From other sources[5] and from all the examples given, it appears that the metre is *mustaf<ilun fā<ilātun mustaf<ilun mustaf<ilun*, with the second hemistich lacking the two final syllables, and with one variation added to those allowed in classical prosody, namely, that the *fā<ilātun* foot may be reduced to *maf<ūlun*, so that the scansion may be represented as follows:

⏓–⏑–|⏓⏑––|⏓–⏑–|⏓–⏑–‖
⏓–⏑–|⏓⏑––|⏓–⏑–|⏓–‖

The very designation of the *kān wa kān*, which may be rendered as 'there was this and there was that', is consonant with the recounting of a succession of occurrences, and al-Ḥillī specifies that it was a Baghdadi invention originally used at least partly for narrative purposes, until a number of worthy gentlemen resorted to the form for more edifying gnomic or ascetic exhortations. The illustrations he gives, however, which are of his own composition, are in a light, witty and mostly amatory vein, and the one transcribed below is the detailed and lively story of a seduction. As is usual both in classical examples of *mujūn* and in present-day folk ballads,[6] it is told in the first person, starts with clever badinage and ends with explicit erotic description.

Since we cannot be certain of the way the Iraqi colloquial was pronounced in the thirteenth century, the transcription follows the text as edited by Hoenerbach, giving consonants the phonetic value they have in classical Arabic, and altering the vocalisation only when variations known to be allowable accord better with the metre.

The Text

jāzat fa qult in ratnī lā budda mā tal <ab ma <ī
    d̲ī la<bahā wa[7] <abat̲hā >ana <rifū >isrāf
min[8] >abṣaratnī tahayyat wa ḥarrakat lī rāsahā
    wa t̲aqqalat mašyathā wa hazzat al- >a <ṭāf
qultū ṣabāḥan mubārak qālat <a[9] man takallamū
    qult in sami < mā >aqul-lū qālat wa >illā nḥāf
wa b yaddahā raṭṭalatnī wa >abrazat lī zandahā
    kannū sabīkah fiḍḍah >aw jawharan šaffāf
raytu s-siwār al-muraṣṣa < wa qad xatam fī zandahā
    wa kulla sā <ah tadīrū wa tafruk al- >ašnāf
fa qultu lā tabriqīnī kat̲īr ana bṣartū d̲ahab
    qālat ṣadaqta wa lākin fīh[10] dakkat aṣ-ṣarrāf
fa qultu bassik samāḥah hād̲ī ẓarāfah bāridah
    qālat wa >ahl al-ḥillah w allah rifā < ẓirāf
>anā mašīṭū l-ḥillah mā raytu fīhā muḥtašam
    qultū wa lā bna s-sunaydī qālat wa lā l-x̲arrāf
qultū fa fī l-muqtadiyyah fī darbakum >aḥšam minū
    li >anna d̲īk al-maḥallah manāzil al- >ašrāf
lā mit̲la d̲ī ḥišmatkī w malḥafatkī l-mumazzaqah
    wa hī qarāmil qarāmil maqṭū <at al- >aṭrāf
qālat li xallī xurā <ak >anā xarajtū mnakkarah
    wa man yurīd al-lūlū lā yunkir al- >aṣdāf
qultū fa ma < d̲ā >amšī narūḥ lī baytanā
    wa našrab al-yawm wa naḥḍir min sā >ir al- >aṣnāf
qālat fa baytī >aqrab wa t̲amma ḥaḍra mrattabah
    qultū >axāf min zawjik qālat min īši txāf
d̲āk al-jakir ṭallaqtū w axad̲tu lak >akyas minū
    <a qadra mā turīdu w xuliq kafāf bi <fāf

lammā ttafaqnā tamaššat w anā ttamašša xalfahā
juznā li baytan muḥaṣṣan wa mā <alayh išrāf
bi ḥuṣra bardī wa baṣrī wa naṭ <a kīšī w maswarah
wa fī ṭabaq qannīnah fīhā qalīl sulāf
>amlat qadaḥ w a <ṭatnī fa qultu ṭābanjā šrabī
ḥassat wa qālat tašrab qultū <ašart ālāf
lammā šaribnā wa ṭibnā wa fawqa fummī fummahā
wa kāna nuqlī minhā bi l-bawsa wa t-tiršāf
maddaytu >īdī >ilayhā wa qultu šīlī l-maqna <ah
fa raytu ša <ra mrajjal kannū janāḥ x̱udāf
wa šiltu <anhā l-qabāḥā w ajlastuhā fawq rukbatī
wa ṣirtu >afruk <ukanhā w aqallib al- >ardāf
>anā >arīd aqlibhā wa zawjahā >aqbal daxal
lammā naẓarnī tašamxar wa >akṯar al- >irjāf
fa qultu w allah flaḥtū hāḏā llaḏī xiftū minū
yaslam min al-liṣṣa qalbī fa yāxuḏu l- <arrāf
>ay sitta mā qultī lī wa ḏī l-quwaydī >ummakī
>annū xurayyif muwāfiq mā ya <raf al- >ixlāf
hiy abṣaratnī nza <ajtū qāmat li wajhū ta <tibū
wa n-naḏl iḏā jā xulqū mā yanfa <ū sti <ṭāf
maddat bi diqnū wa qālat >ay ḥarfa mā dā mṭallaqī
kull il-maḥallah ta <rif hāḏā bi x̱ayra xlāf
hāḏā <arafnī qablak wa kulla mā <indī minū
bahit wa qāla w nālik fa qultu >ī bi l-kāf
xajil wa qāla <ḏurnī >al- <afwa <ind al-maqdurah
fa kull aḥad min ṭab <ū mā ya <jibū yanḥāf
w amlā qadaḥ w asqānī w qāla hāḏā ma <rifah
fa >inna tark al-māḍī min x̱āyat al- >inṣāf
fa qultu w allah yā xī narīd ḥalāwa mjaddarah
wa llā fa ṣābūniyyah jamīlat al- >awṣāf
w axrajtu dīnār f īdī wa qultu xuḏ yā sayyidī
hạḏī l-waẓīfah šax̱lak fa >anta mā tankāf
min ṣāra fī d-darba rijlū qumtū qafaltū s-sāqiṭah
wa šiltu rijlayn sittī ṣārat <alā l- >aktāf
qālat fa hayyā sta <jil qabl an yajī ya <raf binā
qultū <araf wa tax̱ābā wa hū ḏakī <arrāf
w axrajtu dīnāran āxar wa qultu hạḏā ḥiṣṣitū
wa >anti hāḏā naṣībik w axrajtu zawja xfāf
fa qabbalatnī wa qālat bi llāh <alayk lā tanqaṭi <
fa >anta rabb al-manzil wa kullanā >aḍyāf
qultū na <am wa nahaḍtu w aqsamt mā jūz bi darbahā
wa lā baqītu qābil man zawjahā rajjāf

Translation

As she passed by me I thought: If she spot me she will surely sport with me
I know how extravagant her playfulness and trifling are.
No sooner did she see me than she livened, signalled with her head,
Loaded her gait and made her flanks quiver.
I called, 'A blessed morning!' She asked, 'Whom do you address?'
I said, 'Would he but listen ...' She answered, 'Else he would be the loser.'
She gestured[11] *at me with her hand, revealing a forearm*
Like a silver ingot or a translucent gem.
I noticed a bejewelled bracelet as if sealed upon her wrist.
Which all the time she twirled, also toying with her earrings.
I pleaded, 'Do not over-dazzle me – I see it is of gold.'
She answered, 'That is true. Indeed it bears the assayer's mark.'
I said, 'Enough of idle chatter! This is a cooling[12] *pleasantry.'*
She replied, 'And Ḥilla's people are, by God, both noble and engaging.
I have walked the length of Ḥilla and found no call for reticence.'
I taunted, 'Not in Sunaydis'[13] *quarter?' She retorted. 'Not even by the waterwheel.'*
I prodded on, 'In Muqtadiyya, in your quarter, are some more prudish,
For in that area are the dwellings of the noble.
Not of such cachet is your modesty, or your ragged wrap,
For it is only strips on strips, and their fringes are cut short.'[14]
She riposted, 'Restrain your shamelessness! I come out in disguise.
One who reaches for the pearl ought not to shrink back from the shell!'
I led on, 'It being thus and thus, let us make for my home
That we may drink today, and order a diversity of foods.'
She argued, 'Mine is nearer, and the fare already set.'
I objected, 'But I fear your husband.' Said she, 'What have you to fear?
That tyrant[15] *I've divorced, and taken another as much more understanding*
As you may like, for he is fashioned of self-denial and of reticence.'
Having come to an arrangement, she walked on and I behind her,
To a house well-fortified, and yet unguarded,
Furnished with papyrus and Basri mats, a kishi[16] *leather spread, a leather pillow;*
On a platter was a bottle with a remnant of choice wine.
She filled a cup for me. Said I, 'A measure[17] *you must drink.'*
She heard and urged, 'Will you then drink?' I answered, 'Ten thousand times!'
When we had drunk and mellowed, her mouth being over mine,
And I now kissing and now sucking,
I stretched my hand and pleaded, 'This head-veil do remove!'
And I saw hair spread loose that was like a raven's wing.

I stripped her of her undergarment,[18] *sat her on my knee,*
Stroking her belly-fold and kneading her buttocks.
I meant to tilt her then, when there appeared her man – he walked in,
And seeing me, he drew up and uttered many threats.
To her I cried, 'Well done, by God! Just this is what I feared:
My heart escapes the thief, and then falls victim to his spy![19]
Lady, did you not say – and this mother-pimp of yours –
He is a consenting cuckold,[20] *never failing in complacence?'*
She saw I was upset, so drew up, chiding, to his face –
For in dealing with the vile, it is not pleading that avails.
She pulled his beard and railed, 'You wretch,[21] *he is my former husband.*
The entire neighbourhood well knows it, and there is none who will gainsay.
He knew me before you did, and all I have has come from him.'
Perplexed he asked, 'And has he had you?' I interposed, 'Yes, amply!'
He was confused and said, 'Forgive me! Pardon is fitting when one has power,
And by nature no one likes to be imposed upon.'
He filled a cup and gave it me, saying, 'Here's to our acquaintanceship.
Letting bygones be bygones is the ultimate in equity.'
I added, 'By God, brother, we need mujaddara[22] *for a sweetener,*
Or else a sabuniyya of the finest quality.'
With a gold piece in my hand, I urged him, 'Take it, Sir!
This function is truly yours – you will never have to beg!'[23]
The moment he was on the road, I pulled the curtains down
And raised my lady's legs upon my shoulders.
She said, 'Hasten, lest on returning he find out what we're about.'
I replied, 'He knows, but acts the fool though perceptive and aware.'
Another coin I brought out, saying, 'Let this be his share,
And this be yours' – and fetched her a lightsome pair.
She kissed me pleading, 'By God, never desist!
You're master in this house, and all of us your guests.'
I agreed and rose, pledging never to bypass her neighbourhood,
Nor do I own I've cause to tremble from her man.

Notes

1. Reproduced, translated, and studied in Clifford E. Bosworth, *The Mediaeval Islamic Underworld*, 2 vols (Leiden, 1976).
2. Edited, introduced and annotated by Wilhelm Hoenerbach, *Die Vulgärarabische Poetik al-Kitāb al-ʿĀṭil al-Ḥālī wal-Muraḫḫaṣ al-Ġālī des Ṣafīyaddīn Ḥillī* (Wiesbaden 1956) – hereafter referred to as Hoenerbach.
3. Hoenerbach, p. 136.
4. Expounded and illustrated in Hoenerbach, pp. 148–70, the text transcribed and translated above being on pp. 157–62.

5. Hoenerbach, Introduction, pp. 46–7.
6. See *Ballads*, pp. 13–20.
7. In his observations on the linguistic licences of the *zajal*, which he affirms apply to other non-classical forms, al-Ḥillī specifies that to avoid similarity to the classical all desinences should be those of the accusative – Hoenerbach, pp. 135, 18.
8. For *mundu*, which is said to be too classical – Hoenerbach, pp. 30, 80.
9. The text has *<ala*, but here as in line 14 the metre requires only a short syllable. Shortening to *<a* accords with present-day colloquial practice, and parallels al-Ḥillī's assertion that *matā* may be reduced to *mat* – Hoenerbach, p. 32.
10. The text has *fī*.
11. The verb *raṭṭala* is attested in modern colloquials only in the sense of 'patting one's hair' or 'tickling'. It may be read here as meaning that the woman stroked the poet, but it is unlikely even in such a context that she would do so in public (she remains veiled until line 19!), and I take it rather that she waved her hand in a deprecatory fashion, as if to dismiss him.
12. The connotations of this word are pejorative. A possible emendation would be *zā >ida* , 'excessive.'
13. It is evident from the context that the three toponyms in this line and the next refer to quarters of the city, but I have found no references to them or to the social status they connote in either Ibn Baṭṭūṭa's *Riḥla* or Yāqūt's *Mu<jam al-Buldān*.
14. *Xara<a* is a dialectical variant of *xala<a* – Lane, *Arabic–English Lexicon*.
15. The nearest recorded form is *chākir*, which carries a number of derogatory meanings, including 'daring', 'shameless', 'insolent' – Claude Denizeau, *Dictionnaire des parlers arabes de Syrie, Liban, et Palestine* (Paris, 1960).
16. Kish is an island in the Persian Gulf – see Ibn Baṭṭūṭa, *Riḥla* (Beirut,1964), p. 231.
17. The word *ṭabanja* most commonly denotes 'pistol' or 'musket', and is also recorded in the sense of 'cupping glass' – Dozy, *Supplément aux Dictionnaires Arabes* (Leiden, 1881) – hereafter: Dozy. In this context, however, it must mean either a drink or a cup of some kind, with a possible punning derivation (not unusual in present-day folk verse) from *ṭāb in jā*, 'it pleases when it comes'.
18. Not found in any dictionary. Linking it with *qabāḥa*, 'abomination', 'rudeness', suggests a derivation parallel to the English euphemism 'unmentionable' for an undergarment. Less appropriate is Turkish *qabācha*, 'jacket' or 'cloak' – James Redhouse, *Turkish and English Lexicon* (Constantinople, 1921) – hereafter: Redhouse.
19. The usual meaning of *<arrāf* is 'seer', 'fortune-teller', but also 'one who traces stolen or mislaid objects' – Fagnan, *Additions aux Dicttonnaires Arabes* (Beirut, n.d). It is not unreasonable to extend the sense to 'a thief's accomplice' who looks out for what is worth stealing – cf. *midāwirgī* in *Ballads*, p. 104.
20. The root *x-r-f* produces several derivatives associated with dotage; *xurayyif* may therefore be translated 'dotard', but it is more likely to be a diminutive of *xarūf*, 'ram', which in modern usage is a euphemism for a cuckold.
21. The root *ḥ-r-f* has associations with 'pungency', or 'acritude'; also with 'bad luck'. The form closest to the word here is Turkish *ḥurf*, 'ill-luck', 'adversity' – Redhouse.
22. A *mujaddara* is a dish made with lentils and either rice or bulgur; yet the context seems to refer to a dessert, unless *ḥalāwa* is taken to mean not 'a sweet' but – as it also does in modern usage –'a celebratory gift'. A *sạbūniyya* is a kind of jelly made with sesame oil, starch, almonds and honey – Dozy.
23. The recorded words nearest to this are *tinkaff*, 'stretch out the hand', and *tinkafa>*, 'to be defeated'.

8

An Incomplete Egyptian Ballad on the 1956 War

In the course of the field work which eventually led to the publication of my *Ballads*,[1] I made it a practice to ask as few leading questions as possible in order to let my informants reveal their own priorities. What emerged was that among the ballad-mongers who did not specialise in the epic cycle of the Hilālīs, by far the most popular themes were accounts of 'honour crimes' in which fierce retribution is visited upon women who offend against the strict (if unequal) code of conduct still prevalent among the masses. Closely allied were other feats of bravery and violence, mainly motivated by revenge. Following at some distance were ballads of a religious character, either embroidering a Qur>anic story or recounting the deeds of a holy man.

Not once was I volunteered a song celebrating some national event and reflecting the kind of loyalty to the state that is very much in honour among the educated modernists – what Albert Hourani has defined as 'territorial nationalism' to distinguish it from pan-Arabism or pan-Islamism.[2]

One of my informants was Muḥammad Ramaḍān Sayyid Aḥmad, known as Abū Ðrā<, that is, 'the One-Armed'. He was of peasant stock. His first home had been with his mother and stepfather, but when he was about five years old his father – whom he had not known before – claimed him and took him to Uṭūr in the district of Kafr iš-Šēx near Ṭanṭā in the Delta. There he worked in the fields along with his father, and it was when trying to oil a waterwheel while it was turning that he lost his arm. At the age of nine, enamoured of song, he went – without his father's knowledge – to the greatest *mūlid* in Egypt, the one commemorating the birth of as-Sayyid al-Badawī in Ṭanṭā, and there he chanced to meet an uncle of his and persuaded him to take him to Cairo; but fearing that he would be returned to his father, he took to the streets where he made a living as a newspaper vendor. He then attached himself to a succession of folk singers and musicians until he could strike out as a performer on his own. Because the main outlet for folk literature is at the festivals of holy men whose burial places are scattered all over Egypt, most of his career involved travelling about the countryside, but in time he achieved such popularity that he transferred most of his activities to Cairo, where the pickings were greater.

It was there that I had several sessions with him. That was in 1972, during the month of Ramaḍān when Muslims who had fasted all day sought relief and entertainment well into the night. Abū Ðrā< and his troupe, which included several musicians and at least one female singer, occupied the stage in a temporary pavilion erected just outside a coffee shop in the vicinity of the mosque of al-Ḥusayn, the grandson of the Prophet. A modest entrance fee was charged, refreshments could be ordered from the café waiters, and patrons who wanted to honour a companion would send their request to the stage along with an appropriate sweetener, and the performer would oblige even at the cost of interrupting his song.

Abū Ḍrā< was proud of the fact that he had performed six times in the presence of President <Abd an-Nāṣir, who had made him a member of the 'Military Theatre' (*al-Masraḥ al-<Askarī*) – apparently a sinecure – at a salary of Egyptian £30 a month. He therefore seemed to me the likeliest source for the kind of nationalistic ballad which might have rounded off my collection, and I asked him if he had any to offer. He was not clear what I meant, and asked, 'Like what?' I specified: 'Something about one of the recent wars against outsiders.' 'Ah, yes,' he replied. 'I myself have composed one about the Battle of Port-Said,' which had been fought in 1956. He could not undertake to sing it there and then since he was about to take the stage, but at my request he began to recite it into my tape-recorder.

The form it took was that of the *mawwāl ṣa<īdī*, which I have described at some length in my book and even more fully in an earlier article in this book.[3] The metre is basically the classical *basīṭ*, that is, *mustaf<ilun fā<ilun* twice in each hemistich and with the *fā<ilun* foot often reduced to *fa<lun*, but only at the end of a line, whereas in folk compositions the classical hemistich functions as an independent line, and the shortening of *fā<ilun* is allowed wherever it occurs. Not all lines scan perfectly, and in my transcription I faithfully reproduce Abū Ḍrā<'s rendering even when a slight change in vocalisation or an allowable alternative would bring it closer to metrical regularity – as, for example, in line 14 where *<ašrāt li-miyyāt* would scan better than his *u<ašara li-miyya.*

More stringently observed are the demands of the rhyme. When the *mawwāl ṣa<īdī* is used as a lyrical song, it usually consists of a thirteen-line fixed form poem with the rhyme scheme:

a a a bcbcbc z z z (z)a

that is, having a last line that rhymes with the first, but often containing an internal 'z' rhyme as well. For narrative purposes, the entire thirteen-line unit may be used as a stanza, but more commonly (as in the present instance) it is stretched out by adding any number of alternately rhyming sestets before the final tercet, the closing line still rhyming with the first even if hundreds of lines have intervened.

Moreover, it is a matter of pride for the poet to elaborate every rhyme into a polysyllabic and extremely complicated paronomasia, of a kind unrecorded in classical Arabic and known to the folk practitioners as *zahr*, that is, 'flower'. This is achieved by deliberate distortion of the normal pronunciations: vowels may be altered, dropped, lengthened or shortened, gemination is treated cavalierly, and glottal stops are often elided. Even differences of dialect are pressed into service for this purpose. Thus, in the two interlaced sets occurring between lines 56 and 61 of this text, the 'g' sound occurs in words belonging to different registers of

Egyptian Arabic, as will be specified below. In the end, the only stable and readily recognisable element in the pun is the succession of consonants.

It has to be said that the artifice monopolises a good deal of the artist's resources, that the wording of entire lines is often strained as a result, and that the puns themselves are so obscure that some researchers have worked on similar texts without realising that they were faced with a demanding play on words and not with mere repetition.

In my transcription, I reproduce as faithfully as I can the way the words are distorted in order to achieve the wordplay; but I then add – between square brackets – what would be their normal pronunciation.[4]

Here, then, is what Abū Đrā< recited:

MA<RAKIT BUR SA<ID

THE BATTLE OF PORT-SAĪD

>̃ūlū li->ingilṭira >illi lina xadnāh [xaḍḍāna]
Tell England, which is acting scary towards us
baḥrıkum fi s-siyāsa kan x̱awīṭ xadnāh [xuḍnāh]
Deep was your sea in politics, [but] we've waded through!
ma hu l-kanāl kamān kan min ḥa>̃>̃ina xadnāh
Why the Canal was ours by right, and we've seized it.
li l-x̱arbı wayya ṣ-ṣahayna xiṭṭa dābirha [dabbarha]
The West has a plot it has hatched with the Zionists
<ašān niḥārib ma<āhum wi l-kanāl nisibūh [nisībuh]
To make us engage in war with them, and abandon the Canal.
yīgu l-ingilīz <a l-kanāl yiḥtallu g̃al dābirha [da barrıha]
The English come to the Canal to occupy it – you'd think it was their land,
lākin ra>isna gamāl ṣāḥi li-hum nisibūh [naṣṣabūh]
But our President Gamal was awake to them. He was set high.
bi fadl rabbi >̃aṭa<na l-kullı dābirha
Thanks to my Lord, we have extirpated it all.
wi l-<arabi <and il-kifãḥ nāsil is-silāḥ nisibūh [nāsi >abūh]
For an Arab in battle, with weapon drawn, forgets his [own] father.
xaṭab ra>isna fi l-azhar sa nuqātilhum
In the Azhar mosque, our President proclaimed: We shall fight them
l-agl iš-šaraf wi l-karāma wi hiyya ḥurriyya [ḥariyya]
For the sake of honour and self-esteem, which are worth it.
wāḥid li <ašara bi >izn allāh nu>̃ātilhum [ni>ti l-hum]
[Even] one against ten, by God's leave, we shall meet them.
ya mutna šuhda ya <išna <êša ḥurriyya
We shall either die as martyrs or live a life of freedom.
u <ašara li miyya bi >izn allāh nu>̃ātilhum [ni>̃tilhum]
[Even] ten to a hundred, by God's leave, we shall kill them.

wi f bur sa<īd fi l-qitāl ḥaribna biḥurriyya [? baḥriyya]
[In] Port-Said, in battle, we fought a navy
wi bur sa<īd kānit bi d-dammı ḥurriyya [ḥarrī>̃a]
And Port-Said in battle was avid for blood.
il-gēš yimūt <a l-kanāl bi >amrı m il>abṭāl [?il->̃ubṭān]
The soldiers die on the Canal by order of the (?) Captain.
wi saba>̃ il->usṭūl li l-fida>iyyīn yaḥmīha
The fleet hastened to the commandos, to protect them –
<ašara li miyya wi zāyda himmit il>abṭāl [il-baṭṭāl]
Ten to a hundred, the efforts of the evil one increasing.
wi masrı fi >amān wi >̃ām mandūb yaḥmīha [yiḥammīha]
Cairo was safe, but a representative came forth to rouse it.
wi f bur sa<īd it-tarīx bi ymaggid il->abṭāl
In Port-Said, history is glorifying the heroes.
min ša<b wa bulīs wi gēš il->umma yaḥmīha [yā ḥimāha]
[Drawing on] people, police, and army – how inviolate is the nation!
fi bur fu>ād il-maṭār gabbāna wi ddāyir[5] [id-dêr]
In Port-Fuad, the aerodrome, the Gabbana, and the monastery
kullı fir>̃a bi tinzil fi barašuṭṭāt
Unit after unit comes down in parachutes.
fi bur fu>ād il-maṭār gabbāna wi ddāyir [id-dêr]
In Port-Fuad, the aerodrome, the Gabbana, and the monastery.
ṣāḥib id-dinya mīn ya mḥarrar min iššuṭṭāt [iš-šaṭaṭ]
Who is it who controls the world [I ask you] who are free of excesses?
da fi l-qitāl fi l-kanāl kinnu gaḥīm narha [naqarha]
The fighting on the Canal was like an inferno belabouring it.
sāmi< >azīz ir-ruṣāṣ kan ra<dı ṭal>̃itna
One could hear the whizzing of bullets – our volley was thunder.
il-mitrayūz wi l-banādi>̃ bi l->ulūf narha [narāha]
Machine guns and rifles one could see by the thousands.
ḥarb il-fanā> >aw baqā> bi n-naṣr ṭalqitna [ṭallı >atāna]
A war of extinction, or survival with a victory that loomed and came to us.
mu>̃qāwmit iš-ša<bı ṣabbat <a l-<adu narha
The people's resistance poured its fire on the enemy.
ti>̃ūl sibū<a maḥbusīn wi s-s̃awra ṭal>̃itna [>aṭla>̃itna]
You might say they were caged lions that the Revolution released.
min dār >ilā dār u min ḥayy il-qitāl ilā ḥayy
From house to house, and from one embattled quarter to another
yā mā staxāšu l-<ida min hōlı ḍarbitna
How the enemy sought succour from the terror of our blows!
ŧalat fira>̃ li l-ingilīz ma faḍalšı minhum ḥayy
Of three English units not one man was left alive.

ba<aŧulna <ašara firaq ḥakkimit ḍarbitna [dāyir betna]
They sent us ten units that took firm positions round our home.
kan id-difā< mustamīt wi n-nabī >allāh ḥayy [ḥayya]
Desperate was the defence – and God honoured the Prophet!
d aḥna <arab li l-qitāl wi l-ḥarbı ḍarbitna [durbitna]
For we are Arabs – fighting and warfare our wont.
fō>̃ il-manāzil ḥarīm fōq il-midān <almā> [<ulamā>]
On top of the houses were women, [towering] over the battlefield were the ulema,
wi fi š-šawāri< biḥêra min dammı <addīna [>a<ādīna]
And in the streets a pool of our enemies' blood.
bi nḥibbı ḥarb iš-šaraf ḥubb il-<aṭaš <a l-mā>
We love an honourable war as keenly as thirst loves water.
fōq ḍaḥāya l-<adu bi r-rigl <addīna [<addêna]
Over the enemy victims, on foot we crossed.
tinḥiris il-manzala[6] fi >̃aṭ< il-<ida <almā> [<allāma]
May Lake Manzala be guarded, so expert in cutting down the foe,
wi bur sa<id tinšakar ṣaddat <addīna [<udwānna]
And may Port-Said be thanked that turned back aggression
wi galāl disū>̃i nasaf gēš il-<ida filmạyy [fi l-mạyya]
Galal Disuqi blew up the enemy force in the water,
u bi l-madāfi< yidāfi< kull s̃anya >iddini [tdinn]
Defending with cannon which every moment reverberated.
bi ŧnen mudammarāt <and it-tarīx! filmạyy [fallı miyya]
With two destroyers, in a historic moment, he downed a hundred.
gat bawārig li birṭanya ma gūš >iddini [>̃addna]
British battleships came, but did not measure up to us.
infarag iṣ-ṣabāh li l-<urūba min <ama >iddini [>īdin]
The morning brought relief to Arabs from Eden's blindness.
iskindiriyya ma fī-š ṭayyāra bi t-<addī
In Alexandria, not one plane got past.
fi l-mīna nāṣir wi ẓāfir fātiḥ il-mirṣād
In the harbour, Nasir and Zafir had open gunsights.
qāyid <alêh il-gunūd fi n-nār bit<addi [bi tu<add]
[There was] a leader who, under fire, was responsible for the soldiers,
x̱êr iṭ-ṭawābi >alāt il-ḥarbı bilmirṣād [bi l-murrı ṣādda]
As well as fortresses and instruments of war in bitter defence.
yom ṭallat minnu >isra>īl wi faransa bit<addi [bi t-ta<addi]
On the day when Israel and France looked on aggressively,
illi ti>̃arrab bi-tix̱raq w iḥna bi l-mirṣād
Any that came forward was sunk, for we were on the alert.
>aṣl iṭ-ṭayyarāt <andīna wi slaḥna min gawwi [guwwa]
For we had planes, and our weaponry was stored inland

ni<uzha ba<dēn >iza <tada l-<adu nigi līh
For we might want them later, and if the enemy attacked we would step forward to him
min ṭayyarāt mīg sarī<a w naffaṯāt gawwi
Including fast Mig planes and aerial rockets.
li l-xāyin illi <tada[7] bn il-waṭan nigilīh [niglīh]
As for the treacherous national who attacks us, we polish him off.
wi mugrim il-ḥarbı fi l-gam<iyya kan marīḍ g̃awwi
In the [United Nations] Assembly the war criminal was as if seriously ill.
raḥ maglis il->amn yixraṣ bi l-lisān ig̃ilīh [yig̃ūl ēh]
He went to the Security Council but his tongue was silenced – what could he say?
amar iš-šiblı ṭalab igtimā< gam<iyya dawliyya
The lion gave orders, demanded an international meeting
wi kullı mandūb yimas̃s̃il dawlitu fīha [yifīh]
Where each delegate would represent his country and speak out.
ana <arabi aṣīl wi yōm in-naṣrı dawliyya [dawa liyya]
I am a true Arab, and the day of victory to me was a healing draught.
<ala >isra>īl il-karīha l-mōt ḥalāl fīha [fah>̃a]
As for hateful Israel, a gasping death is licit for it.
illi malak ingilṭirra muš rāgil dawliyya [di wiliyya]
The one ruling England is not a man, it's a she!
wi faransa balad il-<agab šuft il-<agab fīha
And of France, the land of wonders, I indeed saw a wonder!
wa>̃fa šu<ūb il-<ālam yiwaggihu l->inzār
The peoples of the world took a stance, addressing a warning.
ṭalabu min ingilṭira wa>̃f il->̃itāl ma rḍūš
They demanded of England a ceasefire – they refused.
di šu<ūb il-<ālam il-ḥurrı t>ayyidna
The peoples of the free world are backing us
w iṭṭallaqu fi l->̃itāl fi ṣ-ṣaffı wayyāna [wayy >annu]
They set forth to the struggle, standing in ranks –Ah, they lamented.
taḥya l-<urūba da n-naṣrı >itḥakkamit <alêh >idna
Long live Arabism! The grasp of our hand is firm on victory
fi l-qurā wi tura maramīh wayyāna
Throughout the villages, and its extent is visible with us.

The well then ran dry!

The recitation was not without a few hiccoughs. Abū Đrā< hesitated a little at line 15, where the rhyme word is either a repetition of the one in line 13 or is a particularly awkward paronomasia, and line 16 may be presumed to be a correction or an alternative, since rhyming lines ought not to follow each other at this point. There was another lapse at line 25, which is a repetition of line 23, and the sestet to which they both belong is left unfinished. There should also be a line rhyming with *filmąyy* between lines 48 and 49. But it is at line 68 that the pattern began seriously to break apart. Both it and the next line are left without rhyming partners. Abū Ḍrā< halted briefly in the middle of line 71, and soon after he had to stop altogether. He called on members of his troupe to help, but none could remember how the ballad ended, and he had to give up.

Now in previous sessions with me, and earlier in the same session, Abū Ḍrā< had recorded without faltering dozens of short folk songs and two full-length narrative ballads, one his own version of 'Šafī>̃a w Mitwalli'[8] – a notorious 'honour crime' based on an event that had taken place in 1925 – and a composition which he attributed to one of his early teachers and which tells the story of a holy man.[9] Yet in this instance, only sixteen years after the event that the ballad was intended to celebrate, his memory had failed him. Surely this indicates that, unlike those other songs, it had dropped out of his repertoire. Coupled with the fact that no other performer had offered me anything comparable, this invites the inference that the patriotic themes which inform so much of the elitist writings of the educated modern Arabs have little currency with the public that is served by the folk literature.

No less weighty and heavy with implications is the evidence here provided of the major role played by memory in the transmission of Arab folk texts. Humans are indeed capable of much greater retentiveness than literate people are inclined to believe. Reliance on memory is very much a part of traditional Islamic education, and among the unlettered it is both necessary and generally expected. Great feats of memorisation are attributed alike to great scholars and to the early *rāwis*,[10] whose oral transmission of pre-Islamic poetry was deemed by such as Ibn Qutayba to be more reliable than the written record.[11]

Some of these feats may well have been exaggerated, but so is Western scepticism concerning them. I owe to Professor L. P. Harvey the information that in sixteenth-century Spain a Morisco narrator of prose romances named Ramón Ramírez, who along with many others had had to profess Christianity but who admitted to having at times observed some Islamic rites, fell into the clutches of the Inquisition in 1595, died while imprisoned four years later, was subsequently convicted of heresy and had his bones dug up and burned. What is significant here is that one of the causes of his downfall was precisely his memory, for his tormentors presumed that it must have been diabolical assistance that 'enabled him to recite long passages from novels of chivalry (and other books) when he did not have the actual text before him'.[12]

To such long-rooted incredulity among Westerners, modern scholarship has added a new dimension. The study of Western folk literature has been much illumined by the Parry–Lord theory of oral-formulaic composition, and scholars are keen to assert its validity and universality. Some, such as Michael Zwettler and James Monroe, have made brave attempts at detecting traces of the technique in early Arabic poetry, and not in the pre-Islamic period alone. The temptation is strong to assume that it is the mainstay of Arabic folk literature also. I have in fact received an invitation to contribute to a special number of the *Journal of Mediterranean Studies*, which sets out not as a proposition to be investigated but as a 'given' from which to start that 'the Mediterranean is a region where folk-poetry, singing, and extemporising in music and words/texts, has both a long tradition and a living presence. Folk-poetry has also been associated with the growth of nationalism and "national identity".' Do the facts bear this out?

Improvisation is, of course, by definition oral composition, although not necessarily formulaic, and there are indeed indications that some Egyptian performers do improvise. It is consistent with the Parry–Lord theory that these are mostly specialists of the Hilālī epic cycle, and at least one of them is reported to have memorised formulaic phrases he did not understand;[13] but the phenomenon is rarer among the ballad-mongers who were the objects of my immediate interest. Even this generalisation, however, is too sweeping, for one finds within the same tradition artists who have different priorities and different skills. Some performers go for musical and metrical regularity, others for the dramatic potential of the story they have to tell. Some are more responsive than others to the mood of their public. The end-products, therefore, can scarcely be expected to conform to one pattern, and I have noted elsewhere some of the variations.[14] But the kind of *mawwāl* presented here, with its demanding puns and complicated rhyme scheme, I have never known to be the result of anything but careful composition and memorisation.

I have in fact heard Abū Đrā< sing unrehearsed compliments to members of his audience, but these invariably consisted of punning tercets. And when I did question him about more extensive improvisation, his response – perhaps making a virtue of necessity – was supercilious: 'Those are games that peasants play. *I* am an artist!'

Of course, oral composition and improvisation are linked but not necessarily co-extensive terms. The fact that an illiterate poet may compose a ballad orally and then commit it to memory has long been recognised, and scholars have sought the hallmark of oral composition – the formula – in poetry that has come down to us in written form, and even in compositions produced long after writing had come into wide use. But the most extensive cases have been made only by stretching the 'formula' almost to include regular grammatical constructions. Of the more stringent kind of formula that could convincingly form a building-brick for a sung narrative, I find little evidence, at least in this kind of *mawwāl.* The verifiable fact is that several of the performers I was able to question had a repertoire of hundreds of songs that they acknowledged they had learned by rote, some picked out of a book, even the illiterate among them calling on the services of literate acquaintances to help them in the process of memorisation.[15] Furthermore, if the mainstay of the oral composer is the possession of a stock of set formulae and if, as is evident, the overwhelming interest of the *mawwāl*-poet is the *zahr*, then it is not irrelevant to stress that I have hardly ever come across the same pun in different compositions.

On these puns I have another observation to offer, not immediately related to orality but relevant to Western assumptions. Western writers on the subject make much of the power of a paronomasia to bring to mind a multiplicity of notions or images that may have a bearing on the context. Such indeed may be the effect on the listeners of a *mawwāl* as they strain to make out the intricacies of the wordplay, but what they rack their brains for is to pick out the form that best fits the slot, and whenever one discusses the matter with the practitioners of the art, they invariably assign a precise meaning to the homonyms at each of their separate appearances. In the present instance, I noticed that Sir Anthony Eden's name in the distorted form in which it occurs at the end of line 49 could also – appropriately in that context – be taken to be *id-dani* (the vile one). When I raised this point with Abū Ðrā<, he conceded that that was also possible, but in such a dismissive way that I was left with the distinct impression that the double entendre had not been in his own mind.

To conclude: I was at the time greatly disappointed not to have a sample of a patriotic ballad to include in my survey of the genre. Yet it is the fact that this particular text had slipped out of its author's memory that I now want to use as a peg for making two far-reaching observations, which are also two earnest appeals to the community of Arabists and Arab scholars.

The first arises from the manifest unpopularity of the theme. Almost inevitably, it is the written literature of the modern Arab elite that reaches out beyond the borders of the Arab world and that penetrates both the ivy-covered walls of Western universities and the ivory towers of even Arab academia. It is easy then to assume that the picture it draws of Arab modernist concerns is also an index of the forces at work in the entire society. A look at contemporary folk literature is a useful, indeed a necessary, corrective to this assumption, and I contend that a study of it *and* of the colloquial forms of the language in which it occurs ought to be an integral part of any programme of modern Arabic studies. There must be an end to 'surveys of modern Arabic literature' that make not even a tangential reference to this other vast field of Arab creativity.

This, in turn, stresses the need to encourage field research in Arab folk literature, and extensive recording of it. The material may not be to everyone's taste, but it has much light to throw on Middle Eastern culture, and possibly on folk arts in general. There is an opportunity here to observe a live phenomenon that has died elsewhere, and the urgency lies precisely in the fact that it too is changing rapidly under changing conditions, and may well be approaching the end of its span.

My second *cri de coeur* is this: even as I welcome all who are willing to labour in this vineyard, I must urge them not to rush into theory, especially not ready-made theories, and least of all theories that assume the universality of whatever conforms with European or Western reality, for the temptation is then strong to bend the evidence to one's pet notions. The subject is immense, the work done in it as yet minimal. A strong foundation of fact is yet to be laid, and generalisations ought to be guarded and confined to the area that has been thoroughly investigated. My own research, specifically in the field of the narrative ballad, has so far uncovered more diversity than uniformity alike in methods of composition and transmission as in the formation and status of the ballad-mongers and the character of their performances.

The academic mind is enamoured of consistency and seeks regular patterns everywhere, but perhaps it needs to be reminded that reality is not always as neat as we should like it. It ought not to surprise even the most cloistered of us to discover that artists are often strongly individualistic and that tradition is seldom monolithic, so that in matters of art even more than in other pursuits, conformity is not necessarily the supreme rule, and the researcher's richest rewards are not always the well-tried recipes.

Notes

1. Oxford, 1989, hereafter *Ballads.*
2. In *Arabic Thought in the Liberal Age* (Oxford, 1962).
3. *Ballads*, pp. 3–34, and Item 2 in this book.
4. On *zahr*, see John Eisele, 'Artificial Punning in the Egyptian Arabic Ballad: A Reinterpretation of Structuralist Poetics', *Language*, 73, 4 (December 1997), pp. 751–69.
5. Newspaper reports mention only three areas in the vicinity of Port-Said where parachutists were dropped: Port-Fuad, the aerodrome of al-Jamil, and the Jabbana. This last word means 'cemetery'.
6. Some parachutists were reported to have fallen into the lake.
7. Possibly a reference to a report that 'an Israeli' named Leonardo Alfred was arrested for signalling with an electric torch during an air-raid.
8. Two other versions of the story are in *Ballads*, pp. 268–322.
9. Named 'X̲arīb'; his story is told in Ballads, pp. 268–322.
10. See George Makdisi, *The Rise of Humanism in Classical Islam and the Christian West* (Edinburgh, 1990), p. 202.
11. *Kitāb aš-Ši<r wa š-Šu<arā>* (Beirut, 1964), Introduction, p. 26; also *Introduction au Livre de la Poésie et des Poètes*, introduction, translation and commentary by Gaudefroy-Demombynes (Paris, 1947), p. 20.
12. L. P. Harvey, 'Oral Composition and the Performance of Novels of Chivalry in Spain', *Forum for Modern Language Studies*, 10, 3 (July 1974), pp. 270–86, especially pp. 272 and 278.
13. Susan Slyomovics, *The Merchant of Art* (Berkeley, CA, 1987), p. 29.
14. *Ballads*, pp. 36–48.
15. *Ballads*, pp. 50–1, 167.

9

An Honour Crime with a Difference

The entire field of Arabic folk literature has long been neglected, not least by Arab scholars whose concern until very recently has been almost exclusively with texts composed in the classical language. Understandably, Western Arabists too have largely confined themselves to material they encountered in Arab written sources. Some interest has finally been awakened in humbler aspects of Arab creativity, the most solid work being done mainly on the folk epic cycles, especially the one that is still alive today: the Hilāliyya.

No less important and no less indicative of the perceptions, priorities and artistic potential of the common people (as against the educated elite) are narrative ballads – usually running to about two hundred lines each – many of which are woven round some contemporary occurrences.[1] The favourite theme is in fact the 'honour crime', the story of a woman who has deviated from the strict code of sexual ethics and thereby placed on a close male relative – usually her father or her brother – the duty of 'washing the family's honour' in her blood. It is three versions of just such a story – the story of Ḥasan and Na<īma – that are presented here.[2] They deal with a crime that took place in 1938, and that differed startlingly from the usual pattern in that it was the man and not the woman involved in the scandal who was killed. And no less startling is the treatment by the folk artists, who for once do not glorify the gory deed but are sympathetic to the lovers – or at least to the male. This radical departure from the ethos of the countryside is most probably due not to a revolution in values, but to the fact that Ḥasan was himself a folk singer.

We shall want to find out how this factor affects the judgement of the three poets; but it would be rewarding to consider first some matters of form peculiar to the *mawwāl* – metre, rhyme and wordplay – which weigh heavily in the way folk poets express themselves.

Egyptian ballads occur in a variety of metrical forms, of which the most rudimentary depend on a simple repetitive rhythm and equally simple rhymes, lending themselves to a certain amount of improvisation. Far more sophisticated is the *mawwāl.*[3] Some of the Egyptian ballad-mongers I have met maintained that the essential feature of a *mawwāl* is that it should not be sung to a set tune; rather, the music should be modulated to fit the sense, and this I hope to illustrate with the last text I shall be quoting in this article. More commonly, it is defined – especially by the more scholarly who rely on written sources – as a composition in the *basīṭ* metre, but it is observable that a few more variations occur in it than are allowed in classical prosody, and that what is only a hemistich in the poetry of the elite always functions as a complete line in the *mawwāl.*

The earliest recorded examples of the *mawwāl* (in a twelfth-century manual of non-classical verse) are all mono-rhyme quatrains, but intricate rhyme schemes have been devised. A single set of any of these rhyme schemes may be the mainstay of a fixed-form lyrical song, or it may be repeated in stanza after stanza of a narrative ballad.

Finally, a feature so increasingly popular that it is becoming a rule is the elaboration of rhymes into a kind of polysyllabic pun achieved by distortions of the normal pronunciation in which anything may happen to vowels, stress, or gemination, only the consonants remaining firm. These contortions may be called consonantal paronomasias. To the native artists, they are known as *zahr*, the term itself being a potential pun for it is primarily taken to refer to 'flowers', but it may also mean 'dice' or 'luck'. The end-products can be so mystifying that some early researchers did not recognise them as puns and assumed them to be repetitions.[4] Yet it is a matter of pride for some folk poets to have every single rhyme blown up into a 'flower', and I have found it necessary when transcribing their compositions to 'open out the flower', as the Egyptian expression goes, by adding between square brackets my reading of how the words would normally have been uttered.

We are now equipped to savour what three folk poets have made of the story of Ḥasan and Na<īma.

The first of the three versions of 'Ḥasan u Na<īma' to be considered here is taken from a cheaply produced booklet, undated but evidently printed before the 1952 *coup d'état* since it bears the imprint of al-Maktaba al-Mulūkiyya, a name that merely lays claim to excellence but that nevertheless has monarchic connotations. The publication is by >Ibrahīm Sulaymān, known as iš-Šēx, and is titled *Kitāb an-Najm al-<Ālī fi l-Fann il-X̱ālī*, 'the Lofty Star of Precious Art'.

It contains several compositions in addition to the ballad I have picked. This is in the form of an Upper Egyptian *mawwāl*, for which the standard rhyme scheme is aaa bcbcbc dedede … zzz (z)a (meaning that the last 'a' line should contain an internal 'z' rhyme), but in this instance the poet has expanded each sestet to an octet of alternating rhymes. The first line read:

1 *yā ṣāḥib il-<a>lı >isma< naẓmı <a nniswān [in-nās wann]*
O man of reason, listen to verse that reverberates among people;
2 *til>̃āh <agīb fi l->adab wi ṭ-ṭa<nı fi nniswān [n-naṣṣı wāni]*
You'll find it a literary wonder – disparaging the text is paltry.
3 *>i<raf ragil gaddı lā tis>al <ala nniswān [n-nās wēn]*
Get to know one man of purpose – do not ask where the many are.
…
208 *šūf il-bawādir bi ta<mil >ēhı yā x̱āwi*
Consider what impulses can do, deluded one!

209 *xirbit buyūt <āl kanum <amrīnı yā x̱āwi [x̱aww]*
Fine houses have been ruined that had been peopled – what loss!
210 *>aktib wi >asṭur w a>̃ul lak ēhı yā xāwi*
I write, I pen, but what shall I tell you, O amateur of verse?
211 *kull il-balāwi lli bi tgīna min in-niswān*
All our misfortunes come from women.

In the intervening narrative, one octet introduces Ḥasan:

12 *ism il-mux̱annī Ḥasan >in-Nims bi kamālu*
The singer's name in its entirety is Ḥasan in-Nims
13 *baladu bani mazār tib>̃a giwār il-minya*
His town is Banī Mazār, which is near to il-Minya
14 *luh ṣūra ḥilwa tizīd <ala l-badr fikamālu [fīk mēl luh]*
His appearance fairer than the full moon, so you incline towards him
15 *ti>ūl da turki lakin fi l->aṣlı milminya [mā luh manniyya]*
You'd say he was a Turk, but of his origin there is no doubt
16 *il-ḥaẓẓı xadamuh wi nāl is-sa<dı fikamālu [fīh kamah luh]*
Luck served him. He attained fortune while blind to it.
17 *wi kān fi lēlit faraḥ mawgūd filminya [fīh il-munya]*
He was present on a wedding night, filled with hope
18 *gum nās wi da<ūh yi>̃īm il-faraḥ bi kamāluh [kam >āla]*
Some came and engaged him to perform at the wedding with so many [musical] instruments
19 *l agl il-mi>̃addar saba>̃ fi l-x̱ēb wilminya [wi l-maniyya]*
All because of destiny unknowably predetermined, and a fated death.

Another two octets tell of his first encounter with Na<īma and the effect he had on her:

28 *ḥasan il-mux̱anni yx̱anni bi n-nax̱am minfō> [min fūh]*
Ḥasan the singer sang out, the melody flowing from his mouth
29 *wi ygīb kalām <āl wi xalāy>̃i kitīr sam<āh [sāwmu m<āh]*
He uttered excellent words, and many made deals with him.
30 *luh waghı ka l-badrı zāyid <a l->amar minfoō> [mīn fā>̃uh]*
His face was like the full moon – more than the moon – who can surpass him?
31 *w ahl il-ḥuẓūẓ wi ṭ-ṭarab kānit hināk sam<āh [sammū m<āh]*
The fortunate who respond to music invoked God with him.
32 *>atāri na<īma bi tunẓur li ḥasan min fō>*
It happened that Na<īma was watching Ḥasan from above
33 *sakan il-x̱arām >̃albiha min ḥubbihā sam<āh [ṣawma<a]*
Passion indwelt her; love made of her heart a hermit's cell
34 *min kutrı nār wagdihā bikyit kitīr minfō> [mīn yifawwa>̃]*
The fire of her rapture made many tears flow – and who brings relief?

35 *ka>innu bulbul wi min fō>̃ iš-šagar sam<āh*
He was like a nightingale which she heard in the treetops
36 *il-ḥaẓẓı zāyid >̃awi fiḍl il-faraḥ li ṣ-ṣubḥ*
Fortune rode high. The wedding lasted till morning
37 *wi na<īma wal<a bi nār il-ḥubbı miḥtāra [miḥtarra]*
And Na<īma was ablaze, heated with the fire of love
38 *ṭil>̃in-nahār wi l-xalāyi> fī hanā liṣṣubḥ [li s-sabḥ]*
Dawn broke, and people were elated with the [songs of] praise
39 *wi na<īma tibkī min il->afkārı miḥtāra*
While Na<īma wept, perplexed with all her thoughts
40 *wi waghı ḥasan ẓahar bān il-gamāl fi ṣṣubḥ [ṣ-ṣabāḥ]*
Ḥasan's face was resplendent, beauty shining in his brow
41 *tunẓur bi <enha wi ti<mil >ēh miḥtāra [mā ḥa tarā]*
Her eyes staring – what was she to do – she was not to see!
42 *nār il-x̱arām ša<lilit wayya n-nisīm fiṣṣubḥ [fa ṣ-ṣabbı bāḥ]*
The fire of passion was livened with the breeze, and the lover was betrayed
43 *w ixtallı minha mizān il-<a>̃lı miḥtāra [maḥḥı ṭāruh]*
The balance of her mind was upset, its frame was weakened.

A different version of the story is recorded on a cassette commercially produced by a firm called Nefertiti, and bought in Cairo in 1979. It is sung by Muḥammad Ṭāhā and consists entirely of 'sevener' stanzas, rhyming aaa bbb a. Here is how the first meeting of the lovers is celebrated, again stressing Ḥasan's honourable behaviour even after Na<īma has declared her passion:

15 *ḥasan il-mux̱anni kān yix̱anni fannı wi layāli [la>āli>]*
Ḥasan the Singer was singing – artistry and pearls
16 *wi yinda<a bi ṭ-ṭarab l afrāḥ wi layāli*
And to delight with singing was engaged for weddings and [musical] evenings
17 *wi da<ūh fi lēla w kānit ḥaẓẓı wilayāli [wallā ya wēli]*
He was called to such an evening – luck departed, alas! –
18 *fi manšiyyit abu ḥanḍal >awwal >̃ismı li l-minya*
In Manšiyyit Abu Ḥanḍal, the first precinct in [the province of] Minya
19 *markaz bani mazār taba< giwār li lminya [l-munya]*
In the district of Bani Mazār, in hope [?of neighbourliness?]
20 *rāḥ il-gada< rāḥ wi >̃aṣdu yux̱lub ilminya [il-maniyya]*
The good fellow went – he went, aiming to overcome a fated death
21 *wi l-xal>̃ı dunya ti>̃ūl ya <ēn ya layāli [lēli]*
All the people joining in the tra-la-la
22 *x̱anna l-karawān wi >alḥān in-nax̱am šabābīk [šabah buka]*
The songbird trilled, and the strains of the melody were like sobs.
23 *ṭil<u l-banāt fi l-<alāli w fattaḥu š-šabābīk*
The girls went up and opened the windows wide.

24 *>ālit na<īma ya x̱arāmi yā ḥasan šabābīk [šabābak]*
Na<īma exclaimed, 'O love of mine, how handsome your youth!'
25 *ba<atit lu mandīl wi >asbāb il-x̱arām mandīl [min dōl]*
She sent him a kerchief – and of such are the bonds of passion!
26 *wi l-ḥubbı l-aglu ttṣāl w illi ḥaṣal mindīl [minnuh ḍall]*
So love was joined, and the outcome was doom.
27 *ḥissak tilūm il-mabāli titūh ma tindal titūh mandīl [mīn yidill]*[5]
Beware of blaming the afflicted: you'll lose your way, and who will guide you?
28 *wi f >̃ōltu yā lēl di nār il-x̱arām šabābīk [šābba bīk]*
With his singing 'tra-la' the fire of passion blazes in you.
29 *lamma ntaha l-faraḥ >̃ām il-x̱arīb rawwaḥ*
The wedding over, the outsider went home
30 *wi l-xal>̃ı nāmit wi nōm il-<āši>̃īn rawwahḥ [rawāḥ]* × 2
People slept – but for lovers sleep is [an arduous] journey.
31 *wi l>̃a<da ḥilyit wi nasīm iṣ-ṣabaḥ rawwaḥ*
The celebration proved pleasant, and the morning breeze gave comfort
32 *na<īma sāhra l-layāli gifnaha ma tlamm*
Na<īma had sleepless nights, her eyelids never closing.
33 *wi garḥ il-muḥabba <igiz <annu ṭ-ṭabīb ma tlamm [tla>am]*
The wound of love defeats the physician – it did not heal.
34 *>iw<a tilūm il-mabāli yā xali titlamm [titlām]*
Beware of blaming the afflicted, you who are whole, or you will [yourself] be blamed
35 *da l-ḥubbı bi d-dammı miš bil-māl >umrawwaḥ [>u mi r-rōḥ]* × 2
Love is purchased with blood, not money, and comes from the soul.
36 *il-ḥubbı xalla na<īma fikriha mašx̱ūl*
Love caused Na<īma's mind to be preoccupied
37 *wi sābit baladha w abūha mi lli ṣār mašx̱ūl [māši yix̱li]*
She left her village, and – because of what happened – her father walked about, boiling
38 *li l-fikrı wi l-<ār wi kalām il-balad mašx̱ūl [muš x̱āli]*
With worry and shame – and the talk of the village was cheap
39 *x̱abit na<īma liha mudda saba< >ayyām*
Na<īma was absent for a period of seven days
40 *bi tšūf ḥabibha l-waḥīd >̃aymā balad >ayyām [>̃iyām]*
She saw her beloved alone and a village up in arms
41 *raḥit lu baladu w >̃ālit lu fāyta būy wayyām [wayy ummi]*
She went to his village and told him: 'I have left my father and mother
42 *wi l-<arḍı minṣān w inta ya ḥasan miš x̱ūl*
My honour secure, for you, Ḥasan, are no monster.'

A very different performance is the one given by Šōg̃i l-G̃ināwi and recorded in the field by the Egyptian poet <Abd ar-Raḫmān al-Abnūdī in the 1970s.[6] It does not conform with the *mawwāl* as prosodically defined, for it has no recognisable metre or rhyme scheme. In fact, some lines are left unrhymed even though they lend themselves readily to punning; line 20, for example, ends in *x̱ulbi*, 'my misery', which could easily be matched with the Upper Egyptian pronunciation of *g̃albi*, 'my heart', but it is not. It does, however, retain – if only in patches – the taste for 'consonantal paronomasias', and it is certainly sung to no set tune. In fact, the singer at times reverts to a speaking voice (as in lines 24–7); but this does not amount to an alternation of prose and verse passages as is known to occur in the performance of some of the epic cycles, for Šōg̃i remains within the same register throughout, the spoken lines end in puns, and it is during the delivery of the last of these lines that he slips back into a singing mode. It is open to speculation whether this text started as a regularly composed *mawwāl* that was then adopted and adapted by an artist more interested in dramatic effect than in metrical virtuosity. Here, at all events, is the passage corresponding to the preceding ones:

14 *il-ḥassı gamīl wi ṣ-ṣūra bizyāda [bi z-ziyyı da]*
The voice was beautiful, and his appearance the same
15 *kama baḥrı ṭāmi wi l-yōm ṭālı bizyāda*
Like a river in spate, so the day was much extended.
16 *il-walad g̃al ya lēl basaṭ il-<ālam winnās [u wannas]*
The lad sang 'tra-la' pleasing all and creating good fellowship
17 *sim<itu na<īma wi jāt wasṭ il-majāl wi n-nās*
Na<īma heard him and came into the gathering, amongst all
18 *maska mandīl wa fi l-mandīl bārīza*
Holding a kerchief, with a ten-piastre piece in it
19 *g̃ālat ya fannān xuđ il-mandīl*
She said, 'Artist, take the kerchief
20 *wi hat li dōrēn <ala x̱ulbi*
And sing me some tunes to ease my misery.'
21 *g̃al il-ismı mīn ya hānim*
He asked, 'What is the name, my Lady?'
22 *g̃alat lu l->ismı na<īma*
She answered, 'The name is Na<īma.'
23 *g̃al yustur <arḍ il-walāya w ḥatta <arḍina<īma [<arḍina <āmma]*
He said, 'May He shield women's honour, and also our honour, collectively.'
24 *il-walad ḥasan g̃al ēh*
The lad, Ḥasan, what did he say?
25 *masak il-mandīl wi g̃āl jabūk min it-tājir ya mandīl wa la štax̱alūk >aṣḥābak*
He held the kerchief and said, 'Were you bought from a merchant, kerchief, or were you worked by your owners?

26 *mēta ykūn il->awān ya mandīl w il-<ēn tundur >ṣḥābak [>aṣḥā bīk]*
When will the time come, O kerchief, when as the eye moistens I shall wake to find you by me?
27 *da nta titḥafiẓ fi j-jēb lama l-<ēn tundur >aṣḥābak [>asḥabak]*
You shall be kept in my pocket, so when the eye moistens I may pull you out.'

It is evident that these performances are not all cast in the same mould. The rigidly formatted pun-laden *mawwāl* calls for enormous linguistic skills, and puts a heavy burden on the performer's memory – for (as I have shown elsewhere)[7] it does not lend itself to improvisation. Such a display of dexterity is not without its price. It smells of midnight oil. The wording is often strained and the sense sometimes forced into blind alleys, or at least into bumpy alleys. One senses, for example, that in iš-Šēx's octets, notably the one beginning with line 36, the two sets of lines sharing the same rhyme were separately composed and only then interlaced. The result is impressive nevertheless. And no less impressive is that it assumes a nimble-minded audience familiar with the technicalities of the form; when, for example, a set of puns is divided – as it is in iš-Šēx's ballad – between a 'doorstep' and a 'skull-cap' occurring more than two hundred lines later, its effect necessarily depends not on an auditory echo, but on a signal initially registered and an expectation finally fulfilled.

And is il-G̃ināwi's plainer performance less admirable? Is not his lyricism entrancing? And is it solely because he is a better poet or is it also because he has shed some of the self-conscious artistry of his rivals that he makes more delicate use of the offer and the careful pocketing of a kerchief to symbolise the placing of Na<īma's honour in Ḥasan's safekeeping?

In this as in many other Arab folk genres, there is not one cast-iron tradition, but room for many styles, and for artists' individual preferences.

Notes

1. I have attempted an exposition of the genre and transcribed some representative Egyptian samples in *Ballads*.
2. Honour crimes are dealt with at length in *Ballads* (pp. 269–350); this includes the full text and translation of one of the ballads discussed here.
3. This is fully described in Item 2 in this book.
4. See, e.g., Nada Tomiche, 'Le Mawwāl Égyptien', *Mélanges Marcel Cohen* (The Hague, 1970), pp. 429–38, and Serafin Fanjul, 'The Erotic Popular Mawwal in Egypt', *Journal of Arabic Literature*, 8 (1977), pp. 105–22. Even a later Egyptian scholar, Kamal Abdel-Malek, misread some of his texts in *Muḥammad in the Modern Egyptian Popular Ballad* (Leiden, 1995), reviewed in *Journal of the American Oriental Society*, 118, 3 (1998), pp. 409–10.
5. A hitch has occurred here. My surmise is that, while singing the line, the performer's mind was racing ahead in search of the next pun for *mandīl*. At first, he recalled only the root he was to use, and uttered a derivative that did not serve the purpose since it introduced an additional consonant, a 't'. He then immediately corrected himself.
6. It is transcribed and translated in full in *Ballads*, pp. 323–50.
7. See Item 8 in this book.

10

Pulp Stories in the Repertoire of Egyptian Folk Singers

When I was collecting Egyptian narrative ballads,[1] mainly in the 1970s and 1980s, by far the most popular were accounts of 'honour crimes', so-called because they celebrated violent deeds committed to avenge the murder of a kinsman as in the story of *l-Adham iš-Šar>̃āwī*,[2] or to punish a woman's offence against sexual ethics as in the many versions of *Šafī>̃a w Mitwalli* and of *Ḥasan u Na<īma*. It was these that one performer after another sang, each in his own words. It was these that the folk singers most commonly offered if the choice was left to them. Even national events, including the wars that have wracked the Middle East since 1948, held the folk poets' attention only for a brief span.[3]

And yet in my collection is a handful of songs that are placed in a contemporary setting, but are of a more universal and less distinctively Egyptian character. They tell at length of dastardly deeds, of the sufferings of their victims and of the eventual triumph of justice, often through the intervention of the police and the courts.

The performers are unquestionably genuine folk singers, the delivery is characteristic of their style and the texts all display, to a greater or lesser extent, their delight in *zahr*, literally 'the flower' which requires rhymes to be inflated into multiple and usually polysyllabic paronomasias achieved by extensive distortion of the normal pronunciation of words. This involves omitting, adding or altering vowels, semi-consonants, glottal stops, and sometimes even the aspirate consonant *hā>*, retaining only the consonants in their correct order,[4] so that the result may be called a 'consonantal' pun. When attempted in every line of a long poem, the effect is seldom achieved without some straining of sense or wording.[5]

Yet of the 'pulp' songs that have come into my hands, all but one are on commercial tapes, produced and marketed by entrepreneurs belonging to, and catering for, a different (or at least a wider) social stratum than the one which is commonly served by Egyptian folk artists; and of all the yardsticks that have been used to delimit Arab folk literature, I have found that the most readily identifiable is the public addressed, consisting mainly of the unlettered and of those who have had a modicum of traditional education without being substantially influenced by Western cultural perceptions.[6] The question therefore arises: How truly 'folk' are these stories?

For a folk artist to sing into a microphone in a well-regulated studio is a far cry from the image one has of a typical performance in close interaction with a circle of *gallabiyya* wearers, perhaps at a *mlid* held in honour of some rural holy man. But occasions for folk celebrations are not exclusively rural. There are well-attended shrines to holy men in the populous quarters of big cities. Itinerant singers flock to locations that offer richer pickings, and the most successful are quick to take advantage of whatever devices may serve their purpose.

More troubling is the evidence of occasional bowdlerisation by cassette marketers of passages that the educated elite may find offensive, such as a reference to the Sudan as 'the land of the slaves', or the assertion that the Prophet sentenced three 'Christian Jews' guilty only of attempted fraud to be burnt alive.[7] Such interventions are rare, however, and do not seem to amount to a systematic – certainly not an officially sanctioned – censorship.

A run through a number of the texts available will bring out both their artistic quality and the cultural perceptions that inform them.

The only one not commercially produced is to be found in the records of the Folk Arts Centre in Cairo. It is sung by Mu<awwa Šams-id-Dīn and runs to 374 lines. Titled 'Šilbāya,' it tells of the unrelieved villainy of a woman of this name. Xālid, the elder of two wealthy brothers, marries her for her looks instead of heeding his mother's advice to look for the well brought-up daughter of a worthy father. Shamelessly, Šilbāya tries to entice Xālid's younger brother Jamīl. He rebukes her, so she complains to her husband that Jamīl has made improper advances to her. Xālid tries to shoot his brother, but his revolver misfires. Jamīl wrenches the gun from him and protests his innocence, drawing a parallel with the Qur>anic story of Yūsuf and Zulayxa. Nevertheless, in deference to his elder brother he abandons home and possessions and sets off into the unknown. On the road, he flags down a taxi and finds himself sharing it with a gentleman imposing enough to be taken for a Bey, travelling with his daughter. They are then attacked by highwaymen who rob the Bey of his money, but when their leader man-handles the young woman Jamīl uses his brother's revolver to good effect. In gratitude, the Bey, who turns out to be a judge, sees to it that Jamīl prospers, and gives him his daughter Layla in marriage. In the meantime, Šilbāya has a son by Xālid, but she falls in love with Kamāl al-Ḥusayn. She steals Xālid's property deeds and his seal, and with her unprincipled father's help she turns him out of his home. She marries Kamāl, and they wallow in luxury but neglect her son Salāma. Although still a lad, Salāma learns his family's true history, so he shoots Kamāl. Šilbāya denounces Xālid and Salāma as the murderers, and both are arrested. Jamīl learns of these events through newspapers, so he and his prestigious father-in-law intervene. Justice is done: Šilbāya is imprisoned, the brothers are reconciled, and their property is restored to them.

Another version of the same story, sung by Muḥammad Ṭāhā, is available on a commercial cassette, and so are quite a few other narrative songs of the same character. One, sung by Yūsuf Šitā is titled 'Karam il-Yatīm'. It recounts – in 357 lines – how Karam being orphaned early in life comes under the care of his uncle, whose rapacious wife schemes to cheat him of his inheritance. She makes his life so miserable that he runs away. A kindly farmer takes him under his wing, and years later gives him his daughter in marriage in defiance of a powerful and aggressive suitor. Now prosperous and well established, Karam returns to his uncle's house to assert his rights; but his uncle has died and his widow and her son claim all the property as theirs. The village headman, however, produces documents that the uncle had entrusted to him. Karam comes into his own, and his stepmother and her son are imprisoned.

In yet another such cassette, Aḥmad >Ismā<īl sings 'Zuhra wi l->Ayyām', Zuhra and [the vicissitudes of] Fate'. Zuhra is the daughter of X̲allāb. Her mother dies and X̲allāb takes on another wife, and by her he has a son called Ṣaddīq. Zuhra's wicked stepmother accuses her of a sexual indiscretion, and in compliance with the code of honour – but not in accordance with custom, which would have him slaughter her and advertise the deed – X̲allāb throws her in a well. A passing gang of bandits hear her moans, pull her out and take her to an isolated desert location as their servant. In time Ṣaddīq has occasion to avenge an uncle's murder, and since the government does not condone 'honour crimes', he runs away to the same isolated location. There he gets to know Zuhra, and 'love had a part in their relationship'. Although there has been no hint that Zuhra has had a lapse of memory, it is only after the scandal is out that she recalls her early life, and tells Ṣaddīq where she was born, who her father is and even that she has a half-brother who shares his name. Ṣaddīq hastens back to his father, tells him what has happened and shoots himself. X̲allāb blames his wife for all those misfortunes, and shoots her and then himself. In this tragic denouement, there is no reference of any kind to Zuhra herself.

A peculiarity of this text is that it is *muzahhar*, that is, the *zahr*, the 'flower' is opened out, the words which are usually distorted to achieve the paronomasias being pronounced as they would be in everyday speech. Thus, in a tercet that sums up the theme of the entire piece, the performer sings:

22 w illi <aksu zahru ma yitḥannāš
For one whose luck is adverse, there is no [celebratory] henna.
imrāt il-<abbı ma tḥinniš
A stepmother has no compassion:
kilmithā <aḍḍit mīt ḥanaš
Her word is the bite of a hundred snakes!

This destroys the punning effect. Even if it is reconstituted in the minds of those who know the rules of the game, the challenge to the percipience of the audience is lost.

Far more polished and worthier of close attention is 'Mas<ūd u Wagīda',[8] sung by the same Muḥammad Ṭāhā to whom we also owe one version of 'Šilbāya'.

For his rendition of this *qiṣṣa*, Muḥammad Ṭāhā resorts to a highly prized and demanding metrical form: he uses the seven-line *mawwāl* as a stanza. This calls for a tercet with a common punning rhyme, another tercet with a new punning rhyme, and a seventh line with a rhyme punning with the first, but also having somewhere within it an echo of the second rhyme. The scheme may be represented as

aaa bbb (b)a.

All this is illustrated in the opening stanza. The *zahr*, however, often necessitates such distortions that I add – between square brackets – the usual pronunciation of what I take to be the intended wording.

> y ahl il-mazāya ma<āya **dōr** xudubālkum [xudūh bi l-kam]
> *People of quality, I have a song – take it in its entirety:*
> mas̃būt riwāya ḥadis̃ **mašhūr** xudubālkum [xaḍab il-kumm]
> *A recorded narrative, a well-known occurrence that stains one's sleeve [with tears],*
> s̃abt ū riwāya <ala l-**ma>̃dūr** xudubālkum [xuđu bālīkum]
> *Recording and recounting a destiny wading into which would try you.*
> >alliftihā w >̃ultiha bi >uṣūl wayyāya [wayya >āya]
> *I composed it and recite it properly, and with a sign:*
> kalām musalsal x̱arām luh >̃ubūl wayyāya [u wi>̃āya]
> *Well-ordered words, of love acceptable and guarded.*
> w ādi ntu >̃a<dīn ya mustama<īn wayyāya
> *And here you are, listeners, sitting with me:*
> >aṣl ir-riwāya tizakki l-<a>̃lı xōđu bālkum
> *The story refines the mind, so be attentive!*

This performer also goes beyond conventional requirements by providing additional internal rhymes, sometimes in a succession of lines as in lines 1–3 (*dr*, *mahr*, *madr*), but more commonly in a pair within a line. These occur not at any specific point within the stanza, but here and there as the opportunity arises, and to these he often gives prominence in his singing by pausing at them. In this text, such additional rhymes are in bold.

Peculiar to this performance is that the stanzaic arrangement is often broken. Folk singers differ in their priorities. Some care more for dramatic effect than for metrical regularity,[9] and it is precisely in the most exciting parts of a long narrative song that prosodic liberties are often taken. But poets who from the start choose the strict form of the *mawwāl* studded with paronomasias are not the ones inclined to stray from it. Indeed, the same Muḥammad Ṭāhā's recording of his version of an 'honour crime', *Ḥasan u Na<īma*,[10] is regular throughout. In this instance, one may infer that the irregularity is due mainly to lapses of memory.

The lapses begin as early as in the second stanza, where the fifth and sixth lines are missing, leaving the fourth line unrhymed and rather lame:

> 8 >il->aslı >̃itnēn y ahl il-ma<rifa >ixwān [>ixā> wānī]
> *It starts with two, O men of learning – a failing brotherhood!.*
> min >ax̱niyā> iṣ-ṣa<īd kānu sawā >ixwān [xuwwān]
> *Wealthy men of Upper Egypt, treacherous to each other.*
> >itfarra>̃ū ba<d abūhum lam ba>̃um >ixwān [xāwyīn]
> *They parted after their father [died], and were no longer close*

ḥaṣal xilāf bēnhum <a šān il-marāš̃ wi ẓrūfhum
A difference sprang between them over their inheritance and circumstances.
...
>illī yišūfhum yi>̃ūl dōla x̲urbı mēš >ixwān
Whoever sees them would say, 'These are strangers, not brothers.'

In fact, although the song runs to 297 lines, only thirteen of its stanzas are perfectly constructed.

The story is told in great detail. The elder brother, il-Harīdī, is a wastrel soon reduced to poverty, whereas the younger, <Umrān, earns the favour of Providence: he prospers, and his wife Šāma presents him with twins, a boy called Mas<ūd and a girl called Wagīda. Out of envy and in the hope of being appointed trustee of his brother's estate, il-Harīdī shoots <Umrān. Unexpectedly, however, it is not to him but to the widow that the authorities award control of the family's fortune. Out of sheer spite, il- Harīdī, hires two criminals, <Uš̃mān and Manṣūr, to kill Mas<ūd.

As may be expected, it is the mother's distress that captures the poet's sympathy, and to it he devotes no fewer than forty-six lines, starting with the two criminals' assault on the house:

>̃am rāḥu bi **l-lēl** wi ḥaṭṭ **is-sēl** rāḥminhā [rīḥ minhā]
So they set out by night and the flood settled in her vicinity,
wi ṭabbu <a **d-dār** ka šu<lit **nār** rāḥminhā [… r ḥamwīnhā]
They swooped on the house like a firebrand they had ignited.
faza<ūha mi n-nōm sa<itha l-<a>̃lı rāḥ minhā
They roused her from sleep, whereupon she lost her reason,
wi xṣūṣi lamma la>̃it ma<ahum silāḥ maḥdūd
Especially as she found that they held sharpened weapons,
wi mlaŧŧimīn waghihum l-agl il-fu<āl maḥdūd [maḥā ḍ-ḍidd]
Their faces masked so that the deed precluded counteraction.
bi tbuṣṣı bi l-<ēn wi burg il-ginān maḥdūd
She scanned with her eyes, but the seat of madness is well delineated.
ma l>̃atšı **mas<ūd** nāyim **mawgūdı** rāḥminhā [rāḥ munāhā]
Not finding Mas<ūd asleep and manifest, her hope departed.
>̃ālit ḍanāya wi nūr il-<ēn mīn šālu
She cried out, 'My offspring, light of my eyes – who took him away?
>ibni ma luš žanbı raḥ yi>̃tal wi lissa ṣx̲ār
My son is guiltless but is to be killed when he is still small
say>̃a <alēku n-nabi l-muxtār wa gamīl
I adjure you by the Prophet, the Chosen and handsome One.'
sa<itha <ušman ḥaḍar <andu l->iman iṭṭayyib [ṭayya bīh]
At that point, >Uš̃man recovered his faith – a twist in him.
wi >̃āl ya šāma ma<āki rāḥ niṣna< iṭ-ṭayyib
He said, 'Šāma, we shall do you a favour

>ibnik balāš ni>̃tilu ḥa naxđu salīm ṭayyib [yiṭṭayyab]
Let us not kill your son, but take him, healthy and prospering
l-agl ittifā>̃na w ta>kīd il-kalām huwwāh [hawā]
Because of our agreement – confirming the terms is our wish:
ḥa ngib lu šandū>̃ li ta>kīd il-kalām huwwāh [hawā]
We shall get him a chest – to confirm our terms at once –
u fi l-baḥrı nirmīh wi xaṭṭ il-masīr huwwāh
And cast him in the river. The plan of action will [otherwise] be the same.
yimkin yiṣūnu l->ilāh wi y>̃āblu bi ṭ-ṭayyib
Perchance God will preserve him and meet him with a favourable greeting.' [Qur>ān 20:61]
wi šāwir li manṣūr <ala šandū>̃ raḥ gābu
To Manṣūr he pointed at a chest. He fetched it.
wi faḍḍa l-hidūm illi fīh bi >dēh raḥgābu [rāḥ gēbu]
He removed the clothes – what was in there, both hands transferred to his pocket.
faraš lu farša yitimm il-fa<l raḥgābu [rāḥ ḥāgbu]
He laid out a spread for him, rounding up the deed, and hiding it.
u šāma tibki tigidd in-nōḥ maḥrū>a [maḥa rō>̃hā]
Šāma was weeping, deeply lamenting – it wiped out her composure.
wi xdudha **l-itnēn** bi dam< **il-<ēn** maḥrū>̃a
Her cheeks despite the tears from her eyes were burning.
bi tbuṣṣi wi t>̃ul luhum min kaddi maḥrū>a [ma ḥ-arū>̃]
She looks and tells them, 'From this travail I shall not recover,
bass il-marū>a >agib lu <u>̃dı wi ḥgābu
But dignity calls for me to bring him a necklet and his amulet',
wara>̃it milādu gabitha wa>̃taha wayyāh [wayyu]
At once she brought his birth certificate – alas for him! –
wi <amalithā-lu ḥgāb wi rabaṭit <u>̃daha wayyāh [wi yā>̃a] × 2
She made it into an amulet, and tied her necklet along with a collar.
wi labbisitu l-<u>̃dı wi darētu mi r-rigāl wayyāh [wa>̃yāh]
She decked him with the necklet, hiding it from the men to save it.
<ammāla tibki tiṣubb il-<ēn mahrū>̃a [immaha r-rō>̃ha]
She kept weeping, her eyes outpouring – composure gone!
<ammāla tibki wi hum wa>̃fīn ḥawalēhā
She kept weeping while they stood around her.
wi maddit >idēha wi ḥaṭṭit mīt ginēh wayyāh
She stretched out her hands and by him she placed a hundred pounds.
ṣārit tibūsu wi twadda<u yāwaladī [yā wēlu da]
She kept kissing him and bidding him farewell – Alas for him, that one!
ṣārit tiwadda< **ibnaha** >illi ḥa-yaxdūh **minnahā**
She kept bidding farewell to her son whom they were wresting from her.
ṣārit tibūsu min il-xaddēn yāwaladī [yā wēlu da]
She kept kissing him on both cheeks – Alas for him, that one!

wi t>̃ul lu yā hal tara rāyiḥ <ala fēn yāwaladī [wa lā diyya]
Saying, 'Where, I wonder, are you going – with no chance of ransoming –
w inta lissa sinnak sana w šahrēn ya waladī
When you are but a year and two months old, my son!
yā retni mā kunt gibtak wa la raḍḍa<tak [riḍīt dē<tak]
Would that I had not given you birth, or borne your loss,
ya ḥabbit **il-<ēn** u mi **n-nahdēn** radda-tak
Or given you suck from my breasts, O apple of my eye.
ya hal tarā min ḥa-tib>̃a tkūn murḍa<tak
Who, I wonder, is to become your wet nurse?
>ana waḍa<tak ḥida r-raḥmān yā waladi × 2
I have placed you in the Merciful One's keeping, my son!'
ṣārit tibūsu wi hiyya f wagdı wi titlāga [>atit lāyğa]
She kept kissing him and was in a passion; she was understandably agitated,
wi d-dam<ı <a **l-<ēn** <ala **l-xaddēn** yitlāga
The tears in her eyes and on both cheeks converging.
wi t>̃ūl ḥa-yirmūk fi baḥrı xawīṭ litlāga [illi yitlagg]
She said, 'They will cast you into a deep and turbulent river.
hayhāt ya **mas<ūd** la>innak lam **ti<ūd** <umrak [<an murrak]
How hopeless, Mas<ūd! You have no way back from your bitter lot.
>ana kān x̱araḍi tikūn <awaḍ il-gidūd <umrak [-ām ir-rakk]
My aim was that you should succeed your [beneficent] forefathers in a year of adversity.
sa>altı rabb il-barāya >innı yiṭūl <umrak
I asked the Lord of all creatures that your life be extended,
w in ṭālı <umrak maṣīr il-ḥayyi yitlāga [yitlağğa]
And if it is, the neighbourhood's lot will be to collect [the benefits].'

Immediately after this stirring passage, il-Harīdi gets his comeuppance: Šāma denounces him to the authorities as a double murderer, and his bad reputation ensures that he is sentenced to twenty-five years of hard labour.

The story can then move on to more attractive themes.

Providentially, the box containing Mas<ūd comes to rest at the feet of a pious old man who has come down to the river to perform his ablutions before prayer. Delighted with his find, he takes the box and the child to his wife Amīna:

yiḍḥak wi >̃āl ya ḥāgga >amīn >̃āl li murātu ya hāgga >amīn da l-farag gā l-na
Smiling he said 'Ḥāgga Amīn,' he told his wife, 'Ḥāgga Amīn, relief has come to us:
bušra <aẓīma w xēr min rabbina gānna [ginya]
Great good news, a boon from our Lord, a reaping!
ba<dı <išrīn **sana** ma šufna **ḍ-ḍana** gānna [gāhna]
After twenty years that we have been denied a progeny, our pride!

buṣṣi ya ḥāgga w šūfi >ēh wayyāya
Look, Hāgga, see what I have with me:
d ana ma<āya x̱ulām zayy il-badrı wayyāya [wayya >āya]
I have a boy like the full moon, with a [providential] sign.'
>̃ālit da ṣabrī wi ṣaḥḥ iṣ-ṣabrı wayyāya [wi >̃uwāya]
She said, 'That is [due to] my endurance. My endurance and strengths
are validated!
rabb il-barāya ḍaman li ṣ-ṣābirīn ganna
For those who endure, the Lord of creation has vouchsafed Paradise.'
>̃alit lu ya ḥagg ḥalliftak yamīn bizzēn [bi >iẕnu]
She said, 'Hāgg, I will have you swear an oath by His leave:
sammi l-walad ṣabri >ana say>̃a <alēk iz-zēn
I adjure you by the Fair One [the Prophet]: Call the boy Ṣabrī [= my fortitude]
la>innu muṣbaḥ wi ṣabāḥu <alēna zēn [zīna]
For he is radiant, and his radiance is an ornament to us.'
wi šalitu fī ḥigraha mi l-farḥı labbanha [li bnihā]
She lifted him to her lap, rejoicing in her son.
rafa<it >idēha li rabb il-<aršı labbanha [labbā n-nuhā]
She raised her hands to the Lord of the Throne; He responded to her virtue.
fattaḥ <yūn ṣudrihā fi l-ḥāl labbanha
He promptly opened the springs of her breast, providing her with milk.
giri labanhā wi ṣār yirḍa< min il-bizzēn
Her milk flowed, and the child suckled both her nipples.

Now known by the name punning with his adoptive mother's exclamation – 'My endurance' – Ṣabrī grows in grace and rectitude, earning wide social approval, so when he announces that he desires to be married someone immediately reports that among his neighbours is a pretty girl called Wagīda. A marriage is arranged. Wagīda and her mother come to take part in lavish festivities, and all seems to be set fair until we come to the crux:

hēli t-tagāli bi-ḍarb in-nāy yāsātir [yissaṭṭar]
Pleasant were the mutual displays, arrayed to the music of the flute.
wi daxal il-<aris li->axẕ il-<arḍ yāsātir [yisātir]
The bridegroom came to claim the inviolable, discreetly.
damm il-<aṣab **ḥann** <a>̃lu **ngann** yāsātir [yissayṭar]
The blood of kinship yearned, his mind was maddened, taking charge.
wi tāh šawābu <an il-maxalī>̃ ma<rifha [ma< <urfihā]
His understanding strayed from [common] creatures and their ways.
wı zax̱ad wagīda bi-šiddit fōr ma<rifha [ma <arrā fīhā]
In his frenzy he elbowed Wagīdā – he bared no part of her,
ka->innu mutrabbi ma<āha wi ṭūl il-<umr wi <arifha
As if he had been brought up with her and had known her all his life.

>awwil ma šafha nadah ya rabbı yā sātir
As soon as he saw her he cried out, 'O Lord, O Veiler!'
u kassar mirāyt **id-dulāb** wi l-<a>̃lı x̱āb hātu [ha ytūh]
He smashed the wardrobe mirror. His mind deserted him, losing its bearings.
wi daxalu r-rigāl yišūfu >ēh il-xabar žātu
The men came into the room to see just what had happened.
wi >̃alit il-ḥagga >amīna da ma hu s-siḥrı wi gawābu
Ḥagga Amīna exclaimed, 'This indeed is sorcery and its counteragent!
<andak ḥigābu w <u>̃du mid-dulāb hātu
You have his amulet and necklet – Fetch them from the wardrobe!'
šāma šafit ibnahā >̃am <a>̃lihā nawwar
Šāma saw her son, and her mind saw the light!
šāma šāfit <u>̃dihā >̃am <a>̃lihā nawwar
Šāma saw her necklet, and her mind saw the light!
wi <irfit li->ann ibnaha malak intahā nawwar [in>̃iwāru]
She understood now that her son was in control, his confusion ended.
wi zax̱raṭit bi **l-faraḥ** >̃am **iṭṭaraḥ** nawwar [nawwār]
She trilled with joy, and blossoms were generated.

The public recognition of Mas<ūd's identity is briefly described, then the story is wound up in two unrhymed lines:

293 w il-ḥamdu li-llāh itgamma< iš-šaml zayyı ma<ā >aḥbāb
Praise be to God! Kith and kin were reunited as if among friends:
>ixwāt wi šāfu ba<ḍuhum bi->amān
They were siblings and could safely see each other.

This is, of course, not a *Tess of the d'Urbervilles* theme, not the story of a great love frustrated by circumstances. It speaks rather of incest narrowly avoided and a family happily reunited, in a milieu where ties of blood have precedence over marriage bonds. Yet the winding up of the story and the closing address to the audience are uncommonly perfunctory and unadorned, almost as if the performer had wearied of the exercise. This and the many lapses from the stanzaic arrangement to which he has shown himself to be faithful in other performances suggest that the piece may not have been a standard, oft-repeated item in his repertoire. It may even have been put together only for this recording.

The evidence seems to be that these themes propagated by new fangled devices are not favourites even among the artists who serve them, or, presumably, among the public for whom they most commonly cater.

Because of this, the artist's creative effort is expended mostly on the wordplay, and the ultimate effect depends on the quality of the singing, whereas the story line is often rather bald and loosely held together, with unclear motivation and loose threads as we have noted in the story of Zuhra. Even in the better crafted 'Mas<ūd u Wagīda', Muḥammad Ṭāhā has enough narrative skill not to leave the fate of il-Harīdi unsettled or to have it jostling the climax, so he dispatches him cursorily before moving on to more exciting themes; yet he offers no explanation why the villain is denounced by Šāma and condemned by the authorities only after the second of his crimes. At best, it may be surmised that it was only from <Ušmān and Manṣūr that Šāma learned of her brother-in-law's perfidy.

Do these stories indicate any shift in the ethos of the common people? It is noticeable that the police and the courts often play a positive role in them, whereas in celebrations of honour crimes, which the law of the land does not entirely condone, the apparatus of the modern state is usually treated as antagonistic or irrelevant, or else it is grossly misrepresented as siding with the perpetrator. Some ambivalence may be detected in the story of Zuhra, for the heroine is depicted as an innocent victim of the code of honour, yet Ṣaddīq is also sympathetically treated, although it is mentioned – casually rather than obtrusively – that he is a fugitive who has committed an honour crime himself. But in both honour and pulp stories, the law and its agencies are brought into play only in a secondary role, when they further the action along lines desired by the narrator.

These pulp stories, therefore, are not a radically new development in Egyptian folk literature. In the hands of a master like Muḥammad Ṭāhā, they may incorporate characteristic folk themes and display no mean artistic quality. The one feature that unquestionably isolates some performances is the *tazhīr*, the 'opening' of the punning 'flower' which we have encountered in the story of Zuhra, for the folk artists are emphatic that they do this only before the '>afandiyya' – the 'modernists' most readily identifiable by their adoption of Western dress – to whom *zahr* is little more than a collection of riddles. Otherwise, what marks these pulp stories out is that they do not twang the deepest nerves in the consciousness of the common folk and appear to be the appanage of a handful of folk artists who have gained access to the big cities and their resources.

But in the final analysis, is this emergence of comparatively new themes to be interpreted as an intrusion into folk arts by those who can pay the piper and therefore call the tune? Or is it a sign that two social strata and the perceptions peculiar to each are coming together?

Tradition is strong in folk literature, but it is far from immutable. If after a remunerative visit to the big city the folk singer takes his new-fangled wares back to his usual clientele and fosters a taste for it, or – better still – if he discovers that his wares can be adapted to the tastes of a wider audience than ever before, folk literature will have been well served.

Time will tell.

Notes

1. Written when I was no longer capable of field work, this piece tries to fill in – by inference from solid information – what might have been gained more directly by live contacts with the producers and immediate consumers of Egyptian folk literature.
2. See Margaret Larkin, 'A Brigand Hero of Egyptian Colloquial Literature', *Journal of Arabic Literature*, 23, 1 (March 1992), pp. 49–64.
3. See Item 8 in this book.
4. There are, of course, no set rules, and folk poets differ in the liberties they take even with some consonants – see, e.g., the punning of *gā l-na* (line 218) with *ganna*. It is also noticeable that *d*, *s*, *t*, and *z* are sometimes interchanged with *ḍ*, *ṣ* and *ẓ*, but usually only in words where there already is a factor favouring pharyngalisation.
5. The practice is mentioned only to be condemned by <Abd-al-X̲anī an-Nābulusī (d. 1731) in his rhetorical work *Nafaḥāt al-Azhār <alā Nasamāt al-Asḥār fī Madḥ an-Nabī al-Muxtār* in his entry on the *tawriya*, 'double entendre'. It is, however, better seen as an attempt at paronomasia, *jins*.
6. See *Ballads*, pp. 79–89.
7. *Ballads*, p. 185.
8. Transcribed and translated by Jenine Dallal in *Journal of Arabic Literature*, 23, 3 (November 1992), pp. 215–35. In the excerpts that follow, my transcription and interpretations sometimes differ from hers.
9. A wide variety is illustrated in *Ballads*. Particularly irregular but effective is Šōg̃i l-G̃ināwī's version of 'Ḥasan u Na<īma', pp. 323–50.
10. Four stanzas of this are transcribed in Item 9 in this book.

11

Karam il-Yatīm: A Translation of an Egyptian Folk Ballad

Egyptian narrative *mawwāls* are so long that they seldom lend themselves to rounded treatment within the confines of an article, and I have myself turned to the same texts more than once to develop different points of interest in them. Even then, I remained aware that I had left in readers' minds questions unanswered, or even unformulated. Among the most basic of these must be questions about the priorities and the skills – perhaps also the inherited conventions – displayed in the poet's gradual unfolding of the narrative.

It eventually occurred to me that I could render a substantial service to readers by making available to them – without comment – an integral translation of one such text drawn from a source not easily tapped from outside Egypt. It would then be open to anyone to ask him- or herself and debate with others whatever issues provoked or stimulated him or her.

For this purpose, the translation need not be accompanied by a transcription of the entire Arabic text; yet when first published, it was. This was done by a student of mine, Ali Obali. I should have liked to involve him in the updating that all the other items in this book have undergone, mainly to ensure that the same system of transcription was used throughout. Alas, all my attempts at reaching Ali failed, and I have no right to reuse his work myself. All factors having been weighed, I find it best to omit Ali Obali's work from the present collection, at the same time pointing out that it is still available in the July 1992 number of the *Journal of Arabic Literature.*

The translation that follows is one of four songs sung by Yūsuf Šitā, recorded on commercially produced cassettes. As is characteristic of Egyptian narrative folksongs, a great deal of the poet's concern is to devise polysyllabic paronomasias, but his way of unfolding the stages of the narrative is also worthy of attention.

Karam il-Yatīm

The pen has traced
Admonition and wise sayings,
And art composed
Melodies and tunes.

A story which people have told and retold –
Some have sung and some have heard it –
A story ... a story the telling of which was a sensation!

You who are oppressed and suffering, probed deep by cares,
Rather than weep and moan to God's creatures: Patience!
Make faith your weapon, and true piety your guard.
Patience is the best and most curative physic, the best provision.
It serves believers well, whose faith is their protection.
It illumines a man's purpose and defends his rights.
Whoever depends on God will never be wronged,
But he who loves himself is forever regretful.
When the time has come for the crop and it has ripened, it is gathered,
And God's blessing, my good man, turns paucity to plenty.
Whoever fears God can demand his reward;
He labours for his worldly needs, and in the afterlife he glories in it.
He will find his deeds piled up before him, reaching up to his neck.
Whoever endures obtains – his sustenance is ever extended;
Submissive to our Lord's testing, he lives happy and contented.
Whoever strives attains his goal – there he is, unmurmuring.
No one's right ever dies provided he be lowly of heart.
You who listen to my art and exposition, do heed it.
I have a fair tale to tell – abide by its moral.
Its hero is Karam the Orphan who, sprung of good roots, has just come to awareness.
Religion is good counsel; then comes deviation,
But patience is followed by relief, very pleasing and fair.
Should you see a man about to err, do him a favour:
Before he strays from the path to follow, warn him!
Karam the Orphan lost his father while still young, unable to speak.
To the wound in his ailing heart, this world's medicine brought no cure.
He trod his life's path while the main road had its own direction.
He tasted the bitterness of Fate, overwhelmed by passion –
And earthly life (as is its nature) intensified its zeal against him.
He grew up deprived – who was there to shoulder his care?
And then his mother died. Alas, he knew no tenderness.
After his mother's death, his uncle was called, and room was made for him.
Qināwī, being his father's sibling, he was commended to his care.
Kinsmen and neighbours came, and they yielded to him.
There were ten acres his father had left as his domain,
Apart from furnishings, houses, and funds from the sale of such.
So Qināwī became thereafter the head of the household,
And his maternal uncles bore witness along with the agnate, and he was appointed guardian.
Now Qināwī's wife, Ḥafīẓa the spiteful, was harsh in her deeds.
She was sterile, and being childless she grieved.

This is why all through her life she acted haughtily.
Like an assailant, she imposed her views upon her husband,
And – lacking good breeding – from that day was jealous.
She envied people's good fortune with excessive rancour.
She always hated others, and by nature was assertive.
The commendation over, I yet have words of splendour.
Qināwī's wife admonished him: 'Be well advised:
The whole possessions shall be ours, to our profit,
Since the boy's upbringing has come into my hands.
Bring the deeds, bring the ownership documents – this is where we are indemnified,
Karam's comfort or discomfort be the ransom –
And when he is a little older we'll employ him as a herdsman.'
Qināwī agreed with his wife. He surrendered to her view,
For he was a weakling always, his beard a ladder for her to climb.
She now had scope, and with her Satan made a compact.
Her husband had been a toy in her hand for months, not days.
Karam was too young to know of the vicissitudes of Fate.
And Ḥafīẓa was ill-natured, with no fear of the reprover's tongue.
She was to subject him to days of privation – save us, O Lord!
From morning till noon he would neither eat nor drink.
From early hours he herded sheep while soaked with dew.
He was doomed to misery, yet from youth he sought the Lord's guidance
She made him lie on the ground; by her deed he was dust-soiled.
She covered him with sackcloth as she deemed, he was clothed.
Yet who, good people, will tolerate the oppression of an orphan?
With the meanest amenity he was content, and under torment he stretched his neck,
So that day after day the poor lad was abased,
Until by the age of ten – what a person! –
He had not known a couple of fair days but that they faded away.
None could he find to save him from torment and assault
His uncle's wife was the cause of his concern, the cause of hatred,
Yet if ever he complained to Qināwī, he would subject him to another bout.
She beat him to excess, abused him, made him stumble.
His garment was in rags, so his body was naked,
Without an undershirt beneath it to hide his private parts – he moaned.
He was poor and resourceless since the tyranny of Fate ruled him,
And placed him in Ḥafīẓa's hands. There was no issue from vexation.
His uncle, on his part, closed his eyes to what was branding him.
He revelled in his property and abandoned him – the shame weighed little on him.

So Karam the Orphan was, in the village, the most wretched of the parentless;
All kinsfolk being cruel to him, the skewing was complete.
Yet guardianship is contingent on tenderness of heart in all that is determined.
Affliction beset him while he was young, still a child,
Deserving no abasement from them. Does one despair?
They ignored the Law of the leader of all Messengers, and his Tradition,
For in his Tradition our master the Prophet commended the care of orphans.
Within himself Karam the orphan said: ‘How can they so abase me
And ill use me? Not for a single day have they indulged me.
They punish me. By constant starving they weaken me.
The best for me is to run away deep in the night,
For they have been false, and turn my days to misery.
Whatever befalls me, I shall endure a not imperfect day
And not stay on reviled. I shall then be congratulated.’
So at night Karam escaped, and none was aware of it.
He abandoned his property in the village. He left behind his father’s house.
The night was cruelly cold. Faintness dizzied him.
Yet he walked on through fields, past villages and villages,
Escaping abasement, escaping insensitive hearts of iron.
With his tears he washed his ancient garment, wetting it.
The want of food, his extreme hunger, weakened him.
As he walked through the night, immersed in darkness,
The sword of Fate rescuing him from grief and from ordeals –
Driven by cruelty from home, and abandoning his field –
He came across a hut among the fields. He entered it.
It was all darkness – no light, its ambience the shades of terror.
Yet such were his weariness and sleep privation that he slept. It suited him,
Having found no spread to lie on, the heavens his only cover.
The owner of the hut was a man called <Abd il-Xēr,
A magnanimous person, by nature altruistic,
And zealous in his husbandry, so his house abounded with blessings.
Early in the morning, at the first light of dawn, still numb,
On his way to tend the maize turning green in his field,
He made a detour by the hut to fetch a plough with which to till,
And found a handsome young boy whose face bespoke good fortune.
The freeborn man went forward and wakened him.
He stretched out his hand to pat him. He shouted: ‘Oh!’
He told him: ‘Have no fear! I am like your father – yes, truly.
Tell me your story, son, and give your view.’
Karam related his story to the old man with a heart that ran with pain.
He spoke his mind, <Abd il-Xēr being a man of sound conscience.
He eased the orphan’s heart, after stroking him,

Saying: 'Son, your tale has cut through my frame.
Listen to a word I have to say that is of the substance of words within me.
Do stay with me, and bring your heart close to what is in me.
Here you shall be like a son to me, living off the choicest.
Working together, your abundance shall grow along with mine.
When you are at your ease, I shall be happy and feel I have done good.
My conscience will be at rest, and my heart constantly comforted.'
He took him to his home that day and treated him most honourably.
He and his wife kissed him in bliss, as in a mother's nest.
He gave him new clothes to wear, and was prodigal in ensuring his well-being.
He told him: 'Abide with me in happiness, my boy.
I have no son. While you are here, I shall build up prosperity.
Let my livelihood be yours forever; then will you perform my funeral rites.
And if I live, my son, I must marry you to >Ikrām,
My only daughter. In honour have I ruled her home,
Bringing her up in perception and knowledge and good taste.
She will be compatible with you, and you must also strengthen the bond.
Forget the past, Karam; concern yourself with what is new.
Always be frank with me. Be serious in purpose,
And your exertion will bring you success, who are of worthy ancestry.
Between the two of us I have secured the bonds of affection.'
He was at the time over ten years of age.
He was true in his love of <Abd il-Xēr and of his tribe.
And in his work he was energetic, deserving ten out of ten.
>Ikrām admired Karam, and her heart inclined to him.
No wonder, for he was bold and high-minded, and filled with the marks of good upbringing,
Honest and manly, with honour on his side.
Whatever he had in hand was by his honesty increased tenfold.
>Ikrām was beautiful, and fair words composed her speech,
Far from all shame, and no disgrace stepped near her.
In the realm of high repute, the pen of happiness had inscribed her.
One of the villagers, a bully among the hefty-bodied –
His name Ḥumēda, and his nature arrogance and criminality –
Came to her father to ask for her hand, offering a high price for his desire.
He responded: 'But >Ikrām has long been promised to Karam.'
He protested: 'How can a stranger to the house wade through it,
And you, <Abd il-Xēr, for all your astuteness, surrender your daughter to him?
How can you agree that this mere boy should have her?
I am Ḥumēda – my name as prominent as a flag up on a staff.
I am a man who always keeps his threatening word,
I swear many oaths: were my body to be placed on a bier,

While I exist, no one would dare give her a fright.'
Firmly answered <Abd il-Xēr in pride
(Though lothe to offend him while a guest in his house)
Saying: 'Each no doubt is free in his decisions.
Yet courteous speech is required, indeed is a religious duty.
Or have you come to realise your ways of thought by imposition?
You have no stake here, so off with you – and there is satisfaction in so doing.'
So he expelled Ḥumēda, who came out angered by the decision.
As he walked, Ḥumēda addressed the Evil One: 'I do not curse you.
To any who oppose me I must do harm – my boon is your outflow!'
He seized his weapon saying: 'Weapon, truly am I your artificer.
Never in my life have I been guided by a brother or a sign,
And all the villagers know who has been attained – Woe!
When I am angry, I do not spare even my father.
By my father's life, <Abd il-Xēr, I shall not let you go!'
Ḥumēda gathered a group that followed him in doing evil,
A gang of malefactors, treacherous, who became highwaymen.
They knew no manliness, and had no dealing with honour.
At the first light of dawn they said: 'Ḥumēda, be our leader.
Bring forth the saws and the knives that are the source of our divisions.
We are heading for <Abd il-Xēr's field – let us go!'
They went and wrecked his orchard and cut down his maize.
Ḥumēda was false, excessively criminal, an oppressor.
He promptly executed his plan, and succeeded in his deed.
He cut down the green shoots, and his weapons wreaked havoc.
The news reached <Abd il-Xēr. He heard of the damage he had done.
Off he went to his field, saw his crop and his enemy before it.
He said: 'Ḥumēda and his filth have wrongfully done me harm.' He loathed him!
'In God I trust for my redress. My Lord is an Avenger, a Mighty One!'
Word reached the headman. He acted immediately in strength.
He reported what had happened to the Prosecution service and the Police.
They made for the field and went about assisting him in reaching a solution.
While investigating, one of them looked intently,
And from a distance spotted Ḥumēda's identity card, pinpointing him.
The Prosecuting Agent said: 'He it is who has done this violent deed!'
He ordered: 'Arrest him and bring him over here at once!'
The investigators searched for him, found him in a house and drew him out.
Seeing them he set off and one ran after, calling out to him.
But never did he take advice from one whose love was true
They were firing at him one round after another,
And set off through the fields, that at the time were clear.
But suddenly Ḥumēda fell down, as if of his own will:

He was dead, killed by a shot from his own friend.
Ḥumēda is dead and gone, and all creatures, the moment he met his fate,
All villagers and strangers alike gloated over him,
For he was a tyrant, and the blood of treachery was his reward.
How many had he killed, taking account of neither young nor old.
To profit from sin was for him a delight and a pride.
His eye was ever greedy, and his vanity deep as a well.
He dug a hole for another, and Fate cast him into it.
As for Karam and >Ikrām, <Abd il-Xēr being a partner to them,
After these events, he called them to him,
And along with Raḥma his wife – 'Let us guide them in consultation' –
He told them what he had in mind and what had taken place:
'From this very day I shall plan for your marriage contract,' he explained.
He sent out invitations. All the guests came, and he was delighted.
Their night was joy to them, and the day as bountiful as dew.
After the wedding they lived together in mutual trust,
And day by day prosperity outstripped the heights.
Their sustenance greatly increased, yielding more good than bad.
Then one day Karam said to <Abd il-Xēr: 'Uncle,
Your goodness overwhelms me, and your favour is intense and pervasive.
But I should like to go to our village in a day or a year
To see my uncle and reassure me concerning the family.
I came to you an orphan, having experienced abasement – such woe!
I attained to honour the day I married your daughter, as soon as you intended.
With all my heart I treasure your affection, and am at one with you.'
He answered: 'Karam, you are indeed magnanimous and perceptive.
You have proved yourself well-rooted and mindful of boons received. Rejoice!
I swear by One who is Unique, the Lord of all creatures, and by His Prophet,
That I shall fulfil your wish, and travel with you.
Come on, my son. Do not change your mind on this.
Let us set off, for stretching time is undependable.
Be content, and beware of self-delusion!'
They journeyed with a will that day, bringing discussion to a close,
And at the end of their march, they reached the village, near Qina.
They stepped in joyfully, to rest from the long trek,
And entered the courtyard to find the ambience set by death's incursion.
Karam walked into his courtyard, to the guesthouse open to all,
Together with his in-law, who had compassed him with bounty.
They sat awhile, in perplexed expectation. Moments passed, the latest being death to them.
And while they sat, patience being their sustenance,
After some time, Ḥafīẓa came in to them.

She entered upon them with someone other than his uncle.
Karam by then had been transformed from his days of woe.
Well-being had greatly altered features once marked by scantiness.
He had become a lion, his frame filled out, stronger than the stag.
She did not recognise him, and at the time she was confused about him.
For time is unstable, now sweet now vinegary.
And she had aged. Faded were the roses of her cheeks and her beauty spot,
Whereas Karam was now excellent, much better than before.
She asked them: 'Who are you, who were headed for abundance?
Tell me your names, who have come upon distress?
You are our guests, but the initiative is ours.'
He answered: 'What has befallen you, Ḥafīẓa? Be alert!
I am Karam the Orphan – remember how my cheek once wetted you!
Days have passed and others come that alter colours for you.
And be aware that I am Karam, the owner of the house.
My uncle Qināwī I do not see – tell me at once!
And what has ushered Shibl into our house? Has its master perished?'
She said: 'And do you come this day to ask where your uncle is?
Your uncle is dead and gone. There is no trace of his existence;
And with him his time has passed away, whether marked by bliss or generosity.
I thought you dead, but here you are as yet, Karam;
And since you are alive, recount – you have been absent for a while!'
He said: 'Ḥafīẓa, my name is Karam as is well known.
My uncle and father-in-law by me is a man of standing, in good odour.
He brought me up in plenty, and I owe him boon and favour.
He married his daughter to me, making happiness truly a gift to me.
The benefit is God's, and on him is gratitude worthily bestowed.
He has come with me today to make sure of my rights,
For in this place my property and rights have long been known.'
Ḥafīẓa said: 'It was Qināwī who saw to everything.
Before he died, he had destined it all to Shibl –
The land, the property, even the court enclosure to its full extent.'
Her words made him alert; he stood out and showed emotion.
The turbid times were over; they had passed, and the air was now limpid:
'If you have witnesses, let them attest. And where are the papers?
Go and get me the papers if indeed he sold them.'
It was Shibl who answered, saying: 'To what point shall I turn you back?
Off with you from here! Go in search of what will please you.
You have a tribunal to go to and present your proof. What answer have you?
And you bring your relative with you! What brings you? Go easy!
I make no fine point in dismissing you! Your stay should not be pleasant!
The house is mine, and nothing pertains to you either there or here.

The land is ours too, as witnesses can testify, not yours!'
Karam left immediately, and off he went to the village headman,
And <Abd il-Xēr accompanied him for support.
When they got to him and wished him long to stay in authority,
After greetings and compliments they told of what had seared them.
He thus learned of Karam's story and listened to his suspicions and accusations.
With a smiling face, he gave attention to their complaint.
He reassured them, and they said: 'Long may you live, Uncle.'
The headman ordered: 'Watchman, go and get me Shibl. Get him up,
And bring Ḥafīẓa too. And be back promptly. Go!
Thus may we find a resolution of this problem, or achieve a reconciliation.'
The watchman set off at once, and quickly he returned,
Reporting: 'Shibl has boldly resisted. He has not come.'
On hearing these words the headman's blood boiled, and he uttered warnings,
And called out: 'Head watchman, bring him to me by force, or else his mother.'
They went and forcibly fetched Shibl, and his mother who had softened.
Openly and boldly the headman questioned him, never weakening.
At that time Shibl got overwrought. His demon ruled him without his taking consciousness of it.
He asserted: 'It is my property. I bought it, and have proofs.
I never knew Karam, nor has he any liens on me.'
The headman heard the case, the averments and the arguments.
He bundled together the papers and the documents he found in his possession,
And said: 'Head watchman, arrest them both,
Ḥafīẓa as well as Shibl, for they are forgers – whoever is twisted moans!
I shall call for the Prosecution service and the Police to come to the residents.
We shall tell them of the case, of what has happened and taken place,
And we shall uncover the secret once they have come and been drawn in.
Truth shall speak out then – there is a procedure for justice,
And they shall be requited as a result of falseness. There is a time for contention!'
He called in the Police and the Prosecution, and they set the pavilion in commotion.
They looked and saw Qināwī's seal on everything they had chosen.
His handprint too they found on everything they saw.
But the headman told the Prosecution: 'I have papers just like these,
Which Qināwī entrusted to me long ago for a purpose:
Ḥafīẓa and Shibl, Sir, have forged these papers.
Qināwī always used to sign all things.
He acquainted me with the orphan's right that I may preserve it.
For he could read and write. I have the valid proof,
And Right wields a sword that pierces the head of Wrong!'

The headman produced the papers he had, and they questioned him.
This was the greatest proof that the Prosecution saw.
Ḥafīẓa was arrested, and her cheating was revealed.
And Shibl too was taken to trial on that day.
The session was speedy. The tenuous was made stringent.
To prison they went, the judge having uttered the sentences.
Ḥafīẓa and Shibl have time to spend in jail – ah, how long!
For Right, having emerged, had its signs and witnesses,
And Falsehood, no matter how high it rise, has no validity or sweetness.
You who would oppress people, your deeds bring down the edifice upon you.
The Lord is there, and He is the wisest of all rulers.
Karam thanked our Lord. For his well-being he is grateful.
His property has been returned to him. How well is the patient one recompensed!
He greeted the headman of their village, Ismā<īl Šākir,
And lived in his village in prosperity, well-being, and happiness,
And his wife >Ikrām with him, in equal plenty and abundance.
At the time he bade farewell to his relative <Abd il-Xēr.
He greeted him fulsomely, adding: ‘Uncle, what else can I say?’
O you who are endowed with reason, make light of cares, be sparing!
Perform good deeds that serve your issue and succession.
Though you be poor, and live in torment and in grief,
You are sure to find contentment after long endurance.

Of Loose Verse and Masculine Beauty

There are many verse forms to which the Egyptian folk singer may resort for narrative purposes. The most demanding is the *mawwāl*, with its set rhyming patterns and elaborate punning rhymes. At the other extreme is the singing to a repetitive tune of mono-rhyme stanzas usually consisting of three lines, but sometimes stretched to four or five if the performer needs space to round off the information he wants to convey. Each of these stanzas is then followed by a refrain in which the accompanists usually join the soloist.

A slight elaboration of this strophic arrangement is the expansion of the tercets by the addition of a fourth line with a distinctive rhyme shared by the closing line of what are now quatrains, so that the arrangement may be represented as:

bbbA cccA dddA ... zzzA

Such a song may (but need not) also have a refrain that shares the binding rhyme.

The resulting pattern is one often encountered in the Andalusian *zajal*, or even earlier in the *musammaṭ* with which >Abū-Nuwās (d. 813) and some of his contemporaries experimented and of which the *murabba<* version has the same rhyme scheme, now a favourite in a great variety of songs.[1]

Yet the trend appears to be for the leading or most ambitious folk singers to turn increasingly to the *mawwāl* with its elaborate rhyme schemes, and their taste for *zahr* is such that some try to expand every rhyme to a multi-syllabic paronomasia achieved by distortion of the normal pronunciation. It is rather refreshing therefore to find that the Hilālī poets of Upper Egypt remain faithful to the quatrain form, as in a version of the story of Yūnis and <Azīza sung by Sayyid aḍ-Ḍuwī of Qūṣ, and recorded in the field by the poet <Abd-ar-Raḥmān al->Abnūdī. The rhymes are straightforward, with no attempt at *zahr*; indeed, they sometimes amount to little more than assonance, for if the final syllable of the line has a long vowel, the accompanying consonants may differ, and there are occasionally lines that do not rhyme at all. As for the binding rhyme, it is merely a long 'oo', easily realisable since such is the plural marker in all verbs, and the shorter 'u' which stands for the third person masculine singular attached pronoun can also be arbitrarily lengthened.

The story line is sometimes jumbled, and one result of this is that the chorus's commentary is not always synchronised with the sequence of events. The song is sung with zest and energy, however, and in places produces a powerful effect.

The narrative is part of the *Riyāda*, the scouting expedition undertaken by >Abū-Zēd il-Hilālī with three nephews of his. One of them is Yūnis, who is famed for his physical beauty. He is also the one entrusted with all deals to be made with the local population. In the vicinity of Tunis, the party runs out of food and ready cash, but they have a very valuable necklace which Yūnis must now try to sell. His uncle cautions him, however:

>ana waṣīk ya wlēd sirḥān
'I urge upon you, son of Sirḥān,
ya handali y abu sēf rannān
O nimble one, with a clanging sword:
tixuššiš sakan in-niswān
Never to enter women's quarters
>il-<ağl iz-zaki a ymayyilūh
Even sharp brains they can derail.
ta<āla yūnis y abu l-<ajāyib
Come, Yūnis, man of wonders,
u y abu ğalbı mmazzağ đāyib
Whose heart is torn and worn out,
u ḥarris min sūğ il <aṣāyib
Beware of the commerce of kerchief-wearers:
ḍiḥku <ala l-jinnı w ḥabasūh
They fooled a jinn and held him captive!'

It is in keeping with this underlying theme and its implied threat that the chorus breaks in at irregular intervals with:

Chorus (bis): >il-hilāli w māl <ala yūnis
The Hilāli inclined to Yūnis.
yunis jamīl wi l-bīḍ <išiğ ūh
Handsome is Yūnis, and the fair ones love him.

Oddly, >Abū-Zēd goes on at some length to specify that it is the cupidity of women that makes them dangerous:

tağūl aḥibbak >amāna w arīdak
She says, 'I love you, in truth I want you!'
lamma yikūn il-ma<āmala f īdak
While there is coinage in your hand.
wi ya mfallis w ạllah l akīdak
But then, 'You're broke? By God, I'll get you!'
<ala filsēn jabūh u waddūh
Over two pennies he's in or he's out.
Chorus >awarrīk šar< in-niswān

Let me expound the women's law:
wi zayy iz-zaman il-mayyāl
Just like inconstant Fate,
wi ma yiḥibbu >illa š-šab<ān
Their love is but for the well-fed;
wa l-mifallis na<alu >abūh
But if he's broke, they curse his father!

Ironically, the story develops the chorus's earlier emphasis on Yūnis's irresistible attractiveness rather than >Abū-Zēd's cynical view of women's priorities.

Yūnis is indeed the object of more feminine attention than is good for him, for the girls dress up as men in order to be able to approach him, and they swear they will never marry another. It is – one may infer – to avoid such contacts that he engages a broker to sell the necklace for him. The bargains proposed, however, do not measure up to this magnificent piece of jewellery, if only because few can afford it. But a key point in the narrative is reached when the decision is taken to offer the necklace for sale to the princess <Azīza, whose father's wealth 'is measured by the bushel'. Her companion Mayy now comes into play:

xađ il-<uḡdı ḡam id-dallāl
The broker set off with the necklace.
<alā <azīza tiwakkal sār
And to <Azīza trustingly he went.
>awwal ma ṭaḡṭaḡ <ala l-bibān
Promptly, when at the doors he knocked,
māyy il-ḥazīna tlaḡḡatūh
Sad Mayy was there to meet him.
>ah w-ādi mayy tijirī bi-niyya
So with a purpose Mayy runs off.
tilḡa <azīza <ala n-namusiyya
She finds <Azīza [shielded] by a mosquito-net.
ḡūmi bīna >amāna ya ṣabiyya
'Up we get, truly, lass!
bēni ma bēnik ra>yı n<idūh
There's something we must privately consider.'
>āh wi <azīza nāzla min fōḡ
And so <Azīza comes downstairs,
>ādi l-mabsam šab<ān zōḡ
Her smiling mouth brimming with sweetness,
tiḡūl >ana lli ḡatalni š-šōḡ
Saying, 'I am the one dying of yearning!'
ḥaṣal li yūnis fi l-ḡaṣrı jabūh
It happened that Yūnis was brought to the palace.

The narrative goes awry at this point, for although it has just been affirmed that Yūnis had been brought to the palace, Mayy next asks the broker for information about the owner of the necklace. He begins to extol his beauty, but abruptly and without any indication of how she comes to be so knowledgeable, she takes over the description in a passage markedly different from the rest of the song. It is made up mostly of rhyming couplets or of pairs of lines of which the first has no rhyme and the second ends in a long 'ā' followed by a consonant, producing what is almost a subsidiary binding rhyme, whereas the 'oo' that punctuates the entire song is temporarily dropped. But what distinguishes the passage most strikingly is that it abounds in powerful imagery. Some of the similes may have features unfamiliar to a foreign audience. Thus, Yūnis's apparently braided hair is compared with a cameleer's rope. And very muscular shoulders are suggested by the image of a swimmer kept buoyant by a pair of dried gourds joined by a rope stretched across his breast, so that the gourds stick up from under his armpits.

The excursus begins with the broker implying that Yūnis is so handsome that he cannot be born of a mortal woman:

g̃alı ya sittī sīd wi jamīl
He said, 'Lady, he is lordly and handsome.
>amma l-ḥawājib na<sanīn
As for his eyebrows, they are languorous.
zurt il-<ajam wi >arāḍi ṣ-ṣīn
I've been to Persia and the lands of China,
ma lgītiš niswān waḍa<ūh
And found no women fit to have borne him!'
mayyı tūl il-kalām wi ḥalātu
Mayy exclaimed, 'Such words, such sweetness!'
>ādi yyāk si yūnis bi-zātu
Such indeed is Master Yūnis in person!
ya dallāl iṭla< rūḥ hātuh
Off, broker, go and fetch him.
ḥag̃g̃il-<ug̃d illa n<iddūh
The price of the necklace we'll count out.'
>āh di mayyı nādat ya <azīza
Ah! Now Mayy calls: '<Azīza,
ya ṣabiyya law šufti yūnis
Oh, lass! If you saw Yūnis
šufti ṭūlu ma<a ma<anīh
And saw his stature and his qualities,
tfūti g̃aṣrik da bi lli fīh
You'd quit this palace and all it holds!
ya <azīza law šufti l-g̃ūra
<Azīza, if you saw his brow

tiḍāwi tgūli bannūra
So shiny, you'd say it was crystal.
ya ṣabiyya law šufti ša<ru
Lass, if you saw his hair,
taḥlif <alēh salab jammāl
You'd swear it was a cameleer's rope.
ya ṣabiyya law šufti <nēh
Lass, if you saw his eyes,
mikaḥḥaln min x̱ēr dalāl
Kohl-painted, yet without coquetry!
ya <azīza law ṣuftı ḥawajbu
<Azīza, if you saw his eyebrows
mašruṭīn l-alif wi l-lām
[Separately] lined, like >alif and lām![2]
ya <azīza da law šufti xašmu
O <Azīza, if you saw his mouth –
mudawwār xātim sulaymān
Rounded like Solomon's seal!
ya ṣabiyya law šufti ktāfu
Lass, if you saw his shoulders –
jōz g̃ar<ı ma<a l-<awwām
Two gourds buoying a swimmer!
ya ṣabiyya law šufti ṣadru
Lass, if you saw his chest,
taḥlif <alēh balāṭ ḥammām
You'd swear it was a bathhouse tile.
ya ṣabiyya law šufti snānu
Lass if you saw his teeth –
lūli wi š-šifaf murjān
Pearls, by lips of coral!
ya ṣabiyya law šufti g̃dūmu
Lass, if you saw his feet –
lohēn ṣabūn f īd il-<aṭṭār
Two bars of soap in the perfumer's hands!
ya ṣabiyya law šufti ḍahru
Lass, if you saw his back –
sikka fāyit fīha jammāl
A road on which a cameleer fares!
fīh ma<na ṣabiyya f ḍahru
There is an image, lass, in his back –
taḥlif <alēh šarṭa mn iz-zān
You'd swear it was a strip of oak.

ya ṣabiyya law šufti ḍahru
Lass, if you saw his back,
lli zayyik yifriš wi ynām
Your like would spread [bedsheets] and sleep.
ya ṣabiyya law šufti baṭnu
Lass, if you saw his belly –
ṭayyit ḥarīr f īd il-wazzān
A roll of silk in the weighman's hands!
ya ṣabiyya law šufti ṣ-ṣurra
Lass, if you saw his navel –
ḥağğa ğa<rit il- finjān
Truly the hollow of a cup!
taḥt iṣ-ṣurra m ağdarš ağūl
Below the navel – how shall I say it?
wāḥid malik wi naṣib lu diwān
A king, and he has set up court!

The chorus now signals the resumption of the narrative in its standard form, including the 'oo' binding rhyme:

Chorus (bis):
<azīza tunādī ya dallāl
<Azīza calls out: 'O broker.
hat-li yūnis kida ğawām
Bring me Yūnis right away!
>ğifil <alēh bi-jadd il-kalām
Lock him with assertive words,
wi l-ḥadd il-<atāba w sayyibūh
So to the doorstep, then let him loose!'

The song then goes on to describe how <Azīza is so infatuated with Yūnis that she holds him in durance, while he – like the biblical and Qur>anic Joseph – resists both blandishments and threats until his fellow tribesmen come to his rescue.

The challenge to one's curiosity and aesthetic judgement is why the passage describing the hero's beauty feature by feature stands out so distinctly from the rest of the text. Would it not have been well within the performer's ability to fit it into the simple prosodic pattern of his song if such had been his priority? On the other hand, if one first came across it in a manuscript, one might well assume it was a specially crafted piece designed to be slotted into any episode featuring a handsome man. If so, one would expect it to have a more regular, more finished prosodic form.

Or – rather than indulge in such speculations – should we not let ourselves be carried away by this outburst of unfettered lyricism?

Notes

1. For a Palestinian sample of such a song, see Jurays Xūrī, ‘yā ẓarīf iṭ-ṭūl: >ux̱niya ša<biyya filisṭīniyya’, *al-Karmil*, 20 (1999), pp. 97–128.
2. I.e., his eyebrows are separate, like the letters >*alif* and *lām* which together spell the definite article *al* (ال) but are never joined.

13

A *Zajal* on the *Mi‹rāj* Attributed to Al-X̱ubārī

This article was drafted and delivered as a companion to a paper by Professor Margaret Larkin in which she surveyed what is known of al-X̱ubārī's career and summed up the character and quality of his writings. This she has since published under the title 'The Dust of the Master: a Mamlūk Era zajal by Khalaf al-Ghubārī' in Quaderni di Studi Arabi, *Nuova serie, 2 (2007), pp. 11–29. I still commend this article to the reader, but since our complementary studies have now been separated, I find it necessary to add within the few pages of mine below the briefest account of al-X̱ubārī's activities as a single sample of his style as a* zajjāl. *This sample comes from al->Ibšīhī Šihāb ad-Dīn Muḥammad,* al-Mustaṭraf fī Kull Fann Mustaẓraf, *vol. 2 (Cairo, 1952), pp. 241–2.*

Urbain Bouriant (11 April 1849–19 June 1903) was an enterprising self-made Orientalist. After an active military career, his scholarly interests caught the attention of the Egyptologist Gaston Maspéro, at whose behest he became a founder member of the Mission Française d'Archéologie Orientale in 1880, then its energetic director from 1886 until he was disabled in 1898. Between 1883 and 1886 he was also in Egyptian Government service as adjunct curator of the Būlāq Museum. Other publications of his, in what became the *Bulletin de l'Institut Français d'Archéologie Orientale*, are translations of Maqrīzī (1364–1442) titled *Description historique et topographique de l'Égypte* and *Monuments pour servir à l'étude du culte d'Atonou en Égypte.* He is also known to have worked on ancient papyri.

The breadth of his linguistic competence and cultural interests was evidenced still further when he published a volume titled *Chansons Populaires Arabes en dialecte du Caire d'après les manuscrits d'un chanteur des rues* (Paris, 1893). It runs to 160 well printed pages and consists of thirty-four verse compositions, all but six of which are in common forms of the *zajal.* The only signs of editorial intervention are minor emendations which in M. Bouriant's judgement were required either by the sense or by the metre, but always with the original text reproduced in a footnote. In addition, a brief notice by the publisher informs us that 'a stroke of luck' had brought the collection to M. Bouriant's hands, that other commitments prevented him from offering more than a sampling, but that an integral edition of 'the manuscript deposited in the Cairo Library, with a translation and commentary', would follow. Alas, M. Bouriant was virtually incapacitated by ill-health in 1895 and he died in 1903 without fulfilling his intentions, and no further information on his extraordinary find has come to light.[1]

So wide is his range that it seems very much in character for him to have jumped at the opportunity of handling folk texts that chance had brought to his notice, although one cannot help being startled at his confidence in dealing with a vernacular form of the language, for which there were few aids at the time. He may well have had the assistance of a native informant.

And although it is a stereotype to assume that a folk artist is necessarily illiterate, it is startling to find such a wealth of material in the possession of a single street singer. Since the editor speaks of a manuscript in a library without specifying whether Bouriant found it or deposited it there, may it be surmised that what he came across was rather a collector's hoard of texts loosely labelled 'street singers' material?'

At all events, what is beyond doubt is that we have here a rare and varied treasure trove of texts dating back at least to the late nineteenth century, lending themselves to several lines of research.

Perhaps the most intriguing is a *zajal* on a very popular theme, the Prophet's ascent to the heavens known as the *mi<rāj*. It consists of forty-nine stanzas in the metrical form most commonly followed by literate composers of *zajal*, as illustrated in the final stanza:

w anā ho l-x̱ubārī <andı >ahl il->adab ۞ li-fannī wi sēlī>̃aṭṭī mā lū wuṣīl
Here am I, al-X̱ubārī. Among the literary
My art and my verve none can attain.
la-qad gubtı đa l-mi<rāg ma<ī yā fahīm ۞ min il-fikrı kulluh fī madīḥ ir-rasūl
With me, O man of understanding, you have gone through this Ascent.
I conceived it throughout, in praise of the Apostle.
>̃a<adtı ŧalaŧŧ ušhur w-anā >agtahid ۞ [u] fī awwil il-maṭla< >aḍīf [luh] w-a>̃ūl
I spent three months exerting myself
Expanding the initial couplet, saying:
ṣalātī wi taslīmī <alā man naṭa>̃ ۞ >ilēh il-ḥaṣā wi-ḍ-abbı sallim wi >̃āl
My blessings and invocations are for him to whom
The pebbles spoke, and the lizard gave greeting and said:
agirnī >igārit xātim il->anbiyā ۞ u fi ṣ-ṣaxrı x̱āḍ il-muṣṭafā bi n-ni<āl
'Grant me the protection of the seal of the prophets,'
And the Chosen One's shoe sank deep in the rock.

Such a *zajal* begins with an introductory couplet, which is repeated at the very end (as it is here) and which determines the binding rhyme for the whole composition, each stanza thereafter having a tercet with a rhyme of its own, followed by a couplet with the same rhyme as the *maṭla<*, so that the rhyme scheme is

AA bbbaa cccaa dddaa ... zzzAA.

The metre in *zajal* is a matter of choice. Here it is a truncated *ṭawīl:*

fa <ūlun mafā <īlun fa <ūlun mafā

∪– – |∪– – – |∪– – |∪– ‖

and in my transcription I enclose between square brackets elements that seem to be required by the metre. More substantial changes are explained in endnotes. That such emendations are needed in addition to Bouriant's is one feature to be considered in evaluating the reliability of the manuscript.

What marks this piece out for special attention is that – as is common among literate *zajjāls*, but rare among folk singers – the author names himself in this last stanza.

Is this attribution to be taken at face value? There was, as Professor Larkin expounded in a companion paper, a man of learning and of letters named Abū <Abd Allāh Xalaf ibn Muḥammad al-X̱ubārī who was active in the mid-fourteenth century. It had become common in his day for men of his standing to compose verse in the vernacular, using metrical forms current in folk literature, but these departures from the literary canon were mostly witticisms not meant to be taken seriously: no literary reputation was built on these alone, and they were often omitted from the poet's collected works. The few fragments of al-X̱ubārī's work that have survived in the works of such compilers as Ibn >Iyās and al-Ibšīhī do indeed display the verbal agility and the mastery of rhetorical devices that were prized by his contemporaries. Among the handful attributed to al-X̱ubārī is a *zajal* expressing the poet's longing for a youth whose duvet is just sprouting on his cheeks: each stanza deriving its vocabulary from a single arbitrarily chosen register – some exploiting naval terminology or the vocabulary of hunting and fishing, others punning on the names of major figures in Islamic history, or the designation given to various non-classical verse forms, yet others enumerating human failings and misfortunes. The plainest illustration is the following stanza with its evident theme:

ḥīn tidabbig iḥmirār xdduh ۞ b-ixḍirār il-<āriḍ >asbānī
When the reddening of his cheeks
Was adorned with the greening at the sides, he captivated me ...
ḍiḥik fa-byaḍḍı wi-tbassam ۞ bi-swidād ša <rī wi >abkānī
He laughed white-brightening,
And smiled at my black hair, making me weep
u ḥīn >aḍḥēt bi-ṣfirār lōnī ۞ >aš<aš >ax̱bar fī hawāh <ānī
And when, turning yellow,
I became dishevelled, grey-haired, abased by love,
>̃āl lōnak qad ṣabaḥ ḥāyil, ۞ u qad abṣar madma<ī ṭūfān
He said; 'Your colour has faded,'
And he saw that my tears were a flood ...
đu>tı tabrīḥ il-x̱arām nādēt ۞ fī hawāk đu>t il-hawān >alwān
I experienced the pangs of love and called out:
'For love of you I've known shades of abasement.'

All this conforms with the practice of his contemporaries, but al-X̲ubārī went further. He is reputed to have compiled a complete, but now untraceable, *dīwān* of his *zajals*. More substantial evidence of his boldness is that he defied a long-established practice by celebrating historical events and praising princes in vernacular verse. One may infer that he lent the genre greater weight than his fellow scholars did, and was prepared to use it for less flippant purposes. Among the literate, no one followed his example. But can it be that he commanded firmer acceptance among the common folk, and that not only his reputation but also a substantial composition of his survived among folk artists for more than five hundred years? We need to look at the work itself for internal evidence.

The narrative is a traditional one, an elaboration of the first eighteen verses of Chapter 53 of the Qur>ān, which emphasises how accessible God was to the Prophet and therefore how reliable the transmission of the divine message was. By some scholars, this is interpreted as the expression of a mystic experience, but the popular imagination has woven it into a story of great wonders, the broad lines of which are firmly established, but the details vary considerably. A version of it was known even in Europe by the thirteenth century, for a detailed Arabic rendering of it that surfaced in Spain was translated on the orders of Alfonso X (1265–84), and it has been surmised that it may even have had some influence on Dante's *Divina Commedia.* Of those translations only one in Old French, dated May 1264, and a Latin one have survived. The Arabic original is lost.[2]

This Andalusian text offers a useful basis for comparison with the one that concerns us here. It has the Prophet tell how he was transported to the Temple in Jerusalem on al-Burāq, a creature that has the form of a horse but the face and faculties of a human. From there he climbs to the heavens on a ladder, visits not only the seven heavens but the eighth, which brings him to the presence of God, and he is then given glimpses of other parts of Creation: seven lands and seven seas, Paradise with its seven ascending levels and Hell with its seven descending ones, from God; and from his guide Gabriel he is given great insights into God's purposes and into many great wonders such as the modalities of the Last Judgment.

The Bouriant text, however, relates in the third person how, accompanied by Jibrīl (sometimes called Jibrā>īl) to accommodate the metre) the Prophet rides al-Burāq to one after the other of the seven heavens, floored successively with smoke (stanza ix), with brass (xiii), with iron, with gold (xv), with silver (xxi), with gems (xxvii), and finally with pearls (xxx). In each, he is received with much deference, sometimes invited to lead the prayers, and all – including the angels and al-Burāq itself – ask him to intercede with God for the forgiveness of their sins. In the seventh heaven, at *sidrat al-muntahā* (the Lote-Tree of the boundary (Q 53:14) Jibrīl takes leave for he has gone as far as he is allowed to go, but the Prophet advances and is welcomed by Mīxā>īl (xxxiii), who is charged with measuring out the waters that the clouds are to release upon the earth, then by Isrāfīl, who is to blow the trumpet on the Day of Judgement. Finally he is admitted where none has been before: to the very presence of God, Who extols him as his choicest creation (xxxix). Invited to express a wish, the Prophet asks God to be merciful to his >*umma*, and this is readily granted. It is only this exchange of words that is reported, whereas the Andalusian text has extensive descriptions of what it calls 'the eighth heaven', of God's writing table and His pen, and not least of God's throne containing the four elements and supported by four angels with faces, respectively, of a man, a lion, an eagle, and a bull, for on the Day of Judgement they will pray for humans, for wild animals, for birds, and for domestic animals. These four angels resemble the 'living creatures' mentioned in Ezekiel 1:10 and Revelations 4:6–10, and are familiar to Christians as symbols of the four evangelists, but are given a very different significance here, implying that (with the unexplained exception of fishes) animals, too, have eternal souls to be prayed for.

Back on earth (xli) according to the Bouriant text, the Prophet's account is readily accepted, except by Abū Jahl, who challenges him to describe Jerusalem where the ascent began, but the doubters – identified as Abū Jahl and the Jews (xliii, 5) – are confounded when at God's behest Gabriel brings them the whole of the city on his back.

Another four stanzas are devoted to the wonders associated with the Prophet and the warlike achievements of some of his principal companions before the concluding *istišhād* we have encountered and its claim to earning merit for praising the Prophet.

The Prophet is indeed extolled both for his noble human ancestry and for his being God's first and noblest creation (xl, 1–2):

> wa qad xāṭabuh rabb il-<ibād il-karīm, ۞ wi >̃al luh xala>̃tak >̃ablı xal>̃ il-wugūd
> *The generous Lord of all creatures addressed him*
> *And said, 'I created you before all that exists,*
>
> wi min >̃ablı xal> il-mā wi xal>̃ is-samā, ۞ u min >̃ablı >ādam yā muḥammad wı hūd
> *Before the creation of water or of heaven,*
> *Before Adam, O Muḥammad, or Hūd.'*

He was, of course, created not in the flesh but as a light from which the sun and moon were derived (xxviii, 3):

> s̃umma xala>̃ min ḍiyāh iš-šamsı wi l->̃amar.

Besides, the deferential exchanges between him and his hosts give ample opportunity – though seldom a precise context – for enumerating his virtues, his achievements, his miracles, and other wonders associated with him.

The narrative structure is self-imposed and the steps are scaled in rather workmanlike fashion, with a few bursts of the imagination in describing some of the angels here and there, with details surprisingly close to those found in the Andalusian text. All of them are said to be of colossal stature, but the fullest portrait is that of <Azrā>īl, who presides over the third heaven (xv, 3–6):

u fīhā malak gālis [wi] luh >alfı rās, ۞ [u] fī kullı rās luh >alfı ṣūra <agab
In it an angel is seated, who has a thousand heads
And in each of his heads are a thousand wonderful likenesses
u fī kullı nāẓir >alfı bāṣir ya>̃īn, ۞ bi->alsun tisabbiḥ rabbinā ẕu l-galāl
In each eye, of a certainty, are a thousand pupils,
And [there are] tongues praising our Majestic Lord,
ilāh[un] ta <ālā mā lahū min šabīh, ۞ wa-lā luh naẓīr yūgad wa lā luh miṯāl
An exalted God who has no like.
No existing equivalent, no one similar.

There are otherwise few visual descriptions. Of the delights of the chosen nothing is said except, repeatedly, that their only sustenance is worshiping the Creator: *wa lā >̃ūtuhum siwā yi <bidu l-bārī*, whereas the Andalusian text paraphrases the relevant Qur>anic verses about the virgins, the food, the dwellings and the gardens awaiting them. By far the most graphic passage in the Bouriant text tells of the torments of the damned, whom the Prophet has occasion to see in the fifth heaven, for it has seven gates looking on to the Fire. So (xxiii–xxiv):

u lamma ṭṭala< ṭāhā <alā >ahl il-<azāb, ۞ u [ḏā] kān ra>̃ī>̃ il->̃albı dam<uh zalaf
When Ṭāhā overlooked those doomed to torment –
He being tender-hearted, close to tears –

li>̃ī fī laẓā šubbān wi fīhā šabāb, ۞ wi fīhā šuyūx qad >ayqanū bi t-talaf
He found in a fire young men full of vigour
And old ones who were sure they were perishing

u fīhā nisā qad ṣullibū bi š-šu <ūr, ۞ wa kullan bi >anwā< il-<ažāb ixtalaf
In it too were women suspended by the hair,
Each person differing in the manner of his torment.

u nās yinhašū fī laḥmı muntin ḥarām, ۞ u [sābū] šiwā ḍānī [yinḍaḥ] ḥalāl[3]
There were some tearing at rotten, unlawful meat
Leaving aside lawful roast mutton oozing juice;

u nās >alsinithum nāzla [fō>̃] iṣ-ṣudūr, ۞ w ahum fī <azāb [hum >̃addı ma] d-dahrı ṭāl
And some whose tongues hung down on their chests.
Here they are in their torment for as long as Time stretches

u nās taḥtı >anyāb il->afā <ī dawām, ۞ u nās fī guhannam yišrabū min ṣadīd
There are some under serpents' fangs in perpetuity
And some in Hell who are drinking pus.

u nās fī guhannam ya >kulū ḍ-ḍarī<, ۞ u nās fī guhannam fī ma>̃āmi <ḥadīd
And some in Hell who eat ḍarī <[4]
And some in Hell in iron restrainers,[5]

u nās fī [guhannam] yusḥabū <a l-wugūh, ۞ yiṣubbū <alēhum mi l-<azāb iš-šidīd
And some in Hell who are dragged on their faces
And on them are poured the severest of torments.

wa lā yisma <ū fīhā wa lā [yixša <ū][6] ۞ u fīhā <a>̃ārib sūd šabīh il-bix̱āl
In it neither do they hear nor are they humbled
And in it are scorpions – black, the equals of mules,

u ḥayyātha >akbar min guzū< in-naxīl ۞ lihum simmı yixra> ṣummı ṣaxr il-gibāl
Its serpents are bigger than the trunks of palm trees,
And have venom that pierces hard mountain rocks.

The next two stanzas specify the crimes that fit some of the punishments. Those eating rotten meat are said to have been adulterers. Those who drink pus and eat *ḍarī<* were wine-bibbers. Those with their tongues hanging low were bearers of false witness. As for the women hanging by the hair, they are said to be the *lāṭimāt*, literally 'those who slapped their faces', I surmise that the condemnation implied is for making an excessive show of distress as is known to happen at funerals, for although custom allows widows to mourn their husbands longer than other relatives, grief must yield to acceptance of God's decree. Yet had the word used been *laṭīmāt*, 'perfumed women', it would have suggested a sin worthier of such a heavy penalty.

The diction throughout is mixture of classical and colloquial, such as is not unusual either in the *zajal* of the learned or the songs of folk poets. One notices, however, formulaic expressions such as are strongly associated with oral composition. The Prophet is never mentioned without some laudatory phrase, and two favourites are *zēn il-<arab wi l-<agam*, 'the best among Arabs and non-Arabs', which occurs four times, and *ḥabīb il->̃ulūb*, 'beloved of [all] hearts', which is used seven times, including twice in the same stanza (viii). For rhyming, too, especially for the *-āl* binding rhyme, facile choices are made. Thus, *rigāl*, 'men', occurs eight times, three of them in tautological apostrophes to the audience: *yā rigāl.* This does not offend against any specified rule of prosody, but what we know of al-X̱ubārī would lead us to expect something more *recherché.*

And yet there are a few passages that bear the mark of an elite poet. One such is a hemistich (xlvi, 5) which is printed:

wa >aṣḥābuhū >ahlu t-tuqā wa t-tuqā

but which I take to be

wa >aṣḥābuhū >ahlu t-tuqā wa n-naqā
his companions are men of godliness and purity

and another (xliv, 5) which reads:

Muḥammad muqarrab muḥtabā mugtabā
Muḥammad is drawn near, wrapped in a garment, favoured

which I take to refer to the fact that the Prophet used to wrap himself in his mantle when receiving inspiration. Both passages contain the kind of embellishment dear to Arab men of letters from the thirteenth to the nineteenth centuries: ‘near paronomasias’ (using words identical in all but one syllable), and in the next passage the last two words also form a graphic paronomasia because in the Arabic script they look alike provided one ignores the dots.

محمد مقرب محتبى مجتبى

The folk poets are no less fond of word play, but they go for *zahr*, that is, full paronomasias achieved by sometimes gross distortion of the normal pronunciation, a practice roundly condemned by the eighteenth-century rhetorician <Abd al-X̱anī an-Nābulusī (d. 1731) in the entry on *tawriya* of his *badī <iyya* entitled *Nafaḥāt al-Azhār <alā Nasamāt al-Asḥār.*

Particularly challenging stylistically is a passage bridging two stanzas (xxx, 4–xxxi, 5), which says of the seventh heaven:

u fīhā malak law yi >zin >allāhu >ilēh, ۞ bala< di l->arāḍī wi l-buḥūr wi-l-gibāl
And in it is an angel who, if God allowed him,
Would swallow these lands, the seas, and the mountains.

bi ṣadruh šabīh id-dīk yi>azzin >azān, ۞ fa tisma< diyūk il->arḍı min x̱ēr miḥāl
In his chest is the like of a rooster that chants the call to prayer
And the roosters of earth hear him without falsity.

tigāwibhu bi t-tasbīḥ >a yā sayyidī, ۞ tisabbiḥ wi tuskut ma< sukūtuh wa qadd
They respond with praise, O my Master,
To his praise, and with silence to his silence, to the same measure.

<aṭā <ilmı mā sa<t il-misā wi ṣ-ṣabāḥ, ۞ u min kuŧrı zuhduh nūr gibīnuh waqad
So [the angel] taught what time is evening or morning,
And so ascetic was he that his brow blazed with light.

u lammā ra>ā ṭāhā nahaḍ luh wi >̃ām, ۞ wi >̃al luh yā tihāmī yā ḥabībī la-qad
And when he saw Ṭāhā he rose to him, he stood
And said, ‘O Tihāmī, beloved of mine, you have

<uṭīt il-hudā wi n-naṣrı ya bn il-kirām, ۞ u yā man bi faḍlu nta>̃alt inti>̃āl
Been given guidance and victory, O son of the noble,
O you who by His favour have progressed indeed

min Adam li Šēṯ l Idrīs li Nūḥ li l-Xalīl, ۞ >ilā đahrı <Abd Allāh firiḥ bak wi nāl
From Adam to Seth to Enoch to Noah to Abraham
And so to <Abd Allāh’s loins, who rejoiced in you and won favour.

The passage is awkwardly constructed. It is grossly insensitive to the purpose and potential of a stanzaic arrangement, for the linking of the call to prayer with cock-crowing usurps the place of the refrain-like couplet at the end of one stanza, then abruptly switches back to the angel's encounter with the Prophet. Linguistic usage also is somewhat strained. For the anomalous use of *qad* at the end of a line there is at least one prestigious classical precedent,[7] but only when the particle is part of a clause the rest of which is suppressed, whereas here it is awkwardly separated from the verb it emphasises. Also strained in order to achieve a paronomasia with the next rhyme word is the phrase *bi sukūtuh wa qadd*, which ought to end as *wa qadduh* … And yet the three rhyming lines – let alone the string of prophets in a subsequent line – bear the mark of a learned author. To begin with, *qad* has no place in Egyptian colloquial Arabic, although used profusely in the hybrid diction of folk compositions, yet *la-qad* is a combination I do not remember encountering in any other non-classical text. As for *waqad* in the sense of 'blazed', it is entirely classical for, as sometimes happens with weak roots, it is treated in the vernacular as if it was a hollow verb, and for 'the fire is blazing' the man in the street would say *in-nār >̃ādit* or *in-nār >̃āyda* – not *wa>̃adit* or *wā>̃da*.

With all this in mind, let us try to reduce the uncertainties that crowd around the genesis of this remarkable text.

Never mentioned in any written source, it appears late in the nineteenth century among the papers of a Cairo street singer, and at the precise spot where convention requires the author to identify himself appears the name al-X̲ubārī. Is this the X̲ubārī we know?

What we have is not a well-drafted manuscript handed down from generation to generation, but a text dealing with a major Islamic theme yet ignored by the literary establishment perhaps because it disapproved of its being cast in a barely tolerated linguistic medium, but welcomed by the common folk, so it passed down from one folk performer to another, sometimes in writing and sometimes orally, and therefore repeatedly recast by defective memories, one version of it eventually recorded by some unknown scribe, whose main concern was to bring the diction closer to standard Arabic.[8]

Awesome though the theme is, the text is not immune from invasions. The vocalists' faulty memory accounts for weak and repetitive rhymes and stale formulae. More invasive are attempts at improvements, such as the rather engaging fanciful notion that roosters on earth echo the morning call to prayer in heaven, inserted by someone – not unlike the scribe who produced the written text – who was acquainted with classical syntax but unappreciative of the stanzaic form. But the naming of comparatively obscure scriptural characters, some of whom do not occur in the Qur>ān, to say nothing of stylistic flourishes such as graphic puns which could scarcely be detected in an oral performance and would certainly be wasted on an illiterate audience, leave no doubt that a scholar had the upper hand in the creation of this text and had no need to draw on folk material in return. It seems almost certain, therefore, that this *zajal* was born as a written composition by a scholarly author.

Might this manuscript have come from the reed-pen of the fourteenth-century al-X̲ubārī? The internal evidence is really too thin to support or deny such a kinship. Had al-X̲ubārī's name acquired such prestige not just among scholars but also among the common people that more than five centuries later a verse composition of his would come to light in a literary Aladdin's cave? This is the more unlikely as this shining light so long sustained appears to have been eclipsed in the next century.

A solution that would be favoured by detective-story writers would be for the text to be a much more recent composition by a namesake, perhaps a descendant of the master; but if so, would he not want to identify himself more precisely and claim credit for what he deemed both a work of art and a meritorious act of faith?

Of tangential relevance here is the role and status of the author among folk artists.

Even at the folk level, there are performers who do not compose, and composers who – either because they are not blessed with a good voice or because it is beneath their dignity to appear in public – do not perform. At least among the professionals, the distinction is clear. In Egypt where all my field work was done, only one who composes is called an artist, a *fannān*; whereas one who sings other people's songs may be called a *muṭrib*, a vocalist, or more disparagingly a *ḥimalī*, a carrier. To the usual folk audience, what matters is the performance, and the performer hardly ever starts by announcing: 'I am going to sing to you a song composed by So-and-So', but if you ask him he will readily tell you from whom he learned the piece, and if the man had been the singer's teacher he would be named with great respect. One such creative artist was Muṣṭafā >Ibrāhīm <Ajāj or <Agāg.[9] He died in the 1930s after a busy and productive life when he seemed to wield some unofficial authority among the professional performers who, forty years later, still remembered him with reverence. But even he did not have his name trumpeted before audiences.

The only one I have known to be so honoured was a certain Ibn <Arūs, whom legend describes as a brigand who mended his ways and composed numberless quatrains urging devotion to God and the practice of good deeds. Yet the name appears to be used not so much as a guarantee of authentic authorship than as the identification of a genre.

Folk artists and their audiences readily accept and use material from any source, including the compositions of the learned, provided these are in a language accessible to them and consonant with their perceptions. So might al-X̲ubārī's name, like that of Ibn <Arūs, have become a label attached to any narrative verse of a devotional nature? There is no specific evidence that this happened, and it would be exceptional for the work of a member of the literary elite to be so well known and so highly esteemed by the common folk, but al-X̲ubārī was exceptional in many respects. And in the end the piece may well prove to be what it claims to be: the unconventionally transmitted composition of a gifted son of his age yet known mildly to stretch the conventions of his age.

I can offer nothing more precise by way of a conclusion than these alternatives, all unlikely but all possible.

Notes

1. See his obituary at the end of *Bulletin de l'Institut Français d'Archéologie Orientale*, 3 (1903) and the introduction of the same Bulletin's *Livre du Centenaire 1880–1980*, pp. xi–xii.
2. Both translations are reproduced integrally and commented on in Enrico Cerulli, *Libro della Scala e la questione delle fonti arabo-spagnole della Divina Commedia* (Vatican, 1949). The possibility of a link with Dante was first mooted by Miguel Asin Palacios, notably in his *Escatologia Musulmana en la Divina Commedia* (Madrid, 1919). Subsequent developments in the controversy were surveyed by Francesco Gabrieli, in 'Ḍaw> jadīd <alā Dāntī wa l-Islām', *Revue de l'Académie Arabe de Damas*, 33, I (January 1958), pp. 36–55.
3. The text has *u tarakū ... yinḍug*. The emendations I offer fit the metre and the sense better.
4. See Qur>ān 88:6. The word is said to be unknown to pre-Islamic Arabs, and is variously glossed as a thorny plant, or one that pasturing animals avoid, a water plant that alters for the worse by long stagnancy, the prickles of the palm-tree, or a thing in Hell more bitter than aloes, more stinking than a carcass, and hotter than fire.
5. Qur>ān 22:21 states that for the denizens of Hell there are 'hooked iron rods', but both the wording of the hemistich and the derivation of *maqāmi<* suggest a somewhat different rendering.
6. The printed text has *yiqša<ū*, 'disperse'.
7. In an-Nābix̱a's *>afida t-taraḥḥulu x̱ayra >anna rikābanā/lammā tazal bi riḥālinā wa ka>an qadī*, 'departure is nigh, except that our mounts are saddled still, yet all but'.
8. For an instance of liberty taken with a folk text, see Gaston Maspéro, *Chansons populaires recueillies dans la Haute-Égypte* (Cairo, 1914), p. 97 where he recounts having to curb his Egyptian subordinates from 'correcting the bad Arabic' of the texts they were recording for him.
9. See Item 4 in this book.

PART 3

Cultural and Social Implications

Two Perspectives on the 'Other' in Arabic Literature

A. The 'Other' in Egyptian Folk Literature

Despite an apparently straightforward title, I have to start with some caveats and reservations, for it is by no means easy to determine what the limits of folk literature are in an Arabic-speaking country. Least of all must it be assumed that it conforms with popular notions of what its European cousins were or are like. Thus, it is only partially true that its compositions are anonymous, or are the creations of illiterate authors, or are confined to the countryside, or are composed and transmitted only orally.

In a book-length study of a single genre in Egyptian folk literature[1] I have argued that the least diffuse of the criteria by which a composition may be judged to be genuinely 'folk' is the public to which it is addressed. This public is at the opposite pole from the minority who have acquired a Western type of education and who produce the 'high' literature too often assumed to be representative of modern Arab societies. The bulk of this public consists of illiterate villagers, but it also includes millions who reside in the poorer quarters of cities, and possibly also a fair number of those who have had a modicum of traditional Islamic education.

An extreme example that I mentioned in my book is that of a prolific versifier who was city-bred, had an Azhar education, made a living as a clerk in the railway yards in Cairo, never performed in public, but either taught his compositions to others or had them printed in cheap booklets. Yet, more than forty years after his death he and many of his works were still remembered with reverence by folk-singers of unquestioned pedigree. The secret is that he not only used the language and conventions of an established folk art, but also conformed with the notions of the common people, so that although he was demonstrably knowledgeable about Christianity, he could – in an embroidery on the Qur>anic story – identify the tormentors of Abraham as Christians.[2]

The fact that Arabic has, on the one hand, a classical form which is still the norm in most of the 'high' literary genres, and, on the other hand, a large number of local spoken forms long considered unfit for serious literary expression, is not enough to determine whether a particular text is or is not 'folk', for the colloquial is gaining a growing measure of acceptance in the modern literary canon. Complicating the issue is the existence of a number of city poets who are neither members of the establishment nor entirely at one with the masses, and who adopt not only the language but also the verse forms of folk literature mainly for satirical purposes. The most famous of these is Bayram at-Tūnisī (1893–1961), and following in his footsteps is the enormously popular >Aḥmad Fu>ād Nigm (b. 1929).

At-Tūnisī, who at one time lived in France, is known mainly through the printed word, in newspapers and magazines. Nigm has been reaching a wider public and has something of the character of an oral poet in that his compositions, sung by Šēx >Imām (1919–95), circulate mostly on audio-cassettes. But these are marked by a much greater and more precise knowledge of national and international affairs than is found among the masses, revealed, for example, when at-Tūnisī caricatures Golda Meir as a toothless old hag and boasts that Arabs now have Russian weapons with which to counter her schemes,[3] or when Nigm mocks the altruistic pretensions of a visiting French president in lines studded with foreign words:[4]

> Valéry Giscard d'Estaing and his good lady too
> Will catch the wolf by the tail and feed all the hungry.
> Wonder, oh wonder, good people, at such gentlemen!
> How very spoiled we're going to be!
> Our lives will be such pure delight;
> Our television will catch colour,
> Societies will be formed,
> And motor cars will fill up
> Not with petrol but with *parfum.*

This must be contrasted with the witness of a rural folk-singer – incidentally one of the few Christians in the trade – who, having served in the first Palestinian war in 1948, vehemently maintains that he had visited the city of Tunis in the Gaza strip.[5]

Although less circumspect or moderate than most members of the Westernised elite in voicing their sympathies and antipathies, the likes of at-Tūnisī are clearly closer to that class in their perceptions and values than they are to the common people, and although I am wary of prejudging issues by excluding material mainly on the ground of its content, I do not consider that their pronouncements form an integral part of folk literature.

In fact, although the influences of the city and of modernism are not negligible, the bulk of what is indisputably folk literature reflects the ethos of a settled agricultural community, yet with a somewhat romantic attachment to Arabism, the fellah taking pride in claiming that he is 'of Arab stock related to the Prophet'.[6] The heroes of three of the enormous epic cycles that have come down to us – *Sīrat Sayf ibn D̲ī Yazan*, *Sīrat <Antar* and the *Hilāliyya* – although the texts are mostly of late composition,[7] are Arabs of the desert and proud of it. The *Hilāliyya*, even though ostensibly dealing with Arab tribes opposed to each other, credits both with noble qualities.[8]

The Arabs celebrate the great among the Banū Hilāl:

> People whose praise God makes resplendent;
> Arabs who bring about no evil, whose intellect brooks no sin.
> They are, in their levies, protectors of the weak.
> And the Zanāta Arabs are freemen,

Their origin being from the Yemen;
Prince-like Arabs as they hurl their spears,
Xalīfa having drawn a Yemeni sword.

Their greatest hero, Abū Zēd, even flaunts his contempt for agricultural pursuits:

Never in my life have I planted vines,
Nor set my hand to feeding date palms.
I know nothing but trials and discomfort;
The day of battle is a feast to me.

Even in stories with a modern setting the qualities that are prized are those associated with Arabs from before Islam: hospitality and generosity; readiness to spring into action at all costs in defence of one's honour; and valour in combat.

It is, of course, nothing unusual to glorify the heroes of the past. In everyday usage, however, the word 'Arab' almost always denotes the Bedouin as against the fellah, and the present-day nomad is viewed in a more matter-of-fact fashion. His distinctive skills are recognised in such proverbs as 'The travelling Arabs know the way to water', or, referring to his reputed speed, 'Wrestle with the Bedouin rather than race him'.[9] On the other hand, a lack of sophistication is implied in the saying, 'Anything is soap to an Arab' (1961), and a byword for resourcelessness is 'like the Arabs' herds, that spend the night ruminating on their own snot' (977). When a poor man makes a show of wealth, he is likened to a Bedouin driving a single camel and shouting to the crowd, 'Watch out for the herd ahead of you! Beware of the herd behind you!' (872).

Such unvarnished references to poverty lead some present-day Arab intellectuals to interpret this folk literature as a movement of social protest. It is true that there is no room in it for the extravagant praise of princes that was once the main concern of elite poets. Often expressed or implied, however, is a conviction that men of virtue and authority can, by dint of heredity or inculcation, ensure a long succession of similarly gifted successors. At the same time, folk artists cannot ignore the stultifying effect of unrelieved exposure to deprivation, as is expressed in this *mawwāl*.[10]

One brought up in hunger makes no true friend;
Taken in by soft words, he invites the foe to strike deals with him.
The child of fornication is truthful when swearing to do ill.
His demon is ever with him, and to his words he hearkens.

Proverbs abound on the humility that befits the poor man, and on the abasement that is forced on him if he should 'walk like a prince'.[11] In fact, the surest foundation for respectability is the ownership of land. Even in a long narrative ballad about a folk-singer, a character who refers to the hero disparagingly as 'Ḥasan the singer' draws the rejoinder:[12]

He is no [mere] singer.
His father has forty-five acres to his name.
His father is headman of Bahnasā al-Xarra.

And yet another proverb asserts that the lowest of creatures are 'the donkey, the dog, the Negro, and the man without land'.[13]

The inclusion of the Negro in this sorry list calls for elaboration. There is no sustained animosity against the black man or deep contempt for him. Indeed, two of the greatest epic heroes – <Antar, an embroidery on the character of the pre-Islamic warrior-poet <Antara ibn Šaddād, and >Abū Zēd al-Hilālī – are black. It is true that they are shown again and again to be underrated by their foes because of the colour of their skin, and the wonder of their deeds is heightened thereby; but they do excite unmeasured and ungrudging admiration.

All the same, the fact that for long centuries most of the slaves were black has left its mark on the consciousness of the common people. The word *<abd* does duty for both a slave and a black man, and the person so denoted is therefore expected to fit a lowly role. A touching and edifying story of Sufi origin has it that the saintly al-Mursī >Abu l-<Abbās, whose shrine is in Alexandria, was a wealthy man who in his lifetime built and endowed a mosque, and appointed a black slave whom he owned, Yāqūt, as its muezzin. But Yāqūt incurred repeated reproof for sounding the call to prayer at times differing slightly from those determined by other muezzins. Not until he was on his deathbed did he reveal that whereas they had to rely on their imperfect senses, he was privileged to hear the angels' call to prayer in heaven. When asked why he had not said so earlier, he replied that had the truth been known, then whenever his voice was heard people's thoughts would have turned to him as the recipient of a great gift instead of to the one who gave him the gift. The story as told to me by a house servant ended with the master praising God who could bestow His favour 'even on a black slave', and building a second mosque to honour his former muezzin.

Similarly patronising is the proverb that asserts, 'Your beloved is whom you love, even if he is a Nubian slave' (521). Other proverbs portray the slave as resistant to training – 'Better to buy a slave than to rear him' (1157) – and secretive – 'They told the slave, "Your master is about to sell you"; he answered "He knows his business"; they asked him, "Won't you run away?"; he answered, "I know mine."' (1691).

As often happens when a minority speaks a little differently from most of the people, black men are derided as making little sense, and a noisy and unruly group is said to be 'like berberines: ten who gabble to one who listens' (873). Often they become the butt of typical ethnic jokes which imply that they are slow-witted. A song that I remember from my childhood affected the imperfect pronunciation of Arabic characteristic of the Nubians, and contained the lines:

Sirīğu s-sandūğı ya muhammād
lakin il-muftāhu ma>āyā

They’ve stolen my money-box, Muhammad,
But the key is still with me.

Similarly, an anecdote represents the stock folk character Juḥā as owning a very profitable water buffalo and a sickly donkey that is more trouble than it is worth. In a moment of impatience Juḥā mutters, ‘O God, take the donkey and leave me the buffalo!’ The next morning he finds the buffalo dead, and the donkey as sick as ever but still alive. Juḥā sits moping at his door, but when he sees a big black man passing by, he hails him with ‘Will you take five piastres to carry a dead donkey and throw it in the river?’ The man agrees, but when taken to the stable he protests, ‘This is a dead buffalo – it weighs much more!’ Thereupon Juḥā turns his eyes to heaven and exclaims, ‘O God! The black slave knows the difference between a donkey and a buffalo, and you don’t?’ The implication is that for a black man to show judgement places him in the same category as – in Dr Johnson’s judgement – the woman preaching and the dog standing on its hind legs.

Another group with whom the ordinary Egyptian is in frequent contact is the gypsies, but they suffer from more intensive and open denigration than the blacks. Although many of them are folk singers and as such may have an admiring following, the Arabic word for gypsies – ‘x̱agar’ – is, to a greater extent than ‘tinker’ is in English, quite simply a term of abuse. Actually, there is little to distinguish them from the bulk of the population besides their rootless way of life, so that it is not impossible for them to ‘pass’ into a community in which they choose to settle; but if known to be of gypsy origin – as is the case of two families of singers who have taken up residence in the village of Bakātūš, some from as early as c. 1890[14] – there are rigid limits to the social intercourse that they may have with other villagers. Conversely, itinerant performers are usually assumed to be gypsies even if they are of peasant stock.

Their condition is such that to be utterly wretched is to be likened to the gypsies’ donkeys, so tired that ‘they bray while lying on their flanks’ (912); yet the gypsy woman is said to ‘lord it over her neighbours’ (1550) because none dare expose themselves to her foul mouth. As for the social status of the gypsies, it is made obvious by such proverbs as ‘Every lane has its gypsies’ (1866), and by an aside in a narrative ballad which tells of a descendant of the Prophet who falls on evil days so that he is reduced to making a living by manual work:[15]

He fell in with people who had no foundation and no standing.
They made him carry stones – they were gypsies, of course!

At the opposite end of the scale are the erstwhile rulers of Egypt, who, since folk literature has a long if sometimes blurred memory, are often referred to as *turkī*, *x̱āzī*, *tatar*, or (recalling their most distinctive function) as ‘soldiers’ (*jindī*). The terms were no doubt once distinctive – *x̱āzī* used to be the common appellation for any of the Mamlukes – but the term is now broadly understood to refer to the one-time elite of Turkic stock.

Proverbs picture the Turk as superb in every sense of the word. He has authority: 'No one dare say, "Soldier, cover up your beard!"' (2123). He is arrogant: 'The Turk goes begging on horseback'. The self-sufficient is like 'the Turk of Tartary who neither misses the absent nor finds fellowship with the present' (976). Yet there may be little more to him than his appearance, for a pretentious person is compared with a character identified only by a funny name and a Turkish title, and is said to be 'like Ba<gar >Axā, with nothing to him except his moustache!' (881).

For all that, the Turks are basically, both for their appearance and their masterful ways, an object of admiration. Even in present-day folk songs a pretty girl is described as 'a Turkish gazelle', and in a lyrical *mawwâl* about a well-watered garden of love,[16] her male counterpart, 'whom the fair ones all desire', is described in the following words:

> The gardener is an *effendi* who calls down blessings on the Prophet every day,
> A Turkish prince with no intention of doing evil,
> Followed by horsemen constantly gnashing their teeth.

Their ways are remembered as harsh: the oppressed are said to be 'like the Tatars' pack horse, with the whip at its tail and a load of worry on its neck' (1011). Yet they are not necessarily the worst. The Egyptian equivalent of 'out of the frying pan and into the fire' is 'She ran away from the Turks only to be met by the Maghrébins' (781). Another proverb which at first blush appears to be a devastating piece of self-criticism reads 'Better the tyranny of the Turk than the justice of the Arab' (481). This, however, appears to be not so much an ethnic slur as the reflection of the experience of villagers who suffered most directly from the exactions of petty indigenous officials, whereas their Turkish superiors had the advantage of remoteness and magnificence. It is the more convincingly so as it is closely paralleled by yet another proverb, 'Better the tyranny of the cat than the justice of the mice' (482).

Again, it is probably because of his remoteness from the village community that the Westerner as such scarcely figures in the folk literature. The title of *xawāga*, which is most commonly applied to Europeans and sometimes to Syrian Christians, looms large in the satirical verse of such as Aḥmad Fu>ād Nigm, where it has been extended to Americans and Israelis and has become a signal for lambasting the imperialist.[17] In folk proverbs, on the other hand, the *xawāga* features mostly as a trader noted for his acumen – 'The *xawāga* told his son, 'Offer every customer what becomes him' (684) – and his commanding position – 'The *xawāga* does not move over to the customer' (685).

British rule was, of course, much more visible in the cities than in the countryside, yet there were occasions when the masses reacted strongly to it, notably in the notorious Danšawāy incident of 1906, when British officers who were out shooting pigeons – which are considered communal village property – got into an altercation with the villagers, as a result of which one officer died. A special court was set up that passed savage sentences on nineteen men, and a public show was made of the hangings and the floggings. In folk ballads that record the event and the horror it occasioned, the English are described as 'acting the Pharaohs after having been a rabble', and the British High Commissioner, Lord Cromer, is named as the prime mover. It is, however, at least partly as Christians that they are reviled, and no less venom is poured on the Egyptian Christian who presided over the court, although there is no mention of the two other judges who were Muslims, one of them the brother of the great nationalist leader Sa<d Zaxlūl.[18]

It is in fact the non-Muslim who is most readily – and usually antagonistically – identified as the 'other' in folk literature, with seldom any distinction between Egyptian and non-Egyptian Christian, or between adherents of any religion other than Islam. The words 'Christian', 'Jew', 'unbeliever' and even 'polytheist' are used interchangeably or even in series. Jesus himself is said to have been victimised by 'polytheistic Jewish Christians'.[19] All alike are cast in the role of villains, as in the story of the 'Christian Jews' who try to cheat an Arab of his fine camel on his way to the Prophet.[20] On earth they are contemptible: a loose woman is said to be available 'to Jews and Christians and street characters' (2044). And what awaits them in the hereafter is clearly implied in proverbs which liken the victim of unrelieved misfortune to 'the unbelievers' blacksmith, who is in the fire both in life and in death' (904); false appearances are 'like the unbelievers' tombs' – a garden above and fire below' (995).

This does conform with the dictum known among the learned that 'unbelief is all one nation', but there can be little doubt that among the common people this view grows out of ignorance rather than a theological position. A folk singer who was asked who the Jews were listed not only Israelis but also the Pharaohs, the Russians, the communists, and the Shia. He ascribed to them characteristically Coptic names, such as Maqar, Dimyān and Faltas, and he asserted that they ate pork and worshiped idols.[21]

Insofar as Christians are distinguished from others, they are reputed to be sly and clannish, as is shown in the proverbs: 'A Copt without slyness is a tree with no fruit' (1720), and 'The church knows its people' (1971). It is in keeping with this that in a ballad which tells of a feud between Muslims and Christians in the village of Bardanōhā, a Copt prominent in the Wafd nationalist party is portrayed as wielding unfair influence in favour of his co-religionists.[22]

More serious is the implication in the epic cycle of aẓ-Ẓāhir Baybars that the native Christians were a source of danger to the Muslims in their wars against the Crusaders,[23] even as the Coptic judge of Danšawāy is represented as doing the bidding of the English.

The fact that at least one-tenth of Egypt's population consists of Christians, that they intermingle with Muslims in all walks of life, and that at a popular level some of their festivals attract Muslims – as does the *mūlid* of Saint George, who is to some extent identified with the intriguing Islamic lore character of al-Xiḍr[24] – gives them a measure of acceptance. A singer beginning his performance with the obligatory praise of God[25] throws in the lines 'Praise Him who created all people, Created both Muslims and Christians', but he then moves on to some amatory verse without further reference to religious denominations. A manifest preference, however, is enshrined in a proverb which makes use of a distinctively Christian name: 'Better our home tares than the selected wheat of Ṣalīb Efendi' (1066). This does at the same time attribute some skill to the Copts, who indeed, like many minorities, do seek the advantages of education and are reputed to be enterprising in their own interests.

The attitude to the Jews is even more inimical. An amusing song which can be dated back to 1893, if not earlier, illustrates the madness induced by love in stanzas of nonsense verse which jumble together the most disparate objects; it contains this revealing passage:[26]

> I saw the donkey fly, having snatched a camel.
> They stretched out boats with tresses hanging loose.
> In war they would serve to fight the Jews.

Some proverbs reveal a fair amount of knowledge about Judaism. To be utterly broke is to be 'more penniless than a Jew on the Sabbath day' (179), and the Egyptian equivalent of 'a voice crying in the wilderness' is 'To whom will you recite your psalms, O David?' (397). Most, however, portray the Jew in very offensive terms. He is said to have 'a clean face, but a cloak like a privy' (1056). He is merciless: 'They needed help from a Jew; he said, "Today is a feast day".' (71) Even his cemetery is 'whiteness covering up ruthlessness' (960). The unreliable are 'like the Jews' messenger – he sets off with no information and comes back with none' (930). Not even his Scriptures are trustworthy: 'The Jews' recitation is two-thirds lies' (996).

He is, however, often portrayed as rich. In a narrative ballad in which Muḥammad's shirt is sold by auction to help a poor man, it is a Jew who outbids all Muḥammad's closest companions,[27] and is then converted by benefiting from its miraculous powers. In fact, the Jew's sharpness in business is proverbial: 'When the Jew is bankrupt, he searches his old accounts books' (2054). Conversely, the depths are plumbed by the poor Jew, who has nothing to enjoy 'in this world or the next' (990).

Conclusion

All this shows how little of the modernism displayed in the 'high' literature has filtered down to the masses. This is true even in the key area of nationalism, local or pan-Arab, which through most of the twentieth century the Westernised Arabs have exalted as a unifying factor, as against the divisiveness of religious confessions.[28] On the contrary, among the common people the strongest bond next to blood relationship is that of a common faith. Indeed, one of the first Arab scholars to turn his attention to folk literature,[29] writing in the 1950s, made this matter of communal loyalty the dividing line between it and the 'high' literature, calling the latter 'nationalistic' and the former 'traditional'.

It is true that in more recent years one hears from some spokesmen of the common people echoes of the values proclaimed by the elite,[30] but mainly in compositions whose ‘folk’ character is at least open to question.[31] A signal example is ‘The Battle of Port-Said’, celebrating an episode in the fighting over the Suez Canal in 1956. It was the work of >Abū Đirā<, a performer of undoubted ‘folk’ pedigree, and it contains such lines as:

Dawn broke for Arabism, dispelling Eden’s blindness …
In the Assembly the war criminal was very sickly;
He went to the Security Council and was struck dumb –
What was his tongue to say?
I am an Arab; on Victory Day I was given an antidote
To wretched Israel, whose death is licit.
The ruler of England is not a man, but a woman.
In France, the land of wonders, I have detected pride.
The world took a stand, issuing a warning.
They asked England to stop fighting; she refused.
The free world joined the fight in our ranks.

Disjointed as the lines are, they show >Abū Đirā< to be comparatively well-informed and, except for the taunt about the queen of England, very much in line with the sentiments of the educated elite. But he has for many years been resident in Cairo; he was appointed by President <Abd an-Nāṣir as entertainer to the troops, and by the time I recorded him in 1972 he could remember only a fragment of the song he had composed. Clearly, it had dropped out of his repertory, whereas still remembered are ballads about Danšawāy, in which Muṣṭafā Kāmil, the politician who made capital of the atrocity story and is known to the educated as the father of Egyptian nationalism, is celebrated by the common people as ‘the pillar of the faith’.

The Westernised intellectual scarcely figures in the folk literature. He almost qualifies – by default – as part of ‘the other’.

Notes

1. *Popular Narrative Ballads of Modern Egypt* (Oxford, 1989) – hereafter *Ballads.*
2. He was Muṣṭafā >Ibrāhīm <Ajāj (d. c. 1936). See *Ballads*, pp. 45–6, 76–7.
3. Kamāl Sa<d, Ṣafaḥāt ḍā>i<a min ḥayāt Bayram at-Tūnisī (Cairo, n.d.), p. 159.
4. My translation of lines quoted by Kamal Abdel-Malek in ‘The Khawāga Then And Now’, *Journal of Arabic Literature*, 19 (1988), p. 178.
5. Susan Slyomovics, *The Merchant of Art* (Berkeley, CA, 1987), p. 64 – hereafter *Merchant.*
6. Ahmed Ammar, *People of Sharqiyya*; and Hamed Ammar, *Growing up in an Egyptian Village*, as reported in Bridget Connelly, *Arab Folk Epic and Identity* (Berkeley, CA, 1986), p. 162.
7. Harry T. Norris (‘Sayf b. D̲ī Yazan and the Book of the History of the Nile’, *Quaderni*

di Studi Arabi, 1 [1989], p. 141) estimates the *Sīra* of Sayf ibn D̲ī Yazan to have been composed between 1400 and 1600.

8. My own translation of a text in Giovanni Canova, 'Hilaliani e Zanata: Considerazioni sulla Sīrat Banī Hillāl', *Quaderni di Studi Arabi*, 7 (1989), pp. 165, n. 6, and 168, n. 18.
9. Proverbs 1385 and 1984 in >Aḥmad Taymūr, *al->Amt̲āl al-<āmmiyya* (Cairo, 1949). Unless otherwise indicated, all other proverbs quoted here are from the same source and are identified by their number as given in that text.
10. Muḥammad Qandīl al-Baqlī, *Ṣuwar min >adabinā š-ša<bī* (Cairo, 1962), p. 17.
11. *Proverbs*, 1616–23.
12. *Ballads*, p. 71. The ballad is that of Ḥasan and Na<īma, which features also in Items 9 and 18 in this book.
13. G. W. Murray, *Sons of Ishmael*, quoted in Connelly, *Arab Folk Epic and Identity*, p. 153.
14. Dwight Reynolds, *Heroic Poets, Poetic Heroes: Composition and Performance in an Arabic Oral Epic Tradition* (New York, 1995), p. 58.
15. 'X̲arīb', in *Ballads*, p. 231.
16. The entire song is to be found in Item 2 in this book.
17. Kamal Abdel-Malek, 'The Khawāga' (see note 4).
18. *Ballads*, pp. 247–58.
19. *Ballads*, p. 76.
20. *Ballads*, pp. 185–225.
21. *Merchant*, p. 61.
22. *Ballads*, pp. 73–4.
23. <Abd al-Ḥamīd Yūnus, *Al-Hilāliyya fī t-tārīx wa l->adab aš-ša<bī* (Cairo, 1956), p. 162.
24. Al-Xiḍr is commonly identified with Moses' companion in the episode narrated in Qur>ān 18:59–81, but he also shares some characteristics of other Middle Eastern legendary heroes. See also *Ballads*, p. 239.
25. Šawqī l-Qināwī, recorded by the poet <Abd ar-Raḥmān al->Abnūdī.
26. See Item 6 in this book.
27. Item 5 in this book.
28. See my 'In a Glass Darkly', *Die Welt des Islams*, 33–34 (1984), pp. 26–44.
29. >Aḥmad Rušdī Ṣāliḥ; see *Ballads*, p. 82.
30. *Ballads*, pp. 74–5.
31. *Ballads*, pp. 74–6, 261–5.

B. The 'Other' in Modern Arabic Prose Writing[1]

If our concern here were solely or chiefly literary, we would have to consider the different levels at which the 'other' impinges on a writer's conscious or subconscious mind: that is, whether the writer is projecting one individual against another, or against his society or some group ideal; or, indeed, whether he is projecting the collectivity with which he identifies against some other. All these projections are to be found in modem Arabic literature, but the present context clearly calls for focusing on the last level I have mentioned: that is, how the Arab writer as an Arab views the group against which he finds it necessary to measure himself. This has in fact been one of the main concerns of Arab intellectuals for at least three generations.

Since the initiative that has led to the present discussion came from the American Academic Association for Peace in the Middle East, this 'other' may have been expected to be the Israeli, the Zionist or the Jew. Indeed, non-specialists all too often assume that the Palestine imbroglio is what looms largest in the Arab mind. To this, a corrective needs to be applied from the start. The fact is that the issues it raises occupy a very small part of modern Arabic literature, except insofar as the Palestinian writers themselves are concerned – and among these it is against the indifference of other Arabs and the supineness of their own leadership that some of their sharpest barbs are directed. This is evident even in the writings of an active member of the Popular Front for the Liberation of Palestine, X̱assān Kanafānī (1936–72), notably in his best-known novel, *Men in the Sun*.[2] Hence, it is against a much wider background that the attitude of the Arab to the 'other' needs to be seen.

Ever since the Prophet established his *umma* (community) in Medina, a common faith had been – theoretically at least – the supreme communal bond and the essential condition of full citizenship. This does not mean that Muslims were uniformly faithful to the teachings of their religion, or immune from the outworking of other social forces, but it was in the name of Islam that initiatives were justified, and it was as unbelievers or heretics that opponents were condemned.

By the eighteenth century, the literature produced was the apanage of a homogeneous educated elite. It was so entirely at one that it poured its energies not into the pursuit of anything new, but into increasingly refined expressions of its traditional values; and it was so seldom challenged that it was scarcely conscious of any 'other'. At most, one encounters an occasional perfunctory curse upon schismatics within the body of Islam,[3] or some veiled barbs by Sufis at the literal-minded interpreters of the Scriptures.[4]

Beginning with the Bonaparte expedition to Egypt in 1798, European powers forced themselves on the attention of the Arabs, and their political and military successes gave their technology, their organisation, the scientific bases of their thinking, indeed, their entire civilisation, a seal of approval which could not be ignored by thinking Arabs. From the 1870s onwards, countless articles in Arab journals began not by arguing but by asserting as a commonplace that Europeans had the upper hand in virtually everything except religion.

Almost inevitably, it was primarily along confessional lines that the Arabs first reacted. The great Islamic reformist Muḥammad <Abduh (1849–1905), even while opening his mind to the need for rethinking the fundamentals of the faith which his generation had inherited, raised the question: 'If Christianity is reputed to be the religion of Peace and Islam the religion of the Sword, how is it that in every clash it is the Christians who emerge triumphant?'[5] The answer he gave was a harbinger of a change of direction: whereas Muslims had fallen away from the true teachings of their religion, Europeans had forged ahead because they were heirs to the Greeks and the Romans.

Had the distinction remained a confessional one, it would have exacerbated issues already existing between Arab Muslims and Arab Christians. A curious incident illustrates this. In 1840, the Christian Buṭrus Karāma (1774–1851) had composed a poem of twenty-three lines, each of which ended with the same word used each time in a different sense. Full of admiration, the governor of Iraq had challenged the poets of Baghdad to do better. One of them had declined the challenge with a churlish: 'Is there a Christian to be deemed eloquent?' Forty years later, another Christian, Rušayd ad-Daḥdāḥ (1813–89), picked up the quarrel and widened it by claiming:

> If the argument refers to eloquence in general, in all languages and under all climes, then by no stretch of the imagination is there anyone who compares with the eloquent Christians writing in European languages, for their lands are resplendent with their intellects, their pulpits are crowded with their orators, and their learned men have filled the earth with books on every art.[6]

It may be worth interjecting at this point that – as Professor Bernard Lewis has shown[7] – it was widely assumed in Europe that Jews were the natural allies of Muslims in their common antipathy to the Christians. This perception was not shared by the Arabs. It is true that Jacob Sanua (1839–1912), a notable pioneer of Arab journalism and of the Arab theatre, allied himself with the Muslim reformists against the Khedive of Egypt and the British occupiers; over his long career, he also drew closer and closer to his public, so that whereas in the first numbers of his journal he signed himself 'Professeur James Sanua' and in his cartoons represented himself in European clothes, he later appeared in Arab garb and called himself 'aš-Šayx Ya<qūb Ṣanū<', even claiming that because of a vow his mother had made during an early illness of his, he had been brought up virtually as a Muslim. This appears, however, to have been an exceptional, not to say an idiosyncratic, case.

What is true is that Muslim Arabs were being made increasingly aware of the challenge of the West, which happened to be overwhelmingly Christian, whereas there was at the time no threat from any Jewish entity. The Jew, therefore, scarcely figured in the educated Arab's image of the 'other'.

And this 'other' was increasingly the subject of both admiration and resentment: admiration of the power he wielded and all that had made it possible; and resentment that this power was used to bring the Arabs into subjection. The combination could be resolved in only one formula: emulation, the adoption of the 'other's' methods as a means of reasserting one's own independence and worth. Initially, the supremacy of religion in the Arab's system of thought caused him to identify the 'other' as 'the Christian'; but as the other refused to conform to the Arab's image of him, he became the formative element in the Arab's image of himself.

An early stage of the process may be detected in the programme which the Muslim Reformist organ *al-<Urwa l-Wuṯqā* set for itself in its inaugural number in 1884. Among its declared aims we find:

> Expounding the duties incumbent on Orientals, failure to perform which would result in decline and weakness;
> Sounding the call to hold fast to the principles of their forefathers, which are indeed the same as those of powerful foreign nations; and
> Refuting the accusations directed at the East in general and at Islam in particular, and the arguments of those who hold that Muslims cannot advance in civilisation so long as they maintain the teachings of their faith.

Noticeable here is the very broad identification with the East as well as with Islam. As against this, the challenger, though unnamed, is more clearly definable, and the validity of his concept of civilisation is implicitly recognised.

It was not long before Arabs who came under European rule, such as the Egyptians, noticed that their occupiers were not greatly concerned with converting them to Christianity; that the occupiers' boast was not faithfulness to God and Gospel, but service to King and Country. The Arabs' boldest thinkers altered their own priorities accordingly, and made it their ideal to strive for the establishment of the nation-state. For some this had pan-Arab connotations, but more often and increasingly it was embraced on the basis of what Albert Hourani has called 'territorial' nationalism.[8] In this the 'other' was an antagonist, but he was also a role model.

The motive force behind this change of direction, and the passion with which it was adopted, are well illustrated in one of the grandiloquent orations of the father of Egyptian nationalism. Muṣṭafā Kāmil (1874–1908):

> I need not draw your attention to the manifestations of lofty patriotism and to the signs of true life which you see in Europe. This great efflorescence proclaims with finest eloquence that it is of the fruits of patriotism; all the justice and order, the freedom and independence, the immense well-being, the great dominion to be found in those lands – all are without doubt among the products of the noble sentiment that causes the members of an entire nation to work for a common purpose and a single aim.[9]

Arab fiction is to an overwhelming degree concerned with Arab problems. I know of only one novel of quality – Ṭāhā Ḥusayn's (1889–1973) *al-Ḥubb aḍ-Ḍā>i<* (1943), a love story with French protagonists – that has an entirely foreign theme in a foreign setting. It is, in most instances, mainly as a contributor to an Arab theme that the 'other' is featured. Thus, the coloniser may be represented as exploitative and his soldiery brutal;[10] but the European at home – as, for example, the hero's friend and mentor in Tawfīq al-Ḥakīm's (b. between 1897 and 1902, d. 1987) *Bird from the East* [11] – is usually seen as cultured and perceptive.

An important corollary of the Arab nationalist thesis has been to play down the role of religion as a social force. This has been fostered by the fact that in the foremost cultural centres of the Arab world, Egypt and the Lebanon, there have been substantial native Christian minorities, so that the doctrine advanced is that one is an Egyptian or a Lebanese first, and a Christian or a Muslim second.

The reality has not always been as idyllic as the modernists would have it; one senses above all a concern not to give offence. One of the earliest attempts at a novel, for example, *Lādilās* (1897), by the poet >Aḥmad Šawqī (1868–1932), has an ancient Egyptian as the hero contending for the hand of a beautiful Greek princess, and part of his ultimate triumph is that he lays the foundations for forty pagan temples; but a Christian contemporary, Jurjī Zaydān (1861–1924), was more circumspect: the heroes of his twenty-two historical romances are all Muslim Arabs. Much later, Muḥammad Kāmil Ḥusayn's *City of Wrong*[12] (1957), a Muslim's novel on Jesus, stops with the sentencing of Jesus to death, thus avoiding the crucifixion, on which Islam and Christianity differ. And in dealing with the violence that had been tearing the Lebanon apart, as in X̱āda s-Sammān's (b. 1942) *Beirut Nightmares* (1976),[13] lovers may be shown as victims of sectarian intolerance, but the persecuting sect is never named.

More positively, Christian and Muslim Arabs are shown to be collaborators in nationalist struggles, as in Tawfīq Yūsuf <Awwād's (b. 1911) *ar-Raxīf* (1939). And the point was never made more explicitly than in a film on Saladin, for which the script was written by Yūsuf >Idrīs (1927–91). In this film, incidentally, Richard the Lionheart is shown as a chivalrous opponent, but the Muslim hero is also given a Christian second-in-command who, when he encounters a woman from the Crusaders' ranks, explains that he looks upon her people not as co-religionists, but as invaders of the Fatherland.

In all this, the Jews scarcely figured until the possibility of the creation of a Jewish state in Palestine attracted Arab attention. When it did, it was easy for the Arab intellectuals to see it in a nationalist light, as yet one more encroachment by a foreign nationalism on their territory, rather than as a religious challenge.

A single exception to this has been <Ali >Aḥmad BāKaṯīr (1910–69), who wrote a series of frankly anti-Jewish plays. The most virulent of these, titled 'God of Israel', argues that from the time the Jews took to worshipping the golden calf, their god has been Satan, and (here BāKaṯīr uses biblical passages more ingeniously than ingenuously) that they have actually interbred with devils.

But BāKaṯīr was in many ways atypical. Born in Indonesia of Arab parents, he grew up in south Arabia and the Hijaz, and did not experience the more open-minded ambience of Egypt until he was twenty-three. He also later fell into public disfavour – not specifically for his anti-Jewish plays, but because his ideology was seen as reactionary – and before his death in 1969 he had to defend himself against the accusation of being a member of the Muslim Brotherhood, which by then was proscribed.

On the whole, the leading Arab writers have been remarkably consistent in distinguishing between Zionism (which has no advocates anywhere in the Arab world), Israel (which only a minority is prepared to accept as a fact of history), and Judaism as a religion or Jews as human beings. Furthering the parallel with the image of the European coloniser, X̱assān Kanafānī distinguishes between the local Jew, who has lived for centuries in amity with his Arab neighbours, and the Jewish immigrant, who is portrayed as an out-and-out usurper.

Lest too rosy a picture be left in the reader's mind, it needs to be said that in Arabic war literature, Israeli soldiers are depicted as brutal murderers and rapists, and in a few instances –perhaps intended to reflect the common people's usage[14] – they are called 'Jews'. Furthermore, no writer has made any notable attempt to enter sympathetically into the dilemma that torments not a few thinking Israelis in their dealings with the Arabs, whereas there have been efforts by Hebrew-language writers to understand the Arabs' predicament. And whereas in the nineteenth and early twentieth centuries Jewish characters appeared only rarely and indeed incidentally in Arab prose writings, this has changed since Zionism has scored practical successes in the region, resulting in the growth of vehemently antagonistic literary works, many of which are unmistakably anti-Jewish.[15] However, these are mostly by third-rate writers. Also worth noting is that most of the derogatory depictions of Jews have come from the pens of Christian Arabs and, indeed, reflect attitudes drawn from the anti-Semitic lore of European Christendom, although it may also be argued that the comparative reticence of Muslims in this respect is due to self-consciousness about charges of fanaticism often levelled against Islam.

Above all, it needs to be stressed that the written corpus under examination here is produced by an intellectual elite for an educated minority. A look at folk literature would show that modernistic values have scarcely trickled down to the masses. There the supreme loyalty, next to ties of blood, is not to the nation-state but to Islam, and non-Muslims of whatever ilk are bundled together as all being equally beyond the pale. The terms Christian, Jew, unbeliever and polytheist are used absolutely interchangeably or in series. In some narratives, the villains are called Christian Jews, and the story of Abraham as told in song identifies his tormentors as Christians![16]

It would neatly cap this presentation if I could represent the stirrings of religious revival among the educated, who often read modern shibboleths (such as socialist values) into the past record of Islam, as a closing of the gap between the elite and the masses, between the high literature and the low. Alas, both the phenomenon and its repercussions in the literature bristle with features that defy simple explanation. It does not derive its inspiration or its vehemence from the grass roots. It is not even, strictly speaking, a traditionalist outcrop, for it claims the right to sweep aside the elaborations of past centuries and to reinterpret the fundamentals of the faith. It has been likened to Protestantism in Christianity. And from the top creative writers, it has evoked no sympathetic echo to speak of.

These writers remain determinedly attached to Western values. Whatever interpretation one may place on Najīb Maḥfūẓ's (1911–2006) allegorical novel on the great Semitic religions,[17] he does treat them all alike. And religious leaders continue to be depicted as inadequate, if not reactionary. For example, Yūsuf >Idrīs, the *enfant terrible* of present-day Arabic writing, has a short story in which an *imām*, while leading prayers, catches sight of a pretty girl of partly European parentage across the street, and abandons his congregation literally at the lowest point of a prostration, with their foreheads touching the ground.[18]

One must admit that such a broad survey inevitably oversimplifies a complex picture, in which there are as many differences of emphasis as there are individual components. Nor are the intellectuals a monolithic group. Among them are Marxists to whom the 'other' is the exploiting capitalist of whatever nationality, although Arab Marxists have had to make accommodations with nationalism.[19] Among them also are feminists, to whom the 'other' is the domineering male. Most of them have claimed a place in the sun by virtue of their contributions to national causes, but at least one – the Israeli Arab Saḥar Xalīfa (b. 1941) – has not pulled her punches in asserting that they have been ill-rewarded for their pains.[20] And a growing number are – like aṭ-Ṭayyib Ṣāliḥ (b. 1929) – expressing concern lest Arab culture be reduced to a pale imitation of that of the West.[21]

Further changes of direction may yet take place, but for the time being, the West remains the dominant 'other', and the high Arabic literature continues to aim at becoming an equal contributor to a culture that, without much consideration of the possible claims of other civilisations, such as the Chinese or the Indian, it views not as regional but global and of universal validity.

Notes

1. This article attempts to summarise and re-arrange information used in three previously published articles: 'The Assumptions and Aspirations of Egyptian Modernists', *Islam: Past Influence and Present Challenge*, ed. Alford Welch and Pierre Cachia (Edinburgh, 1979), pp. 210–35; 'The Treatment of Themes Relating to Christianity and Judaism in Modern Egyptian Drama and Fiction', *Journal of Arabic Literature*, 2 (1971), pp. 178–94; and 'In a Glass Darkly: The Faintness of Islamic Inspiration in Modem Arabic Literature', *Welt des Islams*, 32–4 (1984), pp. 26–44. The reader is referred to these for fuller illustration and documentation. As the subject may be of interest to non-Arabists, further reference will be made, whenever possible, to sources available in a European language.
2. *Rijāl fī š-Šhams* (1963), trans. Hilary Kilpatrick (London, 1978). On Kanafāni, see Muhammad Siddiq, *Man is a Cause* (Seattle, 1984).
3. E.g., <Abd al-X̲anī n-Nābulusī, in his *Nafaḥāt al->Azhār*, p. 226 of the Damascus edition and p. 154 of the Egyptian edition, quotes a line by Ṣafiyy ad-Dīn al-Ḥillī which implies

that <Alī alone among the Companions of the Prophet was entitled to the *imamate*, then comments: ‘He had made plain – God confound him – his false belief which is in agreement with the creed of the Rāfiḍites. God’s curse upon them.’

4. In the widespread use of the conventions of love poetry to express desire for union with God, the stock image of ‘the reprovers’ seems consistently applicable to the *ulemas*. For an example, see poem by al-Xaymī and the commentary thereon in <Alī Ṣāfī, *al->Adab aṣ-Ṣūfī fī Miṣr fī l-Qarn as-Sābi < al-Hijrī* (Cairo, 1964), pp. 267–9.
5. In an article signed also by Jamāl ad-Dīn al->Afx̱ānī, trans. in John Haywood, *Modern Arabic Literature 1800–1970*, (London, 1971), pp. 143–50.
6. Hāšim Yāx̱ī, *an-Naqd al->Adabī l-Ḥadīṯ fī Lubnān* (Cairo, 1968), vol. I, p. 31.
7. *Islam in History* (London, 1973), esp. pp. 124–5.
8. In *Arabic Thought in the Liberal Age 1798–1939* (London, 1962).
9. In <Abd ar-Raḥmān ar-Rāfi <i, *Muṣṭafā Kāmil Bā < iṯ al-Ḥaraka l-Waṭaniyya*, 4th edn, (Cairo, 1962), pp. 110–11.
10. See, e.g., ‘Abd al-Majīd ben Jallūn’, in Vincent Monteil, *Anthologie Bilingue de la Littérature Arabe Contemporaine* (Beirut, 1961), pp. 260–7.
11. *<Uṣfūr min aš-Šarq* (1938), trans. R. Bayly Winder (Beirut, 1966).
12. *Qarya Ẓālima*, trans. Kenneth Cragg (London, 1959).
13. *Kawābīs Bayrūt* (Beirut, n.d.).
14. As in Jamāl al-X̱īṭānī, *Ḥikāyāt al-X̱arīb* (Cairo, 1976), or Sa <d ad-Dīn Wahba’s play, *Ra <s al-<Ušš* (Cairo, 1974).
15. A useful summary of this literature is to be found in three articles published together in *al- <Arabiyya*, XI, 1–2 (Spring/Autumn 1978): Mohammed B. Alwan, ‘Jews in Arabic Literature – 1830–1914’, pp. 46–59; Salih J. Altoma, ‘The Image of the Jew in Modem Arabic Literature – 1900–1947’, pp. 60–73; and Trevor LeGassick, ‘The Image of the Jew in Post World War II Arabic Literature’, pp. 74–89.
16. See *Ballads*, esp. ch. 7.
17. *<Awlād Ḥāratinā* (1959), trans. by Philip Stewart as *Children of Gebelawi* (London, 1981).
18. ‘Did you have to leave the light on, Lily?’, in *Bayt min Laḥm* (Cairo, 1971), pp. 15–35.
19. See, e.g., Anouar Abdel-Malek, *Anthologie de la Littérature Arabe Contemporaine – Les Essais* (Paris, 1965), introduction.
20. Muhammad Siddiq, ‘The Fiction of Sahar Khalifah: Between Defiance and Deliverance’, *Arab Studies Quarterly*, 8, 2 (Spring 1986), pp. 120–42.
21. See Rotraud Wielandt, ‘The Problem of Cultural Identity in the Writings of al-Tayyib Salih’, in *Studia Arabica et Islamica*, ed. Wadād al-Qādi (Beirut, 1981), pp. 487–515. Several of aṭ-Ṭayyib Ṣāliḥ’s works have been translated by Denys Johnson-Davies and published by Heinemann.

15

Maltese: Arabic Roots and Sundry Grafts

A. Cultural Cross-currents in Maltese Idioms[1]

The vicissitudes of history that made Malta part of the Aghlabid domains for more than 200 years, then for even longer centuries the battered but unconquered bastion of Christendom against Islam, have left it a strangely mixed inheritance. On the one hand, its language has obvious, close and today widely acknowledged bonds of kinship with Arabic. On the other hand, not only is there among the common people a conscious antipathy to the Arabs which makes the very word *għarbi* a term of abuse, but almost every manifestation of Maltese cultural life other than the language places it clearly in the stream of European, more specifically Italian, civilisation.

This European affiliation is not merely a veneer taken on by the educated classes, nor is it entirely the result of that penetration of the Near East by the West which began in the nineteenth century and has coloured the life of the Arabs themselves.

It is, of course, most patent in the Maltese literary movement, in that its pioneers were men steeped in the Italian literary tradition, in several instances men with a reputation as writers in Italian before they turned to the native idiom. But Maltese folk literature, too, although not so homogeneous, betrays profound and long-standing European influences. The folktales, for example, are strongly reminiscent of the Arab *ḥaddutah*, with its characteristically luxuriant fantasy – although even in these there are curiously revealing twists, as when the role which in Arab tales is usually filled by a Persian *ḥakīm* or a Maghribī magician is, in its Maltese counterpart, assigned to a German professor.[2] As for folksongs, their metrical forms are Italian, and they are sung to Italian music, usually played on the guitar.

Significant also is the testimony of Fāris aš-Šidyāq, who lived and worked in Malta from 1834 to 1848 and reported at length on the customs, the superstitions, the social demeanour, the mannerisms, even the conventional gestures, of the Maltese. Biased and inaccurate as his observations often were, it is clear that he was reacting to a way of life that on the whole seemed foreign to him, and his final verdict on it was that 'the island of Malta pleases but few Europeans. The reason is that they find nothing novel when they come of it, nothing that cannot be found in their own country – for everything in it is but the refuse of what they possess … Of the Arabs it would please no one. This is because the Maltese all hate the entire race of Arabs and Muslims.'[3]

It is the Maltese language, then, that is the abiding monument of the Arab connection with Malta. The morphology and syntax of Maltese remain remarkably close to, although not identical with, those of Arabic. As for the vocabulary, it appears that some 6,500 words or more of Semitic derivation are still in common use among the Maltese, and, although these are not very many, they are clustered mostly in the primary stratum of the language and are 'enough to express the manifold ideas and contexts of ordinary human life, the world of primitive, elemental ideas, man's natural world of feeling and reacting'.[4] The enquiry suggests itself: what cultural cross-currents may be detected not in isolated words, but in the idiomatic set phrases of the Maltese? It is a first step in such an enquiry that is attempted here.

A first and tentative step it must be, for linguists have paid surprisingly little attention to the study of idioms. Indeed, if the blessing of a well-established scholar is to be sought for this venture, it must be in Professor McIntosh's appeal to linguists not to restrict themselves to the old respectable fields of philology with which linguistics tends to be equated, but to stick their necks out even at the risk of making fools of themselves.[5]

So far as Maltese idioms are concerned, the similarity between many of them and Italian ones was noted by Dr Salvatore Castaldi, who in 1883 published a booklet titled *Maltesismi e Frasi Toscane* in which 456 Maltese set phrases or single words used idiomatically are paired with exact Tuscan equivalents. But of other influences, Dr Castaldi took no note. More directly related to the present study is a suggestion made by Professor Aquilina in an article titled 'Fields of Maltese Linguistic Research' for a detailed study of such loan-translations and *calques*.[6] By way of illustration, he listed twenty Sicilian and Italian idioms, then ten Arabic ones taken from Beaussier's dictionary, all of which made mention of the hand and all of which could be matched from Maltese usage; he thus gave *prima facie* evidence that the crop of loan translations from Sicilian and Italian is more abundant than that from the Arabic of North Africa.

There is an objection to this approach, or rather a difficulty that must be recognised and contended with in any such study. It is that whereas in Italian, as in many other European languages, idioms have been systematically collected, whereas in fact most desk dictionaries record the idioms most commonly in use, Arabic – especially its colloquial dialects – is not nearly so well served. The best collection, that of >Aḥmad Taymūr Pasha,[7] numbers only 336, and the fact that the same idioms seldom recur in the various dictionaries of spoken Arabic – those of Beaussier, Spiro and Barthélémy – suggests how haphazard and incomplete the record must be. A crumb of comfort, however, is that Beaussier's dictionary – which with its North African associations is presumably the most relevant to Maltese – is the most idiom-conscious.

The bias resulting from this under-representation of Arabic idioms could be reduced, though not eliminated, if the procedure suggested by Professor Aquilina was reversed, and one started with a fairly extensive number of Maltese idioms collected with no such intended comparison in mind, and then sought comparable ones in Italian and in Arabic. For the purpose of the present study, all the idioms containing figures of speech related to parts of the body were extracted from K. Fenech's *Idjomi Maltin* (Malta, 1955) and were supplemented from current Maltese dictionaries. This particular group of idioms was selected because it is comparatively easy to trace through the dictionaries, yet may be expected to reveal firm and stable associations of ideas. The number thus brought together was approximately 450. The search for comparable material in Italian and in Arabic was intensified for a smaller number within the group, namely, the idioms which involved the head, face and facial features, by tracing through the dictionaries all the subsidiary words occurring in the idioms; but the additional effort yielded no appreciably different results. In a few instances, I found it necessary to draw on my own acquaintance with Egyptian colloquial Arabic, and to put down as current some idioms that could not be found in printed sources

A further question arises as to whether the Maltese idioms thus collected are not in some measure peculiar to an intelligentsia steeped in Italian or English culture, especially as Fenech illustrates the use of nearly half the idioms in his book by quotations from literary works which may in some instances be the very channel through which these idioms were introduced into the language. But there is in Maltese none of the deep cleavage between the language of literature and the language of everyday speech that we find in Arabic. In fact, Maltese writers show a lively interest in the common concerns and the manners of their compatriots, and they appear faithfully to reflect the speaking habits of the people. Besides the population of Malta is too small and too compact to allow for very extensive variations in usage. Some variations there are nevertheless, as has been pointed out in a study of 'The Lexical Material in Maltese Folklore',[8] and a comparison with idioms extracted solely from folklore – perhaps also of idioms in use among the many Maltese who live or have lived in Arab countries – would be interesting, but for such comparisons there is not, here and now, sufficient material.

It will be recognised, therefore, that such material as we have may be expected to do less than justice to Arab influences, and that any comparison based solely on numbers is subject to obvious reservations.

A fairly representative sample of this material follows. It consists of the idioms relating to the mouth, for which three Maltese words are used: the uncomplimentary *geddum*, literally 'snout'; *fomm*, which is applied mostly to the orifice of the mouth; and *ħalq* to its cavity. The idioms are arranged according to the idea they express. In each instance, the Maltese idiom is followed by a literal English translation and, where the meaning is not immediately clear, by an explanation. Comparable Italian idioms are given on an indented line below, and Arabic ones on another line further indented. For Arabic idioms, a source is indicated wherever possible.[9] If in that source it has been transcribed into Latin characters, the form it has been given is retained.

MALTESE IDIOMS REFERRING TO THE MOUTH

A. Eating, Biting, Swallowing

1. **mimli ħalq**, 'mouthful'

   boccata

   melwı bo>̃>̃uh, etc.

2. **geddumu dejjera fix-xgħir**, 'his snout is always in the barley' (he lives in plenty)

   cf. *mangiare col capo nel sacco*

3. **biskuttini f'halq il-ħmir**, 'sugar-cakes in the mouth of donkeys' (pearls before swine)

4. **tneħħi l-ħobż minn halqek**, 'divert the bread from your mouth' (deny oneself)

   cavarsi (or: *levarsi) il pane di bocca;*

   qadd ma hu kheyyer leqmet le fi temmoh mā hī iluh (Bar), 'he is so generous that the bite that is in his mouth is not for him'.

5. **f'ħalq il-lupu**, 'in the wolf's mouth' (in danger)

   in bocca al lupo

B. Speech

6. **ta' fommu sieket**, 'quiet mouthed'

7. **bil-fomm**, 'with the mouth' (by word of mouth)

   a bocca

   bel-ḥanak (S)

8. **smajtu minn fommu stess**, 'I heard it from his own mouth'

   udire una cosa di bocca (or: *per bocca d'uno*)

   men fommuh (B)

9. **dak li f'qalbek f'fommok**, 'what is in your heart is in your mouth'

   avere sulle labbra (or: *sulla lingua*) *quel che si ha nel cuore*

10. **minn fommok 'l Alla**, 'from your mouth to God' (may your prayer be heard)
    minn fommi 'l barra, 'from my mouth to the outside' (I did not mean what I said)

    cf. *dire ciò che viene alla bocca, aprir bocca e lasciare andare*

    cf. falatet mennī, 'it escaped me'

12. **fommu ta z-zokkor**, 'his mouth is of sugar' (he speaks well)

    cf. *tenere a bocca dolce* (to flatter)

    bo>̃>̃uh bi yna>̃>̃at šahd (A), 'his mouth drips honey' (speaks well)

13. **haġa qiegħda f'ħalqu**, 'something staying in his mouth' (on the tip of his tongue)

14. **ħadlu l-kelma minn ħalqu**, 'he took the word out of his mouth'

    me l'avete levato di bocca

    gazabuh min bo>̃>̃uh

15. **mela** (or: **sadd) ħalqu bl-ilma**, 'he filled his mouth with water' (kept quiet)
    acqua in bocca (mum's the word)

16. **tħit il-ħalq**, 'sew the mouth' (silence someone)
    cucire la bocca

C. Laughter

17. **ċarrat ħalqu**, 'he tore his mouth' (laughed loud and long, esp. in a forced manner)

D. Ill-temper

18. **għamel** (or: **dendel) il-geddum**, 'make the snout' (long face)
    fare il muso, fate grugno
    ṭawwel būzoh, lawā būzoh (S); mbawwez (B)

19. **geddum ta' xiber**, 'snout of a span' (in length)
    baqa' b'xiber geddum, 'remained with a span's length of snout'
    muso lungo un palmo
    būzoh šebrı l->̃uddām

20. **geddum se nieklu l-lejla**, 'it's snout we'll be eating to-night' (said when a member of the company is seen to be in a bad mood)

E. Astonishment

21. **baqa' ħalqu miftuh**, 'he remained open-mouthed'
    rimanere (or: *restare*) *a bocca aperta*

F. Within Reach

22. **taħt geddumu, taħt halqu**, 'under his mouth' (under his nose)
    cf. *sotto il naso, sotto gli occhi*
    cf. >̃uddām būzoh, >̃uddām <enēh

G. Comparison

23. **ħalq il-vopa**, 'mouth of a boops' (said of a large mouth)

It will be readily observed that most of the words used in these as in the other Maltese idioms are of Arabic derivation. Of fifty-eight words for parts of the body which occur in all these idioms, only three are of Italian origin. They are *koxxa*, 'thigh', *mustaċċi*, 'moustaches' and *spalla* with its dual *spallejn*, 'shoulder' – none of them denoting a main part or member, although it is surprising to find the functional *katif* displaced by the Italian *spalla*, especially as a derived form of it occurs in *libsa mkittfa*, 'a tight-fitting dress'. There is also one idiom – *la kap u la kuda*, 'without head or tail' – in which the words for 'head' and 'tail', which elsewhere are always *ras* and *denb*, are given an Italian form.

In idioms, however, they betray a different balance of influences. The figures, for what they are worth, are: out of 257 idioms involving the head or parts of it, sixty-seven can, on the strength of their exact wording or of the figure of speech they express, be matched with idioms both in Arabic and Italian; seventy-five have equivalents in Italian only; and fifteen in Arabic only.

This leaves 100 for which no recognisable matches have been found. Most of these may be presumed to be of native origin; indeed, some of them are demonstrably so because of their local or historical associations. Thus, of a shameless person, 'stone-faced' in the sense that he has none of the mobility of expression that may be taken to denote a sensitive nature, the Maltese say: *Għandu wiċċ l-għatba tal-Kistlanija*, that is, 'he has the face of the door-step of the Castellania', this being a public building (at one time a court) in Valletta. And of a morose person, a kill-joy, one says *Wiċċ Laskri*; the reference being to Jean Paul Lascaris, Grand Master of the ruling Order from 1636 to 1657, and it illustrates how long-lived these idioms can be. Similarly, the Maltese version of 'heads or tails', *wiċċ jew Reġina* (literally: face or queen) – a variant of which has 'queen' in the plural, that is, *irġejjen* – is explained by Fenech as relevant to the English penny, the 'face' being that of the monarch on the obverse, and the 'queen' being the figure of Britannia on the reverse. Also presumably native is an idiom in which a word of Italian origin is used to rhyme with one of Arab origin; it is *Mutu mutu u qrunu f'butu* (silent, silent, but with his horns in his pocket), used in much the same sense as 'Still waters run deep'.

Prominent among these unidentified idioms are simple metaphors associated with the sea. A large mouth is said to be *ħalq il-vopa* – the mouth of a boops, which is a kind of fish. To a drunk with blood-shot eyes, the Maltese apply the cry with which the fishmonger advertises the freshness of his wares: *Għajnu ħamra t-tonn*, 'its eye is red, the tunny'. Of a forgetful person, they say *Moħħu żurżieqa*, 'his brain is a slip-way', and of one with a retentive memory *għajnejh sponża*, 'his eyes are a sponge'. And of a person of small intelligence, whereas an Italian will emphasise the smallness by speaking of 'the brain of an ant', *cervello di formica*, and an Arab of that of a bird, *>aḥlām al-<aṣāfīr*, a Maltese will say *moħħu daqs imħara*, 'his brain is the size of a limpet'.

A somewhat more elaborate example of the same is *Il-qarnita daret għal subgħajha*, 'the octopus turned on its own fingers' for 'to rely on oneself, to fall back on one's own resources'.

The Italian influence throughout is as massive and as obvious as in the samples given above. Many indeed are the Maltese and Italian idioms which have not only distinctive images and associations in common, but in which the Maltese closely follows the wording of the Italian, for example, 'to have one foot *in* the grave', *għandu siequ waħda fil-ħofra*, avére un piede entro la fossa; 'to touch the sky with one's finger' for to attain something highly desirable, *tmiss is-sema b'subgħajk*, toccare il cielo col dito; or 'one *hand* washes the other and both of them wash the face', that is, to be of mutual assistance, *id taħsel l-oħra u t-tnejn jaħslu l-wiċċ*, 'una mano lava l'altra, e le due lavano il viso'. Many also are those in which the turn of the phrase is so peculiar that it cannot be ascribed to a coincidence of thought: for example, *Jiekol minn fuq ras xi ħadd*, 'to eat off the top of someone's head', which like the Italian 'mangiare la torta in capo ad uno' means 'to be taller than, to stand head and shoulders above somebody'. An idiom may even be an allusion to an Italian proverb that has passed into Maltese: for example, 'to wash the donkey's head', *jaħsel ras il-ħmar*, is not immediately intelligible unless it is associated with the saying *chi lava il capo all'asino perde il ranno e il sapone*, 'he who washes the donkey's head wastes both suds and soap'.

One group of such idioms which should be isolated is that which springs from the common faith of the Maltese and the Italians. Some of these are taken out of the Bible, for example, to wash one's hands of an affair is *jaħsel idejh*, and of a hand all too ready to use violence one says *donnha id Malku*, 'as if it were Malchus's hand', for the Malchus who is mentioned in John 18:10 as having had his ear cut off by Peter is also held to be the man who struck Jesus for answering the high priest disrespectfully (John 18:22). Other idioms reflect tenets and practices of the Catholic Church, for example, someone anxiously awaiting something is said to be 'like a soul in Purgatory', *bħal ruħ tal-Purgatorju*, and to make a fresh start is 'to turn the cross over on its face', *radd is-salib għal wiċċu.*

Not surprisingly, there is not a single distinctively Qur>anic echo in Maltese usage, although 'to make someone pass through the eye of a needle', *għaddieh minn għajn il-labra*, which is used in Maltese for 'to dupe someone by a trick that would be obvious to most', recalls a phrase which occurs in Qur>ān (7:38) as well as in the New Testament. It has already been observed by T. Sabbagh,[10] however, that Qur>anic imagery relating to parts of the body is colourless and unexciting, consisting mostly of obvious metonymies.

Evidence of distinctive Arab influence is quite rare. Indeed, the longstanding enmity of the Maltese to the Muslims is reflected in the expression *wiċċ ta' Fatma* for an ugly face – a somewhat cruder and more unkind cut than Shakespeare's 'gipsy brow'. Similarly, if we allow ourselves to stray from the particular group of idioms under examination, we find that *X'it-Torok trid?*, 'What the Turks do you want?', is a close parallel of 'What the devil do you want?' The compliment is, of course, returned, for the Arabic equivalent of 'to waste one's breath' is *yeđđan fe Mālṭah*, 'to sound the (Muslim) call to prayer in Malta'.

It is also noticeable that some associations that are strong in Arabic usage – such as that of the beard with honour and self-respect – are absent from Maltese, for though the Maltese do say of a person or even a thing worthy of esteem that he or it is *bil-mustaċċi*, 'with whiskers', this is precisely the Italian, *coi mustacchi* or *co' baffi* with all its overtones.

The associations that *are* traceable to Arabic usage call for closer examination.

An intriguing idiom is: *Mela jien ta' Buleben?*, literally: 'What! Am I of Buleben?' or rather, more freely translated: 'Do you take me for a Buleben?', that is, 'for a rich man?'. Now the word *leben* is not in use among the Maltese, for in accordance with colloquial practice in virtually all Arab countries except Egypt, Arabs say *ħalib* for 'milk'. The idiom itself appears to be used without awareness of its literal meaning. Fenech baldly asserts in explanation that there was once a very rich family called Buleben, but this is much too facile a surmise, and one for which there does not appear to be any supporting evidence. A literal rendering on the basis of the Arabic suggests that the idea behind it is 'Do you take me for someone that can be milked?'. The variant *Mela ħsibtni li għandi ta' Buleben?*, 'Do you think that I own as much as a Buleben?' further makes it possible to interpret *Buleben* as 'owner of [flocks that produce] milk', that is, 'a rich man'. This would be entirely satisfying were it not that the term *abu laban* is in use in Egypt, where it is taken to be quite offensive, although I was never able to ascertain its meaning even from people who used it. Possibly *leben* here is a euphemism for 'seminal fluid', as it is in the Italian *latte di pesce.* At all events, the obscurity argues for a lengthy history, for it is unlikely – though not inconceivable – that the idiom gained currency while its meaning was indefinite.[11]

There are, of course, clearer and more striking examples of parallelism with Arabic, although it is not contended that these necessarily date back very far. For example, *kiellu wiċċu,*'he ate his face', for to berate someone is exactly matched by *kal wishshuh* (T), and the curious *ħoll xagħrek u ġib iż-żejt*, 'undo your hair and bring the oil', which means 'Do what you intend to do and take the consequences', recalls in part the Arabic *meši* (or: *dāyir)*, '*alā ḥallı ša<ruh* (A) 'going about with his hair undone' for 'doing as he pleases'.

As may be expected, it is in connection with the eye – an organ particularly precious to the Arab – that we find the largest number of contributions to Maltese usage. *Mela għajnu b'xi ħaġa*, 'he filled his eye with a certain thing', that is, was greatly impressed by it – is closely matched by *ma yimlāsb el-'ēn* (S), 'he does not inspire respect'. *Mar għal għajnu*, 'he went (that is, stepped?) on his eye', used in the sense of 'it went badly with him', is common in Arabic in the form of an imprecation: *Xallīh yerūḥ <alā <ēnuh.*[12] *Ma f' għajnu xejn minnu*, 'there is nothing of him in his eye', that is, he disapproves of him, recalls the Arabic *fe <ēnuh* (B) for 'in his good graces'. *Ksir il-għajn*, 'the breaking of the eye', that is, an annoyance, is fairly close to *kasar <ēnuh* (S), 'he humbled him'. Finally, *xortih m'għajnu*, 'his luck is with his eye', that is, is favourable, is matched by š*eyy <alā <ēnuh* (Bar) for 'something to his taste, according to his wishes'.

One also finds interesting associations between congeniality and the blood. In Italian, a person who takes a dislike to another is said 'not to have his blood with him', *non avere il suo sangue con alcuno.* In Arabic, however, it is the intrinsic quality of likeability or its opposite that is expressed in terms of 'light' or 'heavy' blood – *dammı xafīf* and *dammı te>īl* – and there are many elaborations on these, such as *dammuh zey rīš en-na<ām*, 'his blood is like ostrich feathers', *dammuh yiṭarraš*, 'his blood makes one vomit', *dammuh zeyy es-semm*, 'his blood is like poison', or *dammuh yā b ạ̄y*, 'his blood – oh my father!'. Maltese idioms reflect both usages. Expressing dislike are: the somewhat puzzling *ħadu fuq demm id-dars*, 'he took him on the blood of the molar' and *m'għandux demm ma'xi ħadd*, 'he has no blood with a certain person'. Reminiscent of the Arabic is *bniedem demmu jsawtek*, 'a man whose blood scourges you'.

It may well be that here the two sources have enough in common to bolster each other, as presumably they do in the considerable number of idioms that are common to all three languages.

Some of these common idioms are almost inevitable metonymies – such as the usage of 'tongue' for 'speech', of 'brain' for 'intelligence', and so on – for which no indebtedness need be recorded; the others are the result of a widespread interpenetration of ideas.

In some instances, however, it is possible to link the Maltese idioms belonging to this group more closely with one source rather than the other on the strength of some artifice or peculiarity of wording.

Thus, the Maltese form of 'without head or tail', *la kap u la kuda*, has counterparts in Arabic as well as in Italian: *lā rās we lā deneb* (Bar) and *lā rās we lā sās* (B); but the choice of two alliterative and comparatively uncommon words of Italian origin leaves little doubt as to its paternity.

Conversely, a Maltese idiom which makes prominent use of two rhyming words of Arabic origin might have been presumed to be of Arab inspiration, the more so as the rhyme is not a common adornment of these idioms; but so far little direct evidence has been found to support this presumption. The most striking examples are two sayings in which *laħma*, 'flesh' and *għadma*, 'bone' are used antithetically to signify what is desirable and what is undesirable, in much the same way as are the rose and the thorn in English: *min jiekol il-laħma jiekol il-għadma*, 'he who eats the meat must eat the bone', and *daqqa tmissna l'għadma u oħra l-laħma*, 'sometimes we get the bone, sometimes the meat'; yet so far it is only in Italian that the same antithesis has been found: *volere la carne senza l'osso*, 'to want the meat without the bone'. Similarly, there is nothing to show that *żamm ilsienu bejn snienu*, 'he put his tongue between his teeth, that is, 'he held his tongue' is not a native elaboration of *frenare la lingua or mordersi la lingua.* Yet another idiom, *geddumu dejjem fix-xgħir*, which has been mentioned earlier, is related to a proverb: *geddumu fix-xgħir, nesa meta kien fqir*, 'his snout being in barley, he has forgotten when he was poor'; here again the rhyme suggests an Arabic original, the more so as it is perfect in an Arabic pronunciation of the rhyming words *ša<īr* and *faqīr*, but not in modern Maltese where the *ayn* is only a colouring of the 'a' and thus forms a diphthong with the 'i' – yet no such original has been found. In fact, the rhyme has been a surprisingly poor criterion of an Arab connection.

Finally, there is one instance in which identical phrases convey different meanings to Italians and to Arabs. 'To make someone's face red' to an Italian means to make him ashamed. In North Africa, according to Beaussier, it means exactly the opposite, and to shame a person is to make his face yellow, *ṣaffar luh wajhuh.*

Here again, as everything else has led us to expect, the Maltese follow Italian usage. Behind the North African idioms, which seem to run counter to physiological fact, may lie the association – stronger perhaps among a generally sallow people – of a florid complexion with well-being. If so, it may not be irrelevant to add that the Maltese describe a bright, attractive complexion as *wiċċ itajjar in-nar*, '*a* face that sends out fire', even as the North African says of someone of high reputation that 'his face is hot', *wajhuh ḥāmī* (B); so when a Maltese says of a girl *ma'wiċċha tixgħel sulfarina*, 'from her face you can light a match', he is being complimentary, and not comparing her skin to the side of a match-box.

From all this, there may be none but the most obvious and superficial conclusions to be drawn. But perhaps enough has been said to show that idioms – and not Maltese idioms alone – providing as they do collocations and recurring contexts for words, reflect the thinking habits of a people in ways it would not be unprofitable to explore.

Notes

1. Arabists need to know that in Maltese orthography ش is transliterated as 'x'; ح and خ are both pronounced as ح and written as 'ħ'; and ع and غ are both reduced to a colouring of the accompanying vowel and are written as 'għ'. Three other letters of the alphabet appear with dots above: ċ, ġ and ż; they stand, respectively, for ch as in church, j as in jar and z as in zest, whereas the undotted z is sounded as ts in bits.
2. See 'The Fisherman's Son', in *Maltese Anthology,* ed. A. Arberry (Oxford, 1960), p. 26.
3. >Aḥmad Fāris aš-Šidyāq, *al-Wāsiṭah fī Ma<rifat >Aḥwāl Māliṭah* (Istanbul, 1299 AH), p. 17.
4. G. Aquilina, 'Maltese as a Mixed Language', *Journal of Semitic Studies*, 3, 1 (January 1958), p. 63.
5. A. McIntosh, 'The Problem of Language and Literature', lecture delivered to the Ninth Annual Conference of Non-Professorial University Teachers of English, Wadham College, Oxford, 4 April 1959.
6. *Lingua*, 7, 1 (November 1957), pp. 30–45.
7. *al-Kināyāt al-<Āmmiyyah* (Cairo, n.d.).
8. J. Aquilina and J. Cassar Pullicino, *Journal of the Faculty of Arts of the Royal University of Malta*, 1, 1 (1957), pp. 1–36.
9. For these, the following symbols are used throughout: A: >Aḥmad >Amīn, *Qmūs al-<ādāt wa t-taqālīd wat-ta<ābīr al-miṣriyyab* (Cairo, 1953); B: M. Beaussier, *Dictionnaire Pratique Arabe–Français* (Algiers, 1887); Bar: A. Barthélémy, *Dictionnaire Arabe–Français* (Paris, 1935–1954); S: S. Spiro, *Arabic–English Dictionary* (Cairo, 1923); and T: Aḥmad Taymūr, *al-Kināyāt al-<Āmmiyyah* (Cairo, n.d.).
10. *La Métaphore dans le Coran* (Paris, 1943), pp. 137–8.
11. Cf. the use of 'to kick up a shindy' by Americans and others who have never known the old Scottish game of shinty, but who interpret the word – colourfully, though spuriously – as 'shindig', that is, 'rowdy dance'.
12. Cf. *<ēnuh bḥāfruh* as explained by Barthélémy: 'Que son œil soit à son sabot! (afin qu'il marche dessus et perde la vue).'

B. A Curious Maltese Variant of an Arabic Proverb[1]

A rich mine of information long exploited by Maltese scholars is the Maltese–Italian four-volume dictionary compiled in the middle of the eighteenth century by Revd Agius de Soldanis, as yet unpublished but available in MS in Malta's National Library.[2] Its full bilingual title, couched in the somewhat erratic Italianate spelling of the time and reflecting the now exploded theory that Maltese was a Punic language rather than an outgrowth of Arabic, reads:[3]

> Damma tal Kliem Kartaginis I Mscerred fel Fom tal Maltin u/Ghaucin/Maghmula/mel Kanoniku Gianfrangesku Agius Ghauci/Sultana/Raccolta/delle Parole Cartaginesi/ sparse nella Lingua de'Maltesi e Gozitani/I Fatta/dal Canonico Gio. Francesco Agius de Soldanis/Gozitano.

It is, indeed, a painstakingly assembled collection and is all the more valuable for embodying also a great many proverbs and idioms and much other incidental information.

On folio 314 v° of volume I, we find the following three successive entries under the letter 'K':[4]

> *Kordien il p. dal n.s. Kordiena v. Kordiena*
> *In Prov. el Kordien f-scafar ghanein ommu iedher ghazziel ——*
> *nella punta della palpebra di sua madre, sembra Filatore*
> *Kordiena n.s.f. ——*

The word *Kordien* is thus described as the plural of *Kordiena*, although it is actually a collective noun from which the *nomen unitatis* is formed. The reader is then referred to this so-called singular, but no meaning is assigned to it. In between, *Kordien* is recorded as occurring in a proverb, where, however, it appears to be used as a singular, and once again the word is left untranslated.

The blanks are puzzling, for the word is a common one in modern Maltese and means 'a tike', or 'tick'. One can only surmise that de Soldanis' hesitancy was over the precise Italian equivalent to adopt.

The proverb may therefore be transcribed according to present Maltese orthography as: *Il-qurdien fi xfar għajnejn ommu jidher għażżiel.* Its literal translation is: 'The tick on its mother's eyelids appears to be a spinner', de Soldanis' addition of 'at the point of' being unjustified. The proverb is no longer in currency, and its exact application is therefore conjectural, but the implication seems clear that in certain circumstances a creature might appear to be better than it really is.

All the words in this proverb have readily identifiable Arabic originals. These may be transcribed as follows (without any attempt to relate them syntactically):

al-qurrād (pl. *qirdān*)–*fī*–>*ašfār* –<*aynayn*–>*ummuh*–*taẓhar*–*x̱azzāl*

16

Social Values Reflected in Egyptian Popular Ballads

My subject needs to be approached with much circumspection. The whole of Arabic popular literature has suffered not only from neglect, but also from contempt; and now that a handful of scholars have turned their attention to it, some significant issues are being obscured rather than clarified by premature theorising, in which selected facts are made to fit into a preformed frame of literary or social reference. Yet the more closely one looks at this literature with its great diversity and many ramifications, the more difficult it becomes to formulate its distinctive features or delimit its true territory.

In the hope of establishing a reasonably firm foothold, and because I am all too aware of my handicap in trying to study such a subject from a distance, I have limited myself severely to a comparatively small but easily definable genre within popular literature, namely, the narrative told entirely in song or verse, to the exclusion even of such epic cycles as the Hilālī stories that are partly in prose.

The evidence I have come across regarding the origination and transmission of the texts is far from clear-cut or uniform. For the art is indeed practised by men and women who conform with the conventional image of the wandering minstrel carrying songs part remembered and part improvised from one rural festival to another. But there are also men of some education and who may be city-based who are better at composing pen in hand than they are at singing; these may sell their compositions directly to singers (one of them, Azhar-trained Muṣṭafā >Ibrāhīm <Ajāj,[1] has been known to deliver an *ijāza* in time-honoured fashion to whoever memorised 200 quires of his work), or they may publish them in cheaply printed booklets. Yet if – as does happen – their names are held in reverence by the itinerant singers and some of their compositions are remembered a generation after their death, is it not arbitrary to exclude them from the canon of popular literature? It is reasonable to assume that the heart of this literature is in the countryside rather than the city, but how strongly is the contrast to be made? The itinerant singers who travel from one *mūlid* to another do not give the city a miss. Indeed, the most popular – or the greediest – of them find it rewarding to give regular performances throughout Ramadan in cafés or specially erected pavilions in the vicinity of the Ḥusaynī mosque in Cairo. But there they may find themselves next to a state-sponsored group using the same art forms to put forth political propaganda. The more fortunate of the popular singers may themselves receive state patronage. They may also be invited to cut a record or appear on television where they have to adapt to unaccustomed conditions if only

to fit in with a strict timetable. What do they take back to the countryside from these city experiences? Without a wealth of material recorded over a long period, how are we to judge the nature of the changes that are brought about? And if the changes are significant, how are we – without prejudging what may be important issues – to determine whether they amount to a new development in a living art or the corruption of a once pure tradition?

There are issues here that affect the admissibility of some texts as social documents representative of the way of thinking of one social group or another – more issues, in fact, than we can examine in detail here. For my part, I find that nothing concerning popular literature comes closer to being definable than the kind of audience it attracts: villagers of any status, but also town people who have had either a traditional type of education, or very little formal education at all; the hallmark of the overwhelming majority of them is the wearing of the *gallabiyya.* My inclination is therefore to accept as genuinely popular any composition, no matter what its provenance may be, that proves acceptable to such an audience by remaining current for, say, a generation. This criterion has the disadvantage (among others) that it debars us from making any but the most provisional assessments of the contemporary scene. It may also be radically unacceptable to other participants in this colloquium, so I shall make a point of indicating which of the texts I refer to do *not* come from the lips of provincial singers. Finally, it need scarcely be said that no one individual – least of all one who is no longer resident in Egypt – can claim to have anything like a comprehensive view of a literature which is largely oral and on which much fundamental work is yet to be done.

With these many reservations in mind, let me turn to the ballads I happen to know, and set out as objectively as possible the standards that they – and they alone – reveal as governing social relationships. We shall have to read between the lines, for there is very little explicit moralising or philosophising in these stories. I have come across a fable in an undated lithographed booklet in which a bird caught in a net pleads with the hunter to be spared,[2] promising to give him in return three valuable gems. When he is released, he tells his generous captor that the three gems are the letters *ṭa mīm <ayn* which spell out ‘greed’; and very valuable they are since it is to the hunter’s greed that the bird owes its life. But fables are remarkably rare in this type of composition. By far the commonest are embroideries on Qur>anic stories, legends concerning the Prophet and his Companions, and stories of local saints. Not so numerous, but apparently at least as popular, are chronicles of contemporary emotive events, such as honour crimes or vendettas. In stories with a religious tinge, the obvious moral is often drawn that God’s will is not flouted with impunity. In contemporary ones, when the hero’s fortunes are at ebb there are equally conventional reflections on the fickleness of fate and the instability of life. But for the most part, the point is made by the story itself and the artistry of the storyteller.

Let us start with what is expected of the individual before moving to wider and wider circles of involvement.

The behaviour most commonly celebrated is that of the man of honour and unlimited physical courage, ready to spring into instant action to avenge a wrong done to him or his, pursuing his purpose with unflinching determination and utterly reckless of the cost. L-Adham eš-Šar>āwī has only to hear that his uncle has been murdered – the reason is not even disclosed – and he embarks on a series of revenge killings that pit him against the authorities and end in his death.[3] In the very popular story of 'Šafī>ah we Metwalli' or 'el-ḥadša l-Girgawiyyah' the moment Metwalli is taunted with having a sister who has become a prostitute, he must set out to hunt her down and butcher her.[4] In 'Bardanōha' which tells of a vendetta between Muslims and Copts that came to a head in 1942,[5] we see the scorn with which compromise is regarded when the Muslim *<umda* instead of avenging his cousin's death obtains Egyptian £300 compensation for him and offers the money to the victim's daughter.

> The girl took it and said, <Umda, may you live!
> And you, my father's uncle, may you live!
> And you my father's son!
> Here is your money thrown on the ground.
> May all the men live on!
> Because you have become women, shall I sell him to eat bread?'

It is then the victim's maternal uncle, not a fellow-villager but a Bedouin, who exacts a multiple revenge, for he has no compunction about shooting not only several members of the guilty family, but also their chauffeur and an innocent bystander who may prove to be an awkward eyewitness.

There are comparatively few stories with love as the central theme. In these, both male and female beauty are admiringly described. Not surprisingly, there are manifestations of the universal double standard, for a man is sometimes shown boasting of his prowess as a seducer. But resistance to sexual temptation on the man's part is respected if not always expected. This is hardly surprising in the story of Joseph, as published by Muṣṭafā >Ibrāhīm <Ajāj, which follows the Qur>anic narrative but also adds that Joseph eventually married Potiphar's wife after she was widowed, and had several children by her. It is equally obvious in the contemporary story of 'Ḥasan we Na<īma'.[6] Here it is Na<īma who is said to have fallen in love with Ḥasan, and – in a version by >Ibrāhīm Sulaymān iš-Šēx – when her father refuses to marry her to him she goes to his house unbidden; but though she remains there for a fortnight, Ḥasan is careful to spend his time in a café that all may see he is not with her, and when her father comes for her Ḥasan calls in a police officer and a doctor to certify that she is still a virgin. Certainly, of a woman nothing less than the strictest chastity is expected. Thus, in the story of the saintly X̲arīb,[7] as his widowed mother is sailing from the Hijaz back to Egypt, she rouses the lust of the ship's captain but she lets him carry out the threat of throwing her child into the sea rather than submit to him. In fact, the sex-drive features in these ballads more commonly as a threat to honour than in its own right.

Most of the ballads are thus concerned with elemental human forces operating within a framework of long-established and virtually unquestioned priorities. Not one of the stories hinges on an inner conflict, on a choice between two honourable obligations or two painful courses of action. It seems to be assumed that in any situation the right course will be immediately and glaringly obvious to the hero, to the narrator, to the audience, to any right-thinking, noble-minded person. In stories with a contemporary setting especially, the character of the wise counsellor, the elderly spiritual mentor, is noticeably absent. Suspense and tension are created entirely by the obstructions that bar the hero's path and make the pursuit of the right course costly.

But the consensus thus implied is a consensus of opinion only. To judge by these ballads, it was only in the halcyon days of the Prophet and his Companions that men vied with one another in noble and generous behaviour. Our own times are out of joint, and it is anyone's cursed spite to find himself in a position demanding that he set it right. It is very much part of the hero's image that he should safeguard his interests and honour himself by his own valour. He may espouse the cause of the weak and oppressed – as the political leader Muṣṭafā Kāmil is portrayed as doing, springing to the defence of the victims of Danšawāy;[8] – but he himself is never shown to appeal to any constituted authority – not, say, to a council of elders or to any organ of the state; indeed, it does not greatly trouble him if he falls foul of such authorities as did l-Adham eš-Šar>āwī and Metwalli. For if, as we have seen, it is assumed that what is right is self-evident, it is not inconsistent also to assume that it is open to anybody to see to it that the right is made to triumph.

It is also in keeping with this black-and-white view that anyone who refuses to conform with the unwritten code places himself entirely beyond the pale; and the hero who has appointed himself judge, jury and executioner can treat him and even those incidentally associated with them with unmitigated ferocity. There was no limit to the number of unbelievers that such early champions of Islam as <Alī or Ḍirār could put to the sword. In a printed story, we are told of a Bedouin who bred a camel specially to take him to see the Prophet – but on his way to Medina he has the misguided kindness to share his mount with three villains described as 'Christian Jews',[9] one of whom claims the camel as his own and produces the other two as witnesses, so that the Prophet is about to judge in his favour when the camel speaks out the truth; for what is no more than an attempted fraud, the Prophet orders the three Christian Jews to be burnt. L-Adham eš-Šar>āwī takes not one life but several in revenge. As for Metwalli, when he has traced his sister to a brothel he not only slaughters her, but in one version cuts her up and throws the pieces from the balcony for the street dogs to eat.

It remains to be said that it is not only to violent confrontation that the hero may resort. He is also admired for successful ruses and dissimulation, even in circumstances that might have been considered undignified. Thus, l-Adham eš–Šar>āwī in dealing with the police uses ambiguous phrases that mislead without actually telling a literal untruth, and he dresses now as a woman and now as a European. Similarly, the police officer who tracks down the murderers in 'Ḥasan we Na<īma' goes to great lengths to disguise himself as a woman, epilating himself and carrying about everywhere an infant that he has borrowed from an orphanage.

Treachery, on the other hand, is the most heinous mark of villainy. It is almost a convention of the modern stories that, although the prime motive of dark and evil plots may be revenge or envy, they involve suborning close relatives of the victim. Ḥasan in 'Ḥasan we Na<īma' and Ḥesēn in the story of 'Bardanōha' are both led to their death by cousins who have yielded to money bribes.

It will already be apparent that these ballads focus on individuals, and tend to speak of good or evil forces in terms of the moral qualities or failings of these individuals; but it will be no less apparent that the most binding obligations by which the individual is tested arise from blood relationships. If a connecting link is needed, it probably lies in the strong belief not only that qualities are transmitted from generation to generation by dint both of upbringing and of heredity, but also that children may be tainted by their parents' sins. So it is that in 'Bardanōha' Ḥesēn is described as 'having been brought up by his father and having drunk of his mother's milk', whereas the kinsmen who betray him draw the comment: 'By God, one who connives at his cousin's murder must have a mother who strayed.' So it is also that none of the stories of 'honour crimes' are concerned with a cuckolded husband: when a woman errs, it is her father and her brothers who are shamed. Part of Metwalli's dialogue with the judge who asks him why he has killed his sister is instructive in this respect:

> He answered: If you had a tree whose root had cracked a house,
> Which cast its fruit outside, but had its roots in the house,
> Its benefit outside, but bringing shame to the girl –
> Would you, I wonder, cut off the roots, or remain disgraced by your decision?
> He said: 'I should hasten, Metwalli, and fetch a saw;
> I'd fetch an able carpenter with his axe drawn.'
> He said: 'This is why the crime was committed and the shame incurred.'

One story, that of 'Ḥasan we Na<īma', has a number of features that run counter to the general trend, and as such deserve a closer look. The facts on which the story is based are these: Ḥasan was a professional popular singer; Na<īma fell in love with him; and – at least in her father's eyes – compromised herself with him. With the connivance of his son, the father had the young man killed – and this is in itself a most unusual departure from the rule that it is in the woman's blood that family honour has to be washed. Finally, the murderers were tracked down by the police, and imprisoned. Needless to say, the story is handled in different manners by different ballad-mongers. The version by iš-Šēx ends rather cynically:

> So Na<īma alone was left in the house.
> Her menfolk had perished, all because of her –

For a woman can lay a town to ruins and she alone survive,
Boasting: 'By guile against the best of men I have prevailed.'
(For Iblīs has tempted her and she has spread evil about her) –
'Ḥasan is gone, I shall surely love another.'
His mother is grieved and alone weeps over him
Whereas his loved one cares nothing for him.
Consider the omens and what they forecast, deluded one:
Excellent homes are ruined that once were prosperous.
What shall I write, what shall I say, O listener?
All our misfortunes come to us from women.

But another version – by Šawqī l-Qināwī – treats the lovers much more sympathetically, deriving its effects from the pathos of their situation. Certainly, Ḥasan is represented, as I have already mentioned, as strictly honourable in his intentions, refusing to take advantage of Na<īma's virtual offer of herself. But her brazenness is also passed off without a hint of disapproval. Even more startling is her triumph at the end, for when a zealous police officer has discovered the identity of the murderers,

Na<īma trilled with joy and said: 'Thank God I've found a man in the Government!'
He took her to the Prosecution to tell the story of Ḥasan the Singer,
And when she had told the story before the examining magistrate,
He was pleased with Na<īma and asked, 'What sentence shall we pass on the wanted men?
Ten years for each?'
She ripped her shirts and the magistrate stopped and said:
'Don't be upset – you pass whatever sentence you think fit.'

At the trial, she heightens the emotional tension by producing the severed head of her lover, ensures that heavy sentences are passed on her menfolk, and, again at her suggestion, the judge arranges for her to live thereafter under the protection of Ḥasan's father.

It can only add to one's puzzlement to note that the illiberal version comes from the pen of a Cairene writer, and the one that pits daughter against father from the lips of an Upper Egyptian singer. Have we here the first drum-rolls of a women's liberation movement deep in the Egyptian countryside? Or was prejudice turned round in this one case because the murder victim was himself a singer, whose offer of marriage was superciliously turned down precisely because he belonged to that despised confraternity? Is it simply that the artist realised how more effectively his story could be told if sympathies were heavily engaged on the side of the star-crossed victims? At all events, one must note that there is among the common people a sufficient fund of basic human compassion to make it possible for the story of a wayward and tragic love to be presented in this unconventional fashion.

One has to peer unexpectedly hard to catch glimpses of the wider community of which the family is a part. It is a far from egalitarian society. There are frequent references to the power of money to corrupt, to turn the heads of young girls and to buy the services of unprincipled men ready to lead their kinsmen into a death-trap. There is also a clear sense of grievance in ‘Bardanōha’ where it is asserted that the Government appointed a headman over the Copts and another over the Muslims, yet gave the Copt much greater allowances than it did to his Muslim colleague. But except in such an obvious case involving direct remuneration, it is in keeping with the tendency we have already noted of reducing issues to matters of personal morality that the power of money is seen as a temptation for the honourable individual to resist – as did the daughter of the murder victim in ‘Bardanōha’ – rather than as a tool or gauge of social justice.

In fact, three types of men are spoken of without recrimination as enjoying positions of prestige or privilege. The first is the landowner, apparently not only because he is wealthy but also because he is a stable member of the community. It is surely significant that the wandering minstrels themselves, whose rootlessness exposes them to contempt, seem to accept the prejudice as a matter of course. Thus, in al-Qināwī’s ‘Ḥasan we Na<īma’ when the girl’s father tries to trace her to the singer’s native village of Bahnasa l-Xarrah

> A regular watchman met him outside the village,
> And he said: ‘Come, watchman, lead me to the singer’s house.’
> The watchman flared at him saying: ‘Watch your tongue, Uncle!
> He is no singer. His father has 45 acres to his name
> And his father is headman of Bahnasa l-Xarrah.’

Lineage is also deemed worthy of special regard, and ought to set one above menial labour. In the ballad of ‘Xarīb’ we are told the story of the saint’s father, a descendant of the Prophet, in the following terms:

> The *šarīf’s* wealth was stolen – such is the judgement of Fate, what a shame.’
> So he said to himself: ‘Idleness has weakened my body and made me powerless.
> I must seek any means to live by and eat.
> Poverty is an ill thing, a condition that confuses the clear-minded.’
> So he took up with some people who had no basis and no standing.
> They made him carry stones. They were gypsies, of course.

They demeaned a venerable *šarīf* whose ancestry and appearance went back to the Prophet.

Finally, the ungrudging admiration with which the bold and fearsome strong-arm man is regarded seems to stretch into an equally ungrudging acceptance that he is entitled to what he grabs for himself. In ‘Bardanōha’, Ḥesēn of whom it has already been said that he had the qualities expected of one who has had a sound upbringing in a good family,

> Became notorious, recruiting watchmen by force,
> And when notorious he returned to the village and exacted a toll from it.

To lead him into an ambush, his cousins suggest a raid on the cereals-yard, which, like poaching or tax evasion in some Western milieus, seems to be regarded as a sport rather than a crime. He does raise an objection:

> He said: 'We have reached a higher status than to go stealing cereals.
> I have in there eighty ardebs out of our own crop.
> If it is greed that moves you, what is there is no small thing, but plenty.'

But having thus established that it is not greed that drives him, he has only to be taunted with being afraid and he readily embarks on the adventure.

All this may be seen as passive recognition of conditions that have obtained in the countryside for hundreds of years. As for the big city, it looms only in the distance, as it were, exerting the kind of attraction that sophistication has perhaps always held for country folk. So a singer recorded in an oasis in the Western desert who admitted that he had never travelled to the Nile valley nevertheless had a stock of ready-made lines in which Cairo street names were used as rhyme words; and in his version of the Metwalli story, the hero – ostensibly ogling girls, although really searching for his sister – calls out to one of them, promising her 'sweetmeats from Groppi', a luxurious tearoom in Cairo. Sometimes, even titbits of Western lore percolate in unexpected places. In yet another version of the same story, the prostitute is shown entertaining her brother who is in disguise, and she pours out for him *wiski <ala >uṭār*. I was puzzled by this *>uṭār*, but the singer explained to me that 'drink' came in three qualities: the best was in triangular bottles and was called *inzi*; the middle quality was in square bottles and was called *>īg*; and the cheapest and worst came in round bottles and was called *>uṭār*. More familiar with the shape of bottles than with their content, he was favouring Hennessy cognac over Haig whiskey or Otard cognac. Clearly, all this is in the nature of name-dropping; it indicates that there is some prestige in being able to claim acquaintance with city life, but of the penetration of urban or modernistic values there are very few signs indeed.

The agencies of the modern state feature as hazards rather than as positive forces in the life of the people catered for by this literature. It is all too clear that the law of the land carries moral weight only insofar as it coincides with the traditional mores. A police officer may be praised if he furthers the action along desired lines as in al-Qināwī's 'Ḥasan we Na<īma', although here too the praise is in terms of his personal qualities and almost with a hint of surprise – 'Thank God I've found a man in the Government,' is Na<īma's cry. But where there is a clash the fact may be distorted – for example, Metwalli's judge is said to have praised him, released him and confirmed him in his army rank, whereas in reality he was imprisoned – or else the authority of the state is treated as if to fall foul of it was inconvenient rather than reprehensible. L-Adham eš-Šar>̃āwī is neither shamed nor broken by being sent to prison; on the contrary, he defiantly carries on with his vendetta within the prison, dismembering yet another of his enemies under the nose of the authorities; then

> The Government came asking: 'Why did you do this, Adham?'
> He replied: 'What a dead loss of a government you are!
> What did you do when my uncle was killed?
> And here I have killed, O Government, while I was in your own gaol!'

In 'Bardanōha' there is even a hint that those who are prepared to drag the authorities into other people's feuds almost deserve what is coming to them, for when the revenge killings against the family of the Coptic <*umda* have taken place,

> A hundred pities for the ill-luck of a peasant by the canal, returning from his field.
> He said: 'I saw you, who were shooting at the <*umda*.'
> Maḥmūud replied: 'Man, you were going about your business; what concern have you with šēx or <*umda?*'
> He made straight for him and fired a single shot,
> And Ḥesēn's uncle made straight for his head with the rifle butt,
> Saying: 'If you have children orphaned, let the <*umda* settle your account.'

Of course, that same ballad makes open accusations of massive government partiality to the Copts, for not only is the Coptic <*umda* shown to have had preferential treatment from the start, but after his murder Makram <Ubayd, who was Minister of Finance at the time, is said to have presented to the king a plea for exemplary punishment.

> The King took the request and referred it to the master of exalted knowledge, His Majesty the King referred it to the Head of Islam. And the Head of Islam referred it to Naḥḥās.
> When Naḥḥās looked at the papers and saw Makram <Ebēd's signature, calamity was set in motion.
> There was a Christian working in Naḥḥās's office, who interfered in criminal investigations.
> Naḥḥās said to him: 'Off to Banī Mazār, to the police station.
> I want you to multiply the numbers of the accused; then will you be high in my favour.'

On the subject of government, one last detail may detain us for a moment. When l-Adham eš-Šar>̃āwīl was busy outwitting the government, we are told that at one point

> He dressed as a European, and by another road he met them. In Arabic and French, in every tongue he spoke to them.

Is it too facetious to see in this the merest hint that to the masses the machinery of government remains something of a foreign institution?

One must even raise the question: how deeply has nationalism struck root in the Egyptian countryside? In his pioneer work on the whole of popular literature, Aḥmad Rušdī Ṣāliḥ recognises that this is a movement that was born in the city and only later moved to the rural areas.[10] But how far has it actually spread? When speaking to my informants, I generally refrained from asking them leading questions in the hope that they would reveal their own priorities. Not one ballad with a clearly nationalistic theme was volunteered. As a last resort, I did question the singer >Abū Đrā< about this matter, although wary of the genuineness of the material he might offer me since he performs a great deal in the city and receives a regular stipend from the state as an army entertainer. He told me he had himself composed a ballad celebrating the events of the 1956 Suez war;[11] but he did not get very far with the recording as neither he nor any member of his company could remember how it ended. Clearly, whatever vogue it may once have had, it had dropped out of the author's repertoire and did not meet the test of lasting popularity. By contrast, the events of Danšawāy[12] had touched such a live nerve in the consciousness of the people that ballads about it were in circulation a good fifty years after the event.

One version of this, ascribed to the extremely prolific Azharist I have already named, <Ajāj, is a rather wordy composition that inveighs against the English for their ruthlessness and for treating the village 'as if it was their property', specifically against Cromer 'who came asking for excessive compensation', and against 'a Christian judge who deserves beating with a shoe'. Its last line is something of an anti-climax:

> This is indeed something that brings tears to the
> inhabitants and sons of the Fatherland

but it is notable for its use of the word *waṭan.*

Another much more spirited anonymous version starts:

> After judgement had been passed by Governor, sergeant and Pasha –
> Galleons piloted by Cromer, at war with mankind –
> Now do the English act like Pharaohs who once were only riff-raff.

But then, after dwelling on the helpless plight of the villagers, it describes the emergence of Muṣṭafā Kāmil not as a nationalist leader but as 'the pillar of the faith' whose career is cut short when:

> So clever were the Christians they poured poison in his shoe.

Such nationalist sentiment as may be detected here seems at least overlaid with religious consciousness. Taken by and large, the corpus of texts available gives overwhelming evidence that religion retains by far the greatest claim on the allegiance of the masses. Ballads with a religious theme outnumber all others by an incalculably wide margin. Indeed, one could trace in them almost the entire history and destiny of mankind as understood in popular Islam, from the creation of Adam to the Day of Judgement.

There is, however, one unexpected feature of these ballads that ought to make us pause at this point. It is that whereas the religious stories abound in miracles and wonders, those with a contemporary theme are uncompromisingly earth-bound. They are interspersed with invocations and references to the will of God, but apart from an occasional rather faint premonition that something dreadful is about to happen, there is never the slightest supernatural intervention. There is not even a role for the *šēx* as spiritual guide or father confessor. Can it be that the Egyptian man-in-the-field, who is so beset by hard realities in his daily life, likes to dream dreams that he projects into another age or environment, but that in dealing with the here and now he keeps his feet firmly on the ground? Can it be that in facing an immediate crisis his gut reaction – like that of many others with greater pretensions to sophistication – is to 'praise the Lord and pass the ammunition'?

Perhaps it is not for us here to determine how deeply his devotion runs, or how effective it is in directing his actions. What is clear is that the community he recognises as his own is the Islamic brotherhood, and that any non-Muslim is therefore an outsider. In the language of these ballads, the words Nuṣrānī, Yahūdī and Kāfir are virtually synonymous; they may be strung together or used interchangeably. In the story of Abraham, for example, the patriarch's enemies and persecutors are called Naṣārā, and this once again by <Ajāj who, as a man of some education, must have known that his use of the word was, to say the least, anachronistic. There are, of course, many issues in which religious and national loyalties coincide or reinforce each other. 'Bardanōha' shows all too painfully that they may also clash. And when they do, it is the religious label that the ballad-mongers and their public prefer to wear.

Notes

1. See Item 4 in this book.
2. Transcribed and translated in *Ballads*, pp. 121–37.
3. See Margaret Larkin, 'A Brigand Hero of Egyptian Colloquial Literature', *Journal of Arabic Literature*, 23 (2002), pp. 49–64.
4. Version sung by Muḥammad Ṭāhā, on cassette marketed by Nefertiti, *Ballads*, pp. 292–322.
5. *Ballads*, pp. 30, 66, etc.
6. The variants of this story are: (a) a taped performance by Šawqī l-Qināwī transcribed and translated in *Ballads*, pp. 323–50; and (b) a text printed in a booklet by >Ibrāhīm Sulaymān known as iš-Šēx and titled *an-Najm al-<Ālī fi l-Fann il-<X̱ālī* (Cairo, n.d.). See also Item 9 in this book.
7. Recited by >Abū Đrā<, transcribed and translated in *Ballads*, pp. 227–38.
8. Anonymous handwritten text bought from a Cairo bookseller. See *Ballads*, pp. 247–53.
9. Two versions, one in an anonymous and untitled booklet containing several narratives, and the second sung by Fāṭima Sirḥān on a cassette marketed by Nefertiti. See *Ballads*, pp. 185–225.
10. *al-Adab aš-Ša<bī* (Cairo, 1955). *Funūn al->Adab aš-Ša<bī* (Cairo, 1956). *al-Funūn aš-Ša<bīyya* (Cairo, Ministry of Culture, April 1961), No. 34.
11. See Item 8 in this book.
12. On basic facts and two folk compositions on the subject, see *Ballads*, pp. 247–58.

    In June 1906, three British officers went shooting semi-wild pigeons and got into an altercation with the villagers of Danšawāy who considered such pigeons, for which they built dovecots, to be village property. As a result of a beating and/or sunstroke, one officer died. A special court was set up that condemned some of the villagers to hanging, some to flogging, some to imprisonment.

Ultimate responsibility rested with the British High Commissioner, Lord Cromer, although he was out of the country at the time.

From among the Egyptian elite, Muṣṭafā Pasha Kāmil, founder of the Egyptian Nationalist Party, made political capital of the horror widely expressed, although his activity was differently understood by the common people. What drew stronger reactions from the folk poets was that the President of the Court was an Egyptian Christian.

17

Folk Themes in the Works of Najīb Surūr

Najīb Muḥammad Surūr[1] was born in 1932 in the village of >Axṭāb (in the Governorate of Daqahliyya in Lower Egypt) where his father was a tax collector. A poem of his[2] is cast in the words of a man recalling how as a child he was filled with pride when his father was summoned to appear before the village headman, but was shattered when he saw the representative of authority take off his shoe and use it to beat the man standing defenceless before him. If this is meant to record an experience of the poet's, the incident must have been magnified in his imagination for it is difficult to believe that the father would have been so mistreated if he was a state official. The poem, however, is indicative of Surūr's lifelong resentment of authority, which was to cost him dearly.

After completing his primary and secondary education in provincial schools, he enrolled in Cairo University, but during a summer vacation back home he is said to have led a number of students in raiding and vandalising the home of a local Pasha, and to have been severely flogged by the Pasha's henchmen in revenge.[3]

He also tells us in his verse that at the university he studied law – 'the law of the jungle/recited by a gang' – but that he abandoned the course in his last year 'believe me, not because I feared the examination/but that I feared out there a den of serpents/preying on doves.'[4] He enrolled instead in the Higher Institute for Theatrical Arts and obtained its diploma in 1956. In 1958, he was sent on a scholarship to Moscow to further his study of the theatre, and even when other Egyptian students left because of a change in Egypt's political alignment, he stayed on, married a Russian lady and contributed to the Arabic programmes of Soviet television. He became an ardent admirer of the Stanislavski method, but again he left without a degree, implying that it was his professors who were untrue to the master's teaching.[5] And he had to spend a lonely year in Budapest before he was allowed to return to Cairo.

He had his greatest successes in the late 1960s when the Egyptian theatre was particularly active and socialist realism was in vogue;[6] but – contending that the revolution had been betrayed – he was soon out of sorts both with colleagues in the profession and with political authorities. The 1970s saw him sink into alcoholism and mental as well as physical illness, and – except for a spell of teaching in the Institute for Theatrical Arts between 1975 and 1976 – he was reduced to penury, and he is said to have dramatised his predicament by going out barefoot to beg in the street. He died on 23 October 1978.

At his best, Najīb Surūr was a fluent poet in both classical and colloquial Arabic, sometimes boldly mingling the two idioms in compositions that were somewhat facile, but not devoid of verve and of some striking imagery. He had three volumes of poetry published,[7] and he circulated on tape a collection of satirical verses which, because it is punctuated with a certain vulgar invective, is known by a name for which one may derive from al-Mutanabbī's best-known satire on Kāfūr the euphemism *al-waylummiyyāt.* He also on occasion used the folk verse form of the *mawwāl*,[8] but not its themes, his specific references being mostly to al-Ma<arrī, Dante, Shakespeare, Schopenhauer and Cervantes, as well as to the betrayal and crucifixion of Jesus that seemed to him to parallel his own experience. A curiosity in this context is that although a prominent feature of the *mawwāl* is elaborate punning achieved by distortion of the normal pronunciation, he denounced as 'non-Arab, non-Arabic, non-Egyptian, and non-folk' such linguistic and metrical irregularities as the lengthening or shortening of syllables which he detected in popular songs, and which he attributed to a Masonic/Zionist plot.[9]

He was, however, primarily a man of the theatre – not only a prolific playwright, but also a translator of Chekhov's *The Cherry Orchard*, an actor, a producer, to some extent even a theatrical critic, although his criticism – when it is not an exposition of broad principles mainly reflecting Stanislavski, as in his *Ḥiwār fi l-Masraḥ* ('Dialogue on the Theatre') – is all too often animated by his fierce resentments and his personal quarrels. It was above all in the theatre that his poetic verve found its widest outlet, for most of his plays are in fact in verse. So is his one novel, of which more is to be said below.

He subscribed fully to the socio-political passions and perceptions dominant among the intellectuals of his generation, so that his work abounds in denunciations of Zionism, imperialism, colonialism, as well as the local manifestations of injustice that were somewhat simplistically interpreted as deriving from international complicities. He was convinced, for example, that al-Ma<arrī's writings contained a hidden warning against a worldwide Jewish–Masonic plot hatched as early as in Assyrian–Babylonian days (*Juḥā*, pp. 76–98). One of his plays gifted to the Palestine Liberation Organisation and titled *aḏ-Ḏubāb al->Azraq* ('The Bluebottle')[10] consists of little more than a framework for the recitation of long passages from the Protocols of the Elders of Zion, which he evidently believed to be genuine and which he dubbed (p. 177) 'the latest edition of the Talmudic manifesto'. Yet another play, which is a farcical representation of the trial of an artist, carries the revealing title of *al-Ḥukm qabl al-Mudāwala* ('Judgment *before* Deliberation'). His operetta, *Malik aš-Šhaḥḥātīn*, too, written in 1971 at the behest of a friend who had read Brecht's *Dreigroschenoper* and depicting a cut-throat struggle for supremacy between beggars and thieves, takes easy pot-shots at favourite targets, including corrupt officialdom, economic inequality, British rule and Zionism.

Many were the predecessors and contemporaries who projected their own priorities into representations either of the past or of the masses amongst whom modernist values had scarcely percolated – as witness the romanticism of Muḥammad Ḥusayn

Haykal (1888–1956) in *Zaynab*, or <Abd ar-Raḥmān aš-Šarqāwī's (1920–87) class militancy and nationalist fervour in the novel *al->Arḍ* and in plays celebrating heroes from al-Ḥusayn ibn <Alī to <Urābī. Fewer are those who claimed some fragile link with the folk literature long despised by the elite, as in Yusrī l-Jindī's play, *al-Hilāliyya* (1985), which represents >Abī Zayd as fighting only warmongers, or >Aḥmad <Uṯmān's play, *Ṯawra fi l-Ḥarīm* (1961), in which Šahrazād leads a palace revolt.

Surūr's distinctive position, however, is that he acquired – and indeed fostered – the reputation of being particularly close to the perceptions of the common people and appreciative of their literature, as his use of the colloquial and of folk metrical forms attests. Indeed, he ascribed his own formation to his village upbringing, saying in an open letter to a friend (*Juḥā*, p. 148): 'Never mind Italy, France, Germany or any other Eastern or Western state or nation. Come, let us study together in the >Axṭāb Academy. We stayed in >Axṭāb – my village, my teacher, my inspiration, my nurse, my murderer – merely a week (a little less or a little more), and you admitted that you had learned nothing abroad!' Accordingly, his hottest diatribes against older contemporaries, mainly Tawfīq al-Ḥakīm (?1899–1978) and Rašād Rušdī (1912–83), whom he despised for 'their ability to live under any regime, in any social or political or cultural atmosphere', often targeting their 'elitism' even when they appear to draw on folk literature (as in al-Ḥakim's *Yā Ṭāli< iš-Šajara* which echoes a folk song) and may be summed up in his judgement that 'Dr Rašād Rušdī, for all his profuse output, is of all writers most like Tawfīq al-Ḥakīm in that he is most remote from, most alien to the theatre, just as – despite his use of folk topics, themes, and characters – he is most remote from and alien to the people, the most antagonistic to the people, to their reality and their aspirations.'

In fact, the most substantial part of Surūr's own published output has been his use of folk themes. It is on this that the present study concentrates.

Surūr wove a succession of plots round the persons of Yāsīn and Bahiyya. These are characters in a kind of story which usually has some basis in fact and on which folk poets compose long narrative ballads abounding in contrasts of good and evil, in wondrous coincidences and heart-rending experiences that call forth moralising comments indicative of the values prized by the common people.[11] Unfortunately, no version of the folk ballad has come to hand, but the bare bones of the story are known to be that Yāsīn was killed by camel-borne Sudanese warriors while he was serving as a cavalryman under joint British and Egyptian command (presumably in the campaign led by Lord Kitchener in the Sudan at the end of the nineteenth century),[12] and that Bahiyya, his cousin whom he was to have married, was subsequently involved in an apparently unrelated imbroglio that ended with her bearing witness in court against a number of evil-doers.

Surūr gave the title *Yāsīn wa Bahiyya* to a novel which – following the example of Pushkin in his *Eugene Onegin* – he wrote in free verse.[13] Considerations of style are relevant to the present study only insofar as they indicate the extent of Surūr's cultural commitment.[14] Thus, one notes that the dialogue and the folk songs with which the text is studded are entirely in the colloquial. The narrative parts, however, are in the literary idiom, but with an occasional colloquialism to suggest off-handedness or earthiness, as when (p. 14) – having mentioned that Yāsīn has lost his father and his property – the poet raises rhetorical questions in the classical language: 'How were they lost? And why?', then answers in the colloquial: 'It doesn't matter!' There are even times when Surūr's verve and facetiousness drive him to 'translate' one idiom into the other, as when (p. 23) he has naive villagers wondering:

Tell us, fellow Muslims,
Is Paradise electrified?
If not, tell us how it's lit –
Or is it also soot-like murk?

He then offers the puristic reader a restatement of the passage in lofty and remote classical diction, in which the tangy colloquialism *mehabbiba*, which I have rendered as 'soot-like murk' and which implies the grossest loathsomeness, becomes a tame *muẓlima*, 'dark'; and Surūr ends up with the comment: 'As different as heaven and earth – not so?'

Also worth noting is that the author sometimes seems immersed in the culture of the common folk, drawing his imagery from rural life, even referring to the season in terms of the Coptic calendar as most peasants do. At one point (p. 24), for example, he describes Bahiyya as: 'Like a fig on the bough – soft/And fresh/And appetising./Warm was Bahiyya/And shy/Like a bowl of milk/On a cold morning in Ṭība./And mellow./She was like mint – mellow;/Like clover – mellow/Like sweet basil – mellow.' Yet a few pages further on he cannot resist adding (p. 34): 'Why our passion for Venus when Venus is no prettier than Bahiyya?/No, nor more poetic./ She is, to begin with, a foreigner;/Besides, without arms she cannot do a thing!'

More directly revealing of his priorities, however, is the way he has recast the story. His version is set entirely in Buhūt, a village in the X̱arbiyya governorship where, in June 1951, there had been violent incidents on the estate of the Badrāwī-<Āšīr family.[15] Yāsīn and Bahiyya are cousins, in love with each other, and she has been promised to him. The community is tyrannised by the local Pasha. Yāsīn has experienced the bastinado at the hands of the Pasha's servants, and his father has died in jail where he was thrown at the Pasha's orders. His submissiveness runs out when the Pasha demands that Bahiyya come to serve him in his palace – and the fate that awaits her is made obvious by the succession of young women who have preceded her, who have gone in 'light as butterflies and come away laden like waterskins' (p. 79). Eventually the villagers, driven to desperation by the Pasha's exactions, have an altercation with his men and set the palace ablaze. Yāsīn does not lead the action, but figures prominently in it. And when the *hajjāna* – the Camel Corps that was manned by Sudanese, much feared for their use of whips in quelling riots – is called in to visit retribution on the rebels, Yāsīn is one of the victims, shot dead in a manner that is in fact (except for the names of the main protagonists) the only direct echo of the folk ballad.

Surūr was to pick up the theme in a succession of plays, almost entirely in the colloquial. The first was *Āh yā Lēl yā >amar*,[16] a title which literally means 'Oh, the Night, the Moon', and which seems to echo a common refrain or filler in lyrical folk songs, but which – as is hinted in the prologue (p. 29) and is made plain at the end of the action – is meant to suggest the persistence of a glimmer of hope in the night of despair. In this play, Bahiyya is shown gradually becoming less punctilious in keeping a sentimental tryst with her dead lover, at the same time innocently attracting the attention of Amīn, the mechanic of the flour mill, who had been Yāsīn's closest friend – virtually his alter ego. He had stood heroically by Yāsīn's side in their struggle, but has lost faith in the possibility of resistance to oppression. He persuades Bahiyya's father to let him marry her, and takes her to the Suez Canal zone where the British had their last stronghold in the early 1950s. For a while, he is content to work for the British army and draw high wages; but eventually he becomes unsettled and even takes to 'English' liquor (p. 80). His self-respect reasserts itself when he realises that the change in his material condition represents no escape from Buhūt (pp. 86–7): 'The bullet is the same,/And the trigger, and the rifle/And the finger/That squeezed the trigger/Is still the same./Only that one was a berberine;/That one used to say "Ya kalba,"/And the one before me is an Englishman,/A berberine who says "Ya dog!"' He blames himself for having been a dog that wagged its tail at its master's call (p. 85), and although well aware of the cost (pp. 109–11), he joins the *fidā>iyyīn* (the 'self-sacrificing warriors' usually described as 'commandos' in the press). The day comes when Bahiyya and her mother join a throng of women outside a building where lie the bodies of fallen heroes, including Amīn's, but Egyptian soldiers deny them entrance, although one of them, of peasant stock, expresses sympathy (pp. 130, 134) mingled with resignation before the futility of opposing government orders.

During her fruitless wait, Bahiyya has a dream in which a venerable figure in white, referred to simply as *aš-šayx*, takes her to where she can see three youths, each with a rose on his forehead, beckon to her. The first, dressed in green, is Yāsīn; the second, in blue, is >Amīn; the third, unidentified, is in white. They tender towards her the semblance of the moon, and she approaches through a succession of obstacles, but as she stretches her arm to seize the moon she wakens and is back to her helpless stance, but with a chorus proclaiming that dreams cannot be banned.

The intended symbolism is plain, and has been put into words by Jalāl al-<Išrī in his introduction to the play (p. 18):

> Bahiyya is Egypt, Egypt who has been linked to three men: the one dressed in green is the peasant, the one in blue is the (industrial) worker, and the one in white is the soldier who activated the white revolution. As for the red rose, it is of course the revolution, the revolution effected by all of Egypt's sons together – soldiers, peasants, and workers – and obstructed by seas and thorns and fires. But thanks to its well-

> directed revolution, thanks to the wisdom of its elders and the determination of its youth, Egypt was able to overstep these obstacles one by one to come within reach of the moon, or the new dawn.

Oddly, although historically it is the army alone that put an end to the monarchy, there is only very slender prefiguration for its role in the play, for with one ineffective exception the soldiery is shown to be harshly repressing the bereaved women, in obedience to orders from above.

The theme is taken up more explicitly in yet another – a somewhat disjointed – play entitled *>̃ūlūli ēn iš-Šams*.[17] The title ('Tell the Sun Disc') is taken from a song which expresses a lover's solicitude for his beloved (presumably again symbolising Egypt) with the couplet (p. 60): 'Tell the sun disc not to wax hot/For the untamed gazelle is out walking early.'

In this the widowed Bahiyya is in Suez, struggling to support her children and her mother, for the Revolution has not done away with the wolves who batten on the poor (pp. 23–4). The sympathetic soldier who appeared in the previous play is given a name: <Aṭiyya. He is now a civilian who has lost an arm while working on the Aswan dam and has been transferred to an administrative task in which he witnesses corruption at all levels. At intervals in the play he delicately hints at his desire to marry Bahiyya, who, however, has thoughts only for the future of her daughter >Amīna and her son, a second Yāsīn. The latter, fired by the history of Egypt's greatness and its many betrayals, in time becomes an army officer, and he too is made painfully aware of rampant corruption. Suddenly the dead Yāsīn and >Amīn appear to Bahiyya with the cryptic message: 'Beware of five-six!' She tries to pass the warning to the authorities, but is taken to be mentally deranged. Its significance becomes all too plain when the Six Day War begins on the fifth day of the sixth month, and the play ends with Bahiyya and the chorus celebrating with rising exaltation the will to recover from a defeat that has set off a mine long dormant in Egyptian hearts.

Surūr wove yet another play round a different folk theme, about which more information is available. This is the story of Ḥasan and Na<īma,[18] an 'honour crime' the factual basis of which goes back to 1938. Murders perpetrated in obedience to the honour code are favourite material for Egyptian ballad-mongers. In a typical ballad of this kind, a woman besmirches family honour by a sexual indiscretion, and it becomes the duty of her nearest able male relative to butcher her. The action is usually described admiringly and in detail by the folk singer and applauded by his audience – as in the story of Šafī>̃a and her brother Mitwallī.[19] The story of *Ḥasan u Na<īma*, however, differs in several radical respects. In most versions, Na<īma is shown to have made advances to Ḥasan, who is himself a folk singer – a circumstance that presumably accounts for the sympathetic treatment accorded to the lovers. Ḥasan treats her honourably; nevertheless, her father has Ḥasan assassinated, and Na<īma becomes the inexorable avenger who embalms her lover's head and produces it in court to win the judge's sympathy and ensure that her father gets a heavy sentence.

Surūr's play on this theme is *Min ēn Ajīb Nās* ('Where am I to find people?').[20] The title is the opening line of yet another folk ballad, *L-Adham iš-Šar>̃āwī*, where it expresses the singer's wonder whether there are any who will grasp the purport of his message, but in the play the words are also put in Na<īma's mouth (p. 17) as an appeal for someone to whom she can tell the truth of her tragedy.

And how is this truth represented? Here Surūr has retained the broad lines of the folk story, but it is the motivation that has been transformed. Ḥasan is made out to be something of a revolutionary whose songs assail and ridicule the *<umdas*, the government-appointed village headmen, and Na<īma's father is a weakling who at the headman's behest refuses to let Ḥasan marry his daughter and eventually engineers his death (pp. 25–8).

The *<umdas* are, of course, the lowest echelon of power, the one with which the villagers are in immediate contact; but they clearly represent an entire oppressive hierarchy, as is plainly asserted by one character after another. At the top are the British occupiers, though they are but the last in a long series (p. 108). Dependent on them are the expatriate communities – 'hats mounted over the fezes' (p. 52), bent on exploitation (p. 36): 'The snake is always a "mister" (*xawāga*)/And the "mister" is (as voracious) as a crane –/Now a Byzantine, now a Turk/Or a Greek or an Armenian', not excluding the Jews disguised as locals (p. 42). And even among Egyptians, there are those all too willing to play the game according to their rules (p. 107): 'There are Englishmen within us!'. These show deference only to the blue-eyed (pp. 41, 115), and use any measure of power they obtain to victimise the common people. The rot is shown to be pervasive. The political parties of the Right and of the Left alike use the innocents as cat's-paws (p. 116). Literary entrepreneurs will make of Na<īma's tragedy a film or a television serial or a play, and reward themselves by drinking champagne out of ladies' shoes (p. 124). The army itself is not immune for there are wolves in officers' clothing (p. 118), just as there are some in blue overalls overseeing factory workers (p. 107).

The smell of betrayal is evoked more than once (pp. 101, 121), and the sense that this has been a feature of Egyptian history through the ages, already adumbrated by Bahiyya's son in *>̃ūlūli ēn iš-Šam* (p. 54) is now elaborated in a nightmarish scene in which Na<īma, bound with chains and crowned with thorns, is dragged before a ring of sorceresses to be tortured. Clearly intended to be an embodiment of the Egyptian spirit, she is asserted to have been a slave under the Pharaohs and is said to be one with Isis and with Šahrazād, as well as with other heroines of folklore, including Bahiyya (pp. 82–92).

This conjoining of Na<īma and Bahiyya invites us to consider a curious one-act play titled *Ya Bahiyya w Xabbirīni* ('O Bahiyya, tell me!') which Surūr labelled 'a critical comedy'.[21] Here a cocky producer, boasting of his sophisticated foreign training, puts on a play on Bahiyya's marriage to >Amīn in their native village of Buhūt. It is built round his 'vision' that Bahiyya has forgotten Yāsīn, but at this the villagers rebel and put on their own version, which places everyone's concern with social justice uppermost and in fact closely resembles parts of *>Āh ya Lēl ya >̃amar*. Yet at this point in the action a character representing the author – who so far has been browbeaten by the producer, the manager and even the actors – abruptly intervenes to declare that none of this corresponds to the reality, which can be ascertained only from Bahiyya herself.

If this is a plea for objective truth, it raises the issue of how true Najīb Surūr has been to the folk theme. That he has radically altered the story, retaining only the names of the hero and the heroine, is patent. For such cavalier treatment, precedents abound. But in view of his reputed closeness to the common people and his own claim to have been formed by his native village of Axṭāb, one may well ask how truly he has represented these common folk, their perceptions, their priorities, their spirit.

He has skilfully woven into his texts a number of folk songs and folk sayings, and even recorded some odd beliefs, such as that frogs bring water to the dead in their graves (*Šams*, p. 43). He makes poetic use of the notion that the dead may reappear in the guise of some living creature, such as a butterfly to reassure their kinsfolk or as a cat to indicate disquiet of some kind. So as a manifestation of Bahiyya's constancy in love, in *Yāsīn wa Bahiyya* she is represented as faithfully revisiting the site where they used to meet in the hope that Yāsīn may be manifested to her in some guise (p. 81). But the author is not above stretching this limited concept to one belonging to an entirely foreign tradition by blandly asserting that she believes – 'as do all the inhabitants of Buhūt' – in the transmigration of souls (*>̃amar*, pp. 27–8); he even hints in *>Āh ya Lēl ya >̃amar* that her new love is at least partly explained by the fact that she detects in >Amīn several traits distinctive of Yāsīn (p. 101). Similarly, Na<īma is portrayed as preserving Ḥasan's head because – in a parallel to the story of Isis and Osiris – she believes that he cannot be resurrected until it has been joined to his body (p. 24), but is assured by boatmen that if she buries the head in sand, waters it and steps over it twice, God may make her pregnant by him and so preserve his seed (p. 128). There is indeed a superstition that if a barren woman step seven times over a dead body she may then be impregnated, but not by the cadaver.

The greater and more fundamental inconsistency in Surūr's work, however, is in his depiction of a plebeian class in which peasants, industrial workers and low-ranking soldiers have identical perceptions and purposes, all his characters being the product – as he himself claims to be – of village life. He does at various points acknowledge not only the quiescence of the common people, as when boatmen ignore the corpses floating in the river rather than be involved in an investigation (*Nās*, p. 33), but also their submissiveness to authority and their toleration of tyrants, as when the ex-soldier <Aṭiyya admits that he was in a position to shoot King Fārūq, but spared him as <Urābī spared the Khedive (*Šams*, p. 36). There are indications, however, that a new spirit is abroad, and this is humorously expressed by a male nurse from an insane asylum who points out to a colleague that a new madness has spread (*Šams*, p. 135): 'Some kind of hallucination/An endemic hallucination/Something akin to patriotism!'

Now the evidence of the genuine folk literature is that villagers are most easily roused by issues of personal honour and that their supreme loyalties are to kinship and to religious confession, whereas nationalistic themes are all but absent.[22] Surūr's references to religion, on the contrary, are extremely rare and mostly mildly dismissive. Thus, in *Yāsīn wa Bahiyya* (p. 19) he has villagers puzzling over the source of their miserable condition, and the dialogue includes this exchange:

– Ask Šēx >Ismā<īn (the village preacher).
– By God he wouldn't know. He's just like a parrot.
– He's memorised the Qur>ān.
– So what – a gramophone record!

And when Bahiyya is mourning the death of >Amīn, a character identified only as iš-Šēx X̱arīb – which happens to be the name of a holy man buried in Suez, where she was residing at the time – appears to her to offer the comforts of religion, and draws from her a wry response when he describes to her how >Amīn must be revelling in the company of the houris of Paradise (*>amar*, pp. 71–3).

Intent as he is on ascribing to the common people the heroic role of saving Egypt from its tormentors and its traitors, Surūr goes in search of other motivating forces. He speaks through a factory worker who senses in the whole country a rebellious spirit like that of <Urābī (*Nās*, p. 101). And although this has only recently been activated, he represents it as sustained by an extraordinarily lively social perceptiveness and commitment. Thus, Bahiyya's father behaves in a decidedly uncharacteristic manner not only in that he keeps postponing her marriage to Yāsīn year after year,[23] but even more startlingly after Yāsīn's death when he determines that she must forever remain unmarried – 'crucified' is the word he uses (*>amar*, p. 51) – as a reproach to the oppressors. And this earns him the applause of his fellow villagers in *Ya Bahiyya w Xhabbirīnī*, although in *>Āh ya Lēl ya >amar* they persuade him to let her marry >Amīn by quoting the earthy folk song (p. 62): 'Father of the nubile girl, sell her/Before the girl's honour is lost;/Protect your name before she acts/Like a mare that has gone wild./Well-born is your daughter/But even the well-born girl becomes a mare/When she sees young men out there!'

No less noble is >Amīn, who declares that he fell in love with Bahiyya when he saw her in court taking a firm stand for the underprivileged (*Xhabbirīnī*). And an old man boasts to Na<īma of having once headed a band of brigands (p. 66): 'We used to swoop down on a village like falcons/Openly and fully armed/In broad daylight/And what we took to the Pasha's distress we gave to the people./This means we were not stealing/For to steal from a thief is not to steal./He who steals the lifeblood of the people/Is the thief.'

Nowhere is the arbitrariness of Surūr's interpretation more strikingly revealed than in his depiction of Ḥasan as a champion of the poor and the scourge of *<umda*s, whereas in a folk ballad arising directly from a community in which stability and status are best defined by ownership of land, Na<īma's father comes to confront

Ḥasan in his village, meets a watchman and gruffly asks to be directed to the singer's house, whereupon (*Ballads*, pp. 332–3):

> The watchman flared at him: Watch your manners, Uncle,
> He is no (mere) singer.
> His father has forty-five acres to his nameAnd is the šēx of Bahnasa l-X̲arra!

Clearly, Surūr has achieved his purpose only by projecting on to villagers what was politically correct among the intellectuals of his generation, city-dwellers who were subject to different social and political pressures and buffeted by different cultural winds. At the very outset of his *Yāsīn wa Bahiyya*, this son of Axṭāb put the following words on the tongue of the prologue:

> Would that I were Homer,
> Would that I were Virgil,
> Would that I had Dante's lyre
> Or Shakespeare's pen,
> Or the pen of that knight among knights, Byron,
> That I may tell of Buhūt
> That I may tell of Yāsīn, of Bahiyya.

The identity of the poets invoked does not appear to carry any significance other than that they are giants of world literature, for most of them scarcely figure elsewhere in Surīr's writings. And the irony is that the galaxy includes not a single folk or Marxist star.

Notes

1. Works repeatedly cited are fully identified when they first occur, but are then referred to by a single prominent word in the title.
2. 'Al-Ḥiḏā>' ('The Shoe'), in *At-Trājīdyā l->Insāniyya* ('The Human Tragedy') (Cairo, 1967), pp. 12–18.
3. Robert B. Campbell, ed., *Contemporary Arab Writers – Biographies and Autobiographies*, Beiruter Texte und Studien, Band 62 (Orient-Institut der Deutschen Morgenlandischen Gesellschaft, Wiesbaden, 1966), p. 718.
4. In *Luzūm mā Yalzam* (literally: 'Adhering to what must be adhered to', an adaptation of al-Ma<arrī's *Luzūm mā lā Yalzam*, 'Adhering to what need not be adhered to', which unlike Surūr's collection refers not to content but to additional rhyming constraints) (Cairo, 1976), pp. 32, 33.
5. *Hiwār fī l-Masraḥ* ('Dialogue on the Theatre') (Cairo, 1969), p. 195.
6. See Roger Allen, 'Egyptian Drama after the Revolution', *Edebiyat*, 4, 1 (1979), pp. 97–134.
7. In addition to the two mentioned in preceding notes, *Brūtūkūlāt Ḥukamā> Rīš* ('The Protocols of the Elders of 'Riche', in which he satirised the pretentious intellectuals who frequented the Café Riche in Cairo) (Cairo, 1977).
8. See 'Mawwāl li l-Ḥanīn', in *Luzūm Mā Yalza*m, pp. 64–5. On the *mawwāl*, see Item 2 in this book.

9. *Hākaḏā Qāla Juḥā* ('Thus spake [the comic folk character] Juḥā') (Cairo, n.d.), pp. 90, 91). In subsequent notes, this source is abbreviated to *Juḥā*. Surūr's puristic pronouncement on literary language may be an echo of a less condemnatory observation made by al-Jāḥiẓ – see the opening paragraph of Item 2 in this book.
10. This and the next two plays mentioned in this paragraph are to be found in his *al-A<māl al-Kāmila* ('Complete Works') (Cairo, ?1995), vol. 2.
11. One example is 'Karam il-Yatīm', Item 11 in this book; it tells in 357 lines how an orphan ultimately triumphs over the relatives who have ill-treated him and cheated him of his possessions. Another is 'Muḥammad Ṭāhā's *Mas<ūd u Wagīda*', transcribed and translated by Jenine Dallal, *Journal of Arabic Literature*, 23, 3 (November 1992), pp. 215–35; it tells in 297 lines of a brother and sister separated in infancy by evil kinsmen, who are later married to each other but who are saved from incest by the groom's instinct. For a study of the entire genre of narrative ballads, see *Ballads*.
12. <Iṣām ad-Dīn >Abū l-<Ulā, Masraḥ Najīb Surūr (Cairo, 1989), p. 95.
13. Written between 5 December 1962 and 3 February 1964, and published by *Majallat al-Masraḥ* as No. 5 in *Silsilat Masraḥiyyāt <Arabiyya*, July 1965.
14. On some aspects of style and language, and especially on the blending of colloquial and classical in verse form, see Sasson Somekh, 'At-Tašābuk al-Luxawī fī 'Yāsīn wa Bahiyya', *Al-Karmil*, 9 (1988), pp. 35–47.
15. G. Baer, *History of Landownership in Modern Egypt* (London, 1962), p. 221.
16. First published as No. 6 in *Silsilat Masraḥiyyāt <Arabiyya*, now under the imprint of Wizārat aṯ-Ṯaqāfa, al-Mu>assasa l-Miṣriyya al-<Āmma li t-Ta>līf wa n-Našr, Dār al-Kātib al-Miṣrī, January 1968. Reprinted in exactly the same form in January 1980 by Maṭābi< Zēnhum <Uṯmān Muṣṭafā in Šubrā l-Xayma. Page references are to the 1968 edition. The title of this work is hereafter abbreviated to *>̃amar*.
17. Cairo, n.d.; abbreviated to *Šams*.
18. A complete version of the folk ballad is transcribed and translated in *Ballads*, pp. 323–50.
19. Two versions of such a ballad are reproduced in *Ballads*, pp. 269–322.
20. Cairo, December 1975. Reproduced in *al->A<māl al-Kāmila*, vol. 2. Page references are to the earlier edition. The title is hereafter abbreviated to *Nās*.
21. Included in *Ḥiwār fi l-Masraḥ*, pp. 213–94. Hereafter abbreviated to *Xabbirīnī*.
22. See *Ballads*, pp. 65–78. Also Item 8 in this book.
23. This dog-in-the-manger attitude is left unexplained in *>̃amar* (p. 48), but poverty is given as a reason in *Xabbirīnī*.

Elite Treatment of Honour Crimes in Modern Egypt

The Arab elite has often condemned or even more generally ignored folk literature. Even leading modernists like Ṭāhā Ḥusayn (1889–1973) looked upon colloquial forms of Arabic as debased.[1] This in itself made the compositions of the common people unworthy of a serious man's attention except as entertainment. Furthermore, most Arab writers of the twentieth century saw themselves not only as artists but also as agents of cultural and social reform, and shied away from themes that struck them as trivial or reactionary.[2]

The resulting gap is indeed wide between the perceptions of the educated, especially those who have received a Western type of education and have adopted a Western type of dress – the *efendis* – and the *gallabiyya* wearers, who form the great majority of the population in the countryside and the poorer quarters of the cities. And nowhere is the gap wider than on the theme of honour crimes.

These account for most of the violence that occurs in an otherwise peaceable society, for its inherited ethos calls out for blood in two situations that brook no compromise. The first is the *ṯa>r*,[3] which requires a murder to be avenged by a male member of the victim's family. The second demands that a woman who has departed from the strictest standards of chastity to be slaughtered by a near male relative, usually her father or her brother.

The notion that a murdered man's spirit will not rest until he is avenged is common to many cultures, including that of pre-Islamic Arabia. In present-day Egyptian rural society, it is not necessarily the murderer who has to be killed – any male member of his family will do – nor is it a requirement that the new victim be killed in a fair fight. As his death must in turn be avenged, *vendettas* involving entire villages can stretch over generations. Islam provides for the payment of blood-wite to break the vicious spiral, but even this is not wholeheartedly accepted. In a ballad that tells of a feud between Muslims and Christians in the village of Bardanōha in 1943, the daughter of a man killed while raiding an opponent's granary is offered substantial compensation, but she proudly refuses to 'sell her father in order to eat bread', and taunts her menfolk with being women for even entertaining such a deal.[4]

At the folk level, still celebrated in song is l-Adham iš-Šarqāwī,[5] a notorious brigand who was hunted down by the police and shot dead in 1921. The folk artists make of him a hero launched on his violent career by the need to avenge the death of his uncle. That the murderer has been imprisoned is no satisfaction to him, for it places his quarry out of his reach for a while. He starts by slaking his thirst for blood by ripping apart several members of the murderer's family with his bare hands, and when he is himself imprisoned he seizes the opportunity of inflicting the same treatment on the actual culprit, at the same time boasting that he has fulfilled his purpose under the very eyes of the authorities. He then escapes from gaol and humiliates the police force pursuing him by his prowess and his tricks, until he is betrayed and killed by a venal cousin of his.

One of the features of the folk treatment of this theme is that no respect is shown for the law of the land or to the authorities enforcing it. The fact that l-Adham repeatedly fools the police by 'speaking to them in Arabic and French and in all languages' may be an indication that the entire apparatus of the modern state seems foreign to the public served by folk literature.

Radically different values are enshrined in a powerful one-act play by Tawfīq al-Ḥakīm (1899?–1987) titled *>Ux̱niyat al-Mawt.*[6] In this a village woman called <Asākir is living for the day when her husband's murder is avenged, although she knows nothing of what occasioned the crime. Her son <Alwān was only two years old when the tragedy occurred, so she led the village to believe that he had died in infancy and has secreted him to Cairo, never doubting that he would do his duty when grown to manhood. That this will necessarily occasion him to be killed in his turn has no place in her reckoning. Seventeen years later, she is eagerly awaiting his return. Ready for him, rusty but still serviceable, is the actual knife with which his father was slaughtered. But the lad has had an education, has read newspapers and discussed with fellow-students matters of moment. His priorities are not hers. His dream is to awaken the villagers to their rights, to stimulate them into cooperative action to improve their material conditions – not to perpetuate old feuds, not to kill! Horrified at the prospect that 'everyone will spit in disgust at the mere mention of his name' if he fails to do his manly duty, she calls upon another male kinsman to kill him, only to give a great cry of pain when her order is carried out.

The play is remarkable in that it exposes in a few sparse lines of dialogue the immense pressures exerted on members of such a community to comply with an unforgiving tradition, although the implication that a few years of education might transform them is simplistic.

Revenge is, however, a universal motif triggered by a primitive instinct. The folk poet conceives of it only in opposition to cowardice, and it is the likes of Tawfīq al-Ḥakīm who see it as a problem of social conscience. No less stubbornly anchored in the tradition, but more richly laden with the dramatic possibilities of an inner conflict is the demand that if a woman strays in the slightest way from the path of chastity she has to be slaughtered so that family honour may be washed in blood. Unlike the European 'unwritten law' which allowed a betrayed husband to kill his wife and her lover, in traditional Egyptian society the grim duty falls primarily on the woman's father, or failing him on her brother or some other close male relative, the family being held responsible for 'not having brought her up right'. It is this theme rather than the one of revenge that is to be pursued in this article.

In the folk literature, such deeds are celebrated with unstinted approval and unpalliated description of the goriness of the execution. A prime example is a story based on an actual occurrence in 1921, when an army sergeant-major called Mitwalli butchered his sister Šafīqa. On this countless ballads have been composed, in most of which the hero is portrayed as painstakingly tracing his sister to a brothel, presenting himself to her in disguise as if he was a prospective customer, and after the deed proudly advertising that he has done his duty, and defiantly appearing before a judge who in fact compliments him and confirms him in his army rank.

Almost as popular is the story of Ḥasan and Na<īma. This also is based on an actual crime, one that took place in 1938. The facts are exceptional in that once the woman's father was convinced that her honour had been compromised, he arranged to have not her but her lover killed. An even more startling departure from the norm was that Na<īma then set about visiting vengeance on her own menfolk. Possibly because the father's action was as much a breach of the code as the initial love intrigue, but even more probably because Ḥasan was himself a folk singer, the lover – but not always his beloved – is treated sympathetically in most versions of the folk ballad recounting the event. A more detailed treatment of this episode and its development is in Item 9 of this volume.

In the 'high' literature, the theme was first broached by Ṭāhā Ḥusayn in a novel titled *Du<ā> al-Karawān.*[7] In this, a peasant girl forced to flee her village because of her father's scandalous life finds a livelihood in the city as a housemaid, but her employer – a young engineer – seduces her. Finding herself pregnant, she is on her way back to her village but is intercepted by her uncle who slaughters her. Her sister then determines to avenge her by a subtle scheme. She is to enter the service of the young engineer, entice him and then deny him. Her manoeuvre succeeds inasmuch as he does fall in love with her, but by then she realises that she has also fallen in love with him, and they find that they need each other in order to redeem the past.

Without straying into broad considerations of literary criticism, one may point out that the novel falsifies an integral feature of the society to which it ostensibly relates, for it is not true that village women would be driven out because of their menfolk's misdeeds, and when they themselves fall foul of the standard expected of them, it is certainly not back to the village that they would go. These intrusions into the plot were presumably intended to magnify the iniquity of the double standard by which men and women are judged; but they are not vital to the author's ultimate purpose of celebrating the triumph of love over intolerance and vengefulness.

A comparable treatment of the theme is to be found in Yaḥyā Ḥaqqī's novelette titled *al-Būsṭajī.*[8] This is set in Upper Egypt, where concern for the defence of honour is reputed to be at its fiercest, and involves the Coptic community, for the code does not derive from the teaching of any one religion. Jamīla, who is the apple of her father's eye, is nearing the end of her secondary schooling. She falls in love with the brother of a classmate, and yields to him in a moment of passion. Xalīl's intentions are not in doubt, and he goes through the elaborate formalities of asking for her hand in marriage. Through an accommodation address, Jamīla maintains a clandestine correspondence with the young man who is starting a teaching career now in Cairo, now in Alexandria. When she discovers that she is pregnant, she tries – with her mother's complicity – to hide her condition from her father. But the negotiations between the families are lengthy, and the interference of the local postmaster, who escapes boredom by opening the most interesting letters that come under his hand, causes her to lose contact with her lover, so she is unable to alert him to the urgency of her plight. The time inevitably comes when her father discovers her shame, and she can only tremulously await the inevitable. The end is signalled with the tolling of a knell on the church bell, 'brass giving tongue to the ultimate of human sorrow and pain'.

This story was made into a film of the same title.[9] Apparently catering for a public that looks for strong rather than subtle effects, it departs from Yaḥyā Ḥaqqī's conception in some respects. The main one is that – like Ṭāhā Ḥusayn in his novel – it stresses the double standard prevalent in society by portraying Jamīla's father not as a man whose paternal love has to be subordinated to an unyielding ethos, but as a lecher who rapes his housemaid yet who pursues his erring daughter into the street, stabs her, then ostentatiously parades her bloodstained body before his stone-faced fellow villagers.

Other writers drew directly on specific stories told by folk poets, allowing themselves much freedom in reinterpreting them. The first was <Abd ar-Raḥmān al-Xamīsī in what was conceived as a radio serial,[10] and was in fact broadcast. Not surprisingly, it is eked out with none-too-subtle retarding actions, so that it runs to 226 closely printed pages. The bare bones of the plot, however, are that Na<īma is pursued by her cousin <Aṭwa, a bully with a reputation as a night prowler and a killer. Her father Mitwalli is portrayed as a weak character of no firm principles, but he has a relative, <Abd al-Ḥaqq, who acts as his adviser and his conscience. Asserting that she has no choice in the matter, Mitwalli readily agrees to let <Aṭwa marry her, but the wedding has to be postponed because Na<īma's mother had died less than a year before. In the interval, Na<īma meets Ḥasan who has come to her village to sing at a wedding. She makes her interest plain, and he comes to ask for her hand in marriage, but he is rudely rejected because of his low social status as an itinerant singer. Na<īma sends him word that she wants to run away from her father's house; he gallantly comes to her rescue and takes her to his home where she stays under his mother's eye, her honour unsullied. Metwalli follows, and is courteously received. He finds that Ḥasan is highly respected in his village and has the backing of its headman; so he agrees to let the lovers marry, but insists that his daughter should first return home with him. Back on his own territory, however, and under pressure from <Aṭwa, he goes back on the agreement, gives Na<īma a thrashing and confines her to the house. Not satisfied with this, <Aṭwa and an accomplice lie in wait for Ḥasan and his drummer on their way to a singing engagement and shoot at them; they are wounded, but not killed. <Abd al-Ḥaqq

presses Mitwalli to honour his pledge to Ḥasan, pointing out that <Aṭwa is bringing nothing but trouble and ill-repute to the family, whereas Ḥasan has refrained from denouncing him to the authorities. Infuriated, <Aṭwa sets <Abd al-Ḥaqq's crop on fire. Meanwhile, Ḥasan has recovered, and is planning to take manly action of his own. He gathers information on <Aṭwa's movements, captures him and his main acolyte, flogs them, shames <Aṭwa by shaving off his moustache, and leaves them both tied up in the field they had put to the torch, to be discovered and derided by the villagers. With a gang of miscreants, <Aṭwa then spins a more complicated web: Ḥasan, who is due to catch a train to sing at a wedding in a village close to Na<īma's, is to be waylaid by someone pretending to be the groom's brother, offered to be taken to his destination by car, and led into an ambush where he is to be tortured and killed. The first steps of the plot are successfully undertaken, but the plotters have been overheard by the village simpleton who makes no secret of what is afoot. <Abd al-Ḥaqq alerts the authorities, so the ambushers are ambushed by a force of a hundred policemen and are put in irons. Metwalli now insists that Ḥasan be his honoured guest, to celebrate both the wedding at which he is to sing and his own to Na<īma.

Not quite so free and certainly more subtle is the handling of the same story by Šawqī <Abd al-Ḥakīm, a prolific writer with a wide interest in folk literature. His one-act play of the same title[11] – first staged in 1964 – starts with Na<īma still living with her parents, in the very house where they killed her lover twenty years earlier. They are drumming into her that she is a partner in their crime, both by having provoked it and by having been a passive witness of it. Ḥasan's ghost makes a brief appearance, and he also is said to bear some responsibility for having gone to his death knowing what to expect. Eventually outsiders intervene, mainly in the person of a woman called a *sā>ila*, a word which means both a beggar and a questioner, probing the reasons for the characters' inaction. An oppressive sense of immovability is maintained until the very end when three old village women come to reassure Na<īma that there was nothing she could do anyway, but provoking her on the contrary to proclaim:

> The path … the path! We march on without looking backwards, back to the dead behind us. We do not listen to what they said. We just say, 'That's their lot. It was written!' And so we keep silent about evil. We slink along the walls. We hide things from one another. We hide what we have inside us. But, no! I cannot live with the rest of you, or with the dead, holding evil in my arms and saying, 'It is written!'

The same author has a comparable play on Šafīqa and Mitwalli in which very little action takes place. Instead, a number of characters – Šafīqa, who every night awaits a visit from her brother, Mitwalli, who does turn up but is visible only to her, her apprehensive friend Hanādī and her sorrowful father – give vent to their memories and perceptions, mostly without inter-communication, but building an atmosphere of doom deriving from the workings both of fate and of the social compulsions.

In 1975, students of drama in the Academy of the Arts, under the direction of Dr Laila Abou-Saif (1941–),[12] wrote and produced another play bearing directly on the same story. In it, Šafīqa is shown to have been seduced by Diyāb, fully expecting that he would marry her, only to be told bluntly that her social status is too far below his. She has no choice but to run away and adopt a way of life which, 'like any other, ends in death'. Yet even while entertaining men she shows that she holds her father and her brother in high honour and yearns for the security she once had under their protection. When finally confronted by Mitwalli she begs for forgiveness, but she also presents a reasoned defence:

> I was young and found no one to stand by me … Diyāb the headman's son … fooled me with sweet words, then he abandoned me. I was afraid my father would find out and you would kill me. I was at a loss what to do … All the people I met were black-hearted – no one gives you a piastre without wanting a piastre in advance … I could not find work to support me – I was never trained for anything!'

Mitwalli stabs her nevertheless, then immediately kneels by her, agonising over his deed. He then straightens up and tells the audience that he had to kill her 'so I could raise my head among people and say that Mitwalli is a man beyond reproach'. The stage is darkened then relit to show Mitwalli standing silent in the cage reserved for the accused in Egyptian courts; and a panel of judges is seated with the audience in a silent invitation to pass judgement.

A film with the same title but very different in tenor was produced in 1978. The scenario was attributed to Ṣalāḥ Jāhīn (1930–86). In this the action is transposed to the 1860s, bringing in the theme of the exploitation of the Egyptians by their 'Turkish' overlords, with British imperialists waiting for an opportunity to intervene. Mitwalli is represented not as a sergeant-major, but as a draftee so incensed at the way Turkish officers and NCOs ill-treat Egyptians that he knocks down a bullying superior and is severely flogged.

The camera then turns to a glamorous Šafīqa, hard-driven by poverty now that her aged father has been deprived of his son's labour. She resists the temptation of an easy life dangled before her by a procuress, but when she falls in love with the son of the village headman, she agrees to meet him in the procuress's house. During one of their trysts, the puritanical villagers set fire to the procuress's house, and both lovers are driven out to Asyūṭ where they find shelter with a relative of the procuress, herself a brothel-keeper.

Šafīqa still refuses to share the life of the dancers-prostitutes, but is driven by boredom to join them when they are hired to liven a party given by a wealthy man called Ṭarabīšī, who has adopted European ways and hobnobs with highly placed English men and women. She is driven to further cynicism when her lover plays the gigolo to an Englishwoman, and she becomes the mistress of Ṭarabīšī, who introduces her to the high life of London and Paris, where political secrets are common currency.

A scandal breaks out concerning the number of workers digging the Suez Canal who have died of thirst. Afraid of being held responsible for this Ṭarabīšī asks her to seek favour with a Turkish pasha by sleeping with him. Sinking further into cynicism, she takes part in an orgy in the course of which she humiliates Ṭarabīšī under the Pasha's gloating eyes.

At several key points in the progress of her corruption, Šafīqa has a phallic vision of Mitwalli stabbing her in the belly with his bayonet. And finally disgusted and resentful, she goes back to her now deserted village home to await her fate.

In the meantime, Ṭarabīšī and the pasha are pictured overseeing the execution of an Egyptian they have managed to make the scapegoat for the canal deaths, and the pasha pointedly remarks that Šafīqa knows too much.

Mitwalli comes back into the picture when he spots his sister's likeness and name tattooed on Diyāb, who has also been drafted into the army. Mitwalli promptly deserts and heads for his village. Šafīqa sees him and goes out to meet him on a deserted street. They stop and stare at each other, giving no indication whether brotherly love and understanding or the traditional code is to prevail. But a carriage draws up behind Mitwalli, a volley of shots is fired, Šafīqa falls down dead, and the carriage drives away with only the back of two European hats showing.

The imposition of so patently extraneous a theme on a core problem of Egyptian society is only slightly less arbitrary when a similar treatment is applied to the story of Ḥasan and Na<īma, where the victim is not a woman but a man. This is what is done by Najīb Surūr (1932–78) in his play, *Minēn ajīb Nās.*[13] Although he persistently claimed to be a product of village life who truly represented the values of the common people, Surūr reflected the priorities common among the intellectuals of the 1970s when he made of Ḥasan a satirist of village headmen, who are themselves the cat's paws of an entire hierarchy of exploiters of the people, including the native political establishment as well as their foreign puppet-masters. It is at their behest that Ḥasan is silenced. Their corrupting influence is said to have been endemic through the ages, and Na<īma's role as the avenger makes her the embodiment of Egypt's eternal spirit.

Most of the writings I have had the opportunity to survey belong to the third quarter of the twentieth century, when the Egyptian elite was very widely won over to Western values.

To them honour crimes were an embarrassing survival from a bygone age, and many chose to ignore or even deny them. Attempts to tie so long-rooted a phenomenon to the evils of colonialism were too specious to gain acceptance. The bolder writers who took the bull by the horns were the ones to get a sustained hearing, although they sometimes sounded as if they were detached observers rather than native members of the society where the problem has been endemic, and not among the lowest of the low alone. In the memoir to which I have already referred (if only in a note) Laila Abou-Saif recalls that after she had staged her challenging play she asked her assistant what he would do if his sister took the same path as Šafīqa had done, he replied, 'I would not be able to show my face in the neighbourhood if I did not kill her.'

From the stern critics of the late twentieth century, there are calls for remedial action to be taken by state authorities, but no effort to enter the minds of the perpetrators or to investigate the forces that shape their motivation. The next generation, however, produced some writers intent on probing for themselves the social and psychological realities of their own people, and without addressing themselves specifically to honour crimes they brought their insights to bear on the realities of life in the lower strata of their society. Prominent among them was Yūsuf Idrīs (1927–91), who in his fiction dealt with such topics as a young village girl's loss of innocence not through an indiscretion of hers but by being subjected to the brutal testing of her virginity intended to clear her of a false rumour. Most relevant to our topic is a short story titled 'an-Naddāha'.[14] In this, a village couple fall to the siren call of the big city, hoping for a more gracious life than they have known. But when the husband gets a job as a doorman in a block of flats, they find themselves caught up in an unaccustomed pace of living and cowed by the socially superior tenants, Westernised in dress and in customs. When one of these tenants forces his attentions on the wife, she finds herself yielding to what seems to her an inevitable fate, and even experiencing some enjoyment in it. And when the husband bursts upon the scene, he first sets off in pursuit of the young man but soon loses him in the milling crowd, then returns to his wife so disoriented that he cannot act on the initial urge to kill her, throwing her also into turmoil as, hour after hour, she awaits her fate:

> She tries to speak, but he shut her up with a whimper, the whimper of a wounded animal.
>
> And having nodded off for a moment and then been brought back to consciousness by a man's low moan, she was nearly driven mad, unable to believe what was registering, seemingly in her imagination: Was that a man sobbing and weeping? Could he be weeping? Would he have done so had he been in the village? Was he also cursed, had Cairo defeated him, undermined his will and his nature …?

The man then packs up to take his family back to the village, but the wife slips away, choosing to stay in Cairo.

The story is at best tangential to our theme. The parallels with an honour crime are not exact; but the hints thrown speak loud.

Notes

1. See my *Ṭāhā Ḥusayn: His Place in the Egyptian Literary Renaissance* (London, 1956), pp. 99–100.
2. See my *Overview of Modern Arabic Literature* (Edinburgh, 1990), ch. 10.
3. Colloquially pronounceed *tār.*
4. See *Ballads*, pp. 30, 66. The book also contains full texts and translations of two versions of the ballad of 'Šafīqa we Mitwalli' and one version of 'Ḥasan u Na<īma', to which several references are made below.
5. A *mawwāl* in his honour is transcribed, translated and analysed in Margaret Larkin, 'A

Brigand Hero of Egyptian Colloquial Literature', *Journal of Arabic Literature*, 23, 1 (March 1992), pp. 49–64.

6. First published 1950. Translated by Denys Johnson-Davies as 'The Song of Death', in Tewfik al-Hakim, *Fate of a Cockroach and Other Plays* (London, 1973), pp. 78–94.
7. First published in 1942. Translated by A. B. as-Safi as *The Call of the Curlew* (Leiden, 1980).
8. Translated by me as 'The Postmaster', in *Blood and Mud* (Pueblo, CO, 1999).
9. Scenario and dialogue by Ṣabrī Mūsā, with the collaboration of Dunyā l-Bābā, published in book form in Cairo (1974).
10. *Ḥasan wa Na<īma*, No. 76 of the series titled *al-Kitāb aḏ-Ḏahabī* (Cairo, July 1960).
11. Found in several collections of his works, including *Malik <Ajūz wa Masraḥiyyāt Uxrā* (Cairo, 1996). This also includes his 'Šafīqa w Mitwalli'.
12. For a description of the performance and of the circumstances surrounding it, see her memoir published under the name of Laila Said, *A Bridge through Time* (New York, 1985), pp. 126–33.
13. 'Where am I to Find People?' (Cairo, December 1975). For a fuller exposition of Surūr's use of folk material, see Item 17 in this book.
14. In a volume of the same name, published in Cairo, ?1978, translated by Catherine Cobham as 'The Siren', in *Rings of Burnished Brass* (London, 1984), pp. 98–122.